Oxford Guide to Plain English

THIRD EDITION

Martin Cutts

OXFORD
UNIVERSITY PRESS

OXFORD
UNIVERSITY PRESS

Great Clarendon Street, Oxford ox2 6DP

Oxford University Press is a department of the University of Oxford.
It furthers the University's objective of excellence in research, scholarship,
and education by publishing worldwide in

Oxford New York

Auckland Cape Town Dar es Salaam Hong Kong Karachi
Kuala Lumpur Madrid Melbourne Mexico City Nairobi
New Delhi Shanghai Taipei Toronto

With offices in

Argentina Austria Brazil Chile Czech Republic France Greece
Guatemala Hungary Italy Japan Poland Portugal Singapore
South Korea Switzerland Thailand Turkey Ukraine Vietnam

Oxford is a registered trade mark of Oxford University Press
in the UK and in certain other countries

Published in the United States
by Oxford University Press Inc., New York

First published as The Plain English Guide 1996
Published as the Quick Reference Plain English Guide 1999
Second edition published 2004

Third edition published 2009

British Library Cataloguing in Publication Data

Contents

TO IVOR AND JOAN CUTTS
for all their support and encouragement

Acknowledgements

My thanks go to those who have given help and advice on parts of this new edition. Chapter 23 draws heavily on the practical knowledge of Janet Pringle, a Canadian expert on the needs of low-literacy readers, who also commented in great detail on the draft of that chapter. Sarah Carr, Plain Language Commission associate, commented on chapter 10 and conducted several readability tests for me. Christina Gleeson, Plain Language Commission associate, spent many hours extracting word-frequency data from the sources. I remain grateful to Monica Sowash, who conducted the focus-group interviews for the original edition in 1995. Throughout, my wife gave constant help and support.

Several organizations have allowed me to include parts of their printed documents, so I'm grateful to the Local Government Ombudsman for an example in chapter 2; Calgary Sexual Health Centre, Canada for examples in chapter 23; Norwood for an example in chapter 23; and the following organizations for examples in chapter 24—Enfield Homes, Winkworth Franchising Ltd, YHA (England and Wales), St Albans District Council, Sunderland City Council, Yorkshire Water, and Enquire (Children in Scotland). The 'Nebraska' examples on pages 179 and 180 are quoted from www.useit.com with permission.

About the author

Martin Cutts co-founded Plain English Campaign in 1979 and remained a partner there until 1988. He is now director of clearest.co.uk ltd, which owns the trading name Plain Language Commission. The company provides editorial and training services in the plain-language field and runs the Clear English Standard accreditation scheme for documents and websites. His other books include *Lucid Law* (2000), Clarifying Eurolaw (2001), and *Clarifying EC Regulations* (co-author Emma Wagner, 2002), which are all available on free download from www.clearest.co.uk. He lives in Whaley Bridge, near Buxton, Derbyshire.

Starting points

Nearly a century ago, a legendary Cambridge University professor told his students to write in a clear style and avoid inflated language. Plain English, he said, was the difference between 'He was conveyed to his place of residence in an intoxicated condition' and 'He was carried home drunk'.

Today, Arthur Quiller-Couch's lesson is as relevant to business and official writing as it was in 1913. I recently saw a notice saying:

> In the event of an emergency evacuation of these premises should you require assistance to facilitate your evacuation would you please advise your host or reception on arrival.

This is writing that stands on a pedestal and tries to sound posh. It could simply have said:

> Visitors: if there's an emergency, will you need help to leave the building? If so, please tell reception or your host now.

Writing plain English isn't easy: you have to think hard about what you're going to say, why you're saying it, and who'll be reading it. But generally your readers will prefer it. Probably they won't even notice, and that's one definition of good writing.

Wherever you look, there's a daily dribble of officialese, legalese, and quango-speak. My postbag includes an acknowledgment from an insurance firm that I've sent some money, which says:

> The said aggregate further single premium shall be apportioned equally among the existing Policies and consequently in relation to each such Policy the Further Minimum Sum Assured secured by the part of the said aggregate further single premium apportioned thereto shall be a sum equal to the aggregate Further Minimum Sum Assured specified in the Schedule divided by the total number of the existing Policies the Further Participating Sum Assured so secured shall be a sum equal to the aggregate Further Participating Sum Assured so specified divided by the total number of the existing Policies and the amount of the further single premium paid under each of the existing Policies shall be a sum

equal to the further aggregate single premium so specified divided by the total number of the existing Policies

That's a single unpunctuated sentence of 132 words—not even a full stop at the end. Rampant legalese.

The post also includes a bank letter, dated 10 July. The italics are mine but the words are theirs:

I am *writeing* to you *in regards to* a cheque that was paid into your account on the 7th May. *Unfortunetly* this credit was paid into your account a second time by mistake on the 8th May. Hence, today, *(10th May)* we will be debiting your account for the sum of £843.00. I apologise for the *inconveniance* this has caused you.

So many errors (including today's date) in so short a letter. Does it matter? Does the bank care? There's also a letter from the so-called director of quality of a college, copied to me by a student who has used its grievance procedure, which includes the statement:

From the plethora of letters that have been received from you [...] it is impossible to determine the gravamen of your complaint.

The student asks me whether 'plethora' and 'gravamen'—along with 'preliminary procedural representations', 'preliminary representations on points of procedure', and 'preliminary representations'—are acceptable in a letter like this. He says: 'My opinion is that he's deliberately trying to confuse me.'

A resident of central Wales sends me a 49 000-word consultation paper from the Welsh Assembly, asking if I can make sense of it as he'd like to complete the questionnaire. It includes sentences like:

The whole hierarchy from waste minimisation through collection, recycling and residual dispersal has spatial implications.
The diversity of Central Wales' environment also offers unrealised economic potential if developed sensitively and knowledge based industries, new environmental technologies and sustainable forms of high-quality tourism, both inland and at the coast, can be encouraged.

And finally my postbag includes a charity's briefing paper written in fluent quango-speak:

The 'onion model' ... set out ... the Government's vision of what was needed to achieve whole system change. Recent tragic events have demonstrated

that there is an urgent need for still greater integration at every layer of the 'onion' in frontline delivery, processes, strategy and governance. At the level of service delivery in particular there remains significant practical, philosophical and resource barriers to full integration. Further legislative changes at governance level alone will not automatically make it easier to address these barriers.

Unclear writing flourishes partly because few public figures are brave enough to say they don't understand. Such confessions are so rare that they make the news. In 2007, Judge Peter Openshaw was presiding over the trial of three alleged 'cyber-terrorists' when he had to ask prosecutors to explain terms like browser, broadband, and dial-up: 'The trouble is I don't understand the language. I don't really understand what a website is... I haven't quite grasped the concepts.'

A similar admission came in a local parish council meeting in 2006. Councillor Alan Wilkinson said a report from Teesdale District Council was 'incomprehensible to any normal person' and its reference to 'involuntary exclusion from the world of work' meant nothing more than 'unemployment'. Warming to his theme, he said: 'Nobody talks like this; nobody reads books written like this. Frankly it's a turn-off, and it's not surprising that we are having trouble attracting new members.' The 18 000-word report gloried in the title 'Sustainability appraisal scoping report for the local development framework core strategy'. It included statements like 'There is a high level of social capital and community cohesion assisted by a strong foundation of participatory community activity and associated support organisations' and 'The more rural wards also suffer from high levels of employment deprivation.' (In other words, 'In the countryside, few people have jobs.') Not all the councillors agreed with Wilkinson, though. One stoutly defended the authors: 'This is just the way council reports are written, and if you want to be a councillor then you need to understand that. If you go to France, they speak French. Here in the council, we speak like this.'

Guidance not rules

This book is about how to avoid writing French when you intend to write English. It focuses on 'essential information', a loose description that includes business and government letters, emails, and reports;

consumer contracts; product instructions; leaflets and forms on tax, health, welfare, and legal rights; and rules, regulations, and laws. These things may seem humdrum compared to the mighty works of literature but they help to oil the engines of industry, commerce, and administration. They provide information that, if misunderstood or half understood, disadvantages people, oppresses them, or—at the least—wastes their time and money. The book has one main aim: to help you write and set out these documents more clearly. It does this by suggesting 25 guidelines often used by professional editors. They're summarized on page xxvi.

I say guidelines, not rules. There's a guideline to aim for an average sentence length of 15–20 words, but there's no rule banning sentences of more than 20 words. There's a guideline to use words your readers are likely to understand, but there's no rule banning obscure terms as long as you explain them to the uninitiated.

So this isn't a simple recipe book. Writing will still be hard work—perhaps the hardest work you do—but the guidelines should make it easier. The book is not, of course, about writing novels, plays, poetry, or newspapers.

The examples I give are genuine apart from the obvious fictions I've created, mainly in chapter 16. I've changed words only to avoid identifying authors or to add essential context. For some examples, I've provided rewrites. These are not meant to be the sole or perfect solutions. There are many ways of saying the same thing; if you can improve my versions, that's fine.

No writing can truly be regarded as clearer or better until users' performance proves it. Several times I mention the value of testing high-use documents with likely users, to see whether they can follow the information and act on it. I've taken my own advice by testing the clarity of some of the 'before' and 'after' examples. A focus group of 35 people rated them for clarity, giving a score out of 20. The group included police officers, firefighters, librarians, unemployed people, teachers, pensioners, booksellers, gardeners—and one person who described herself as a dogsbody. It wasn't representative of the population but gives a useful snapshot of readers' views.

In general, the focus group preferred the versions that heeded my guidelines, rating them significantly clearer than the originals. That doesn't prove these versions would be better understood in real life, but it's a strong indicator. The results, shown at relevant points in the text, persuade me to recommend the guidelines more confidently.

What has motivated me and others to work in the plain-English field is that clearer documents can improve people's access to services, benefits, justice, and a fair deal. If people understand what they are asked to read and sign, they can make more informed choices and know more about their rights and duties. They might even see more clearly what business and government are doing. Plain English should, I believe, become an accepted part of plain dealing between consumers and business, and between citizens and the State. I hope this book will help it do so.

What is plain English, anyway?

The guidelines will help you create plain-English documents. But what is really meant by plain English? Is it anything more than a campaign slogan and a brand name for businesses selling editing and document-design services? Undoubtedly, it's a woolly term. As no formula can genuinely measure the clarity of a document, I would rather describe plain English than define it. Plain English (or plain language, as it's often called) refers to:

The writing and setting out of essential information in a way that gives a cooperative, motivated person a good chance of understanding it at first reading, and in the same sense that the writer meant it to be understood.

This means pitching the language at a level that suits the readers and using good structure and layout to help them navigate. It doesn't mean always using simple words at the expense of the most accurate or writing whole documents in kindergarten language—even if, as some surveys claim, about seven million adults in the UK and 70 million in the US read and write below the level at which their skills are useful to them in their daily life (functional literacy).

The UK's National Literacy Trust website suggests that the average reading age among adults is about 13, or three years below school-leaving age. Not high, but at least it's well above functional-literacy level. This means that documents for a mass audience need to be pitched at about reading age 13, and plain English can help with this.

Plain English embraces honesty as well as clarity. Essential information should not lie or tell half-truths, especially as its providers are often socially or financially dominant. For example, insurance and pension companies should not hide their charges beneath a mass of detail. A health leaflet should not withhold facts that political, religious, or minority groups might find unpalatable. Products claiming green credentials should not use duplicitous labels like 'recyclable', since almost anything can be recycled, or 'harvested from sustainable forests', since all forests are sustainable and what matters is whether they are indeed sustained, and how.

Plain English is not an absolute: what is plain to an audience of scientists or philosophers may be obscure to everyone else. And because of variations in usage across the English-speaking world, what is plain in Manchester may be obscure in Mumbai or Maine. Similarly, what is plain today may be obscure in a hundred years because language preferences, readers' prior knowledge, and readers' expectations alter over time.

The book focuses on the written word. Of course, speakers as well as writers can get themselves in a tangle. Having partly disrobed the singer Janet Jackson during a concert on US nationwide television in 2004, exposing her star-encrusted nipple, Justin Timberlake called the whole thing a 'wardrobe malfunction'. In 2003 US defense secretary Donald Rumsfeld made himself seem even more brainy than usual by declaring:

> Reports that say that something hasn't happened are always interesting to me, because as we know, there are known knowns; there are things we know we know. We also know there are known unknowns; that is to say we know there are some things we do not know. But there are also unknown unknowns—the ones we don't know we don't know.

That at least can be deciphered after close study. Less appealing are weasel words. The UK's justice minister Jack Straw, challenged about why his Human Rights Act seemed to be working in favour of terrorists and other criminals, told a newspaper in 2008:

In due course I could envisage that there could be additions made to work in the issues of responsibilities.

This has no meaning—or perhaps it has any meaning that anyone cares to give it, making it the opposite of plain English. As Humpty Dumpty says in Lewis Carroll's *Through the Looking Glass*: 'When I use a word, it means just what I choose it to mean, neither more nor less.'

Progress towards plain English

United States developments In the late 1960s and early 1970s the seeds of a modern plain-English revolution were sown. Consumer groups used the mass media to publicize and ridicule examples of obscurity in legal documents and government forms, calling for plain language or plain English. In 1974 Siegel & Gale, a pioneering document-design company, worked with Citibank in New York to write a loan agreement that customers and staff could understand. The Citibank loan note was so striking it was publicized across America. At federal level, it led to the Magnuson-Moss Act requiring guarantees to be in plain language. At state level, it led to laws requiring leases and consumer contracts to be clear, first in New York State in 1978 and then in many others—to the dismay of some lawyers.

The fact that obscurity could be oppressive had been shown in the 1960s when civil-rights activists challenged a Louisiana statute requiring black (African-American) people to interpret difficult passages from the constitution before they were allowed to vote. 'We hold,' said John Minor Wisdom, the judge, 'that this wall, built to bar negroes from access to the franchise, must come down.' In 1971–2 the American National Council of Teachers of English formed a Public Doublespeak Committee to highlight deceptive language by public figures, and since 1975 has given its annual George Orwell Award for honesty and clarity in public language.

In 1978 President Carter signed executive order 12 044 requiring regulations to be written in plain English. In 1998 President Clinton issued a memorandum, 'Plain Language in Government Writing', which said:

The Federal Government's writing must be in plain language. By using plain language, we send a clear message about what the Government is doing,

what it requires, and what services it offers. Plain language saves the Government and the private sector time, effort, and money.

Plain language requirements vary from one document to another, depending on the intended audience. Plain language documents have logical organization, easy-to-read design features, and use:

- common, everyday words, except for necessary technical terms;
- "you" and other pronouns;
- the active voice; and
- short sentences.

The Clinton memo then directed heads of executive departments and agencies to use plain language in all new documents that explained how to get a benefit or service 'or how to comply with a regulation you administer or enforce'. Regulations were excepted from this, but the memo also required that plain language be used 'in all proposed and final rulemakings published in the *Federal Register*'. Both the Carter and Clinton edicts died when the presidency changed hands, but their influence continues.

In 1998 the Securities and Exchange Commission (SEC) instructed corporations to write key parts of stock and bond prospectuses—especially the cover page, summary, and risk factors—in plain language. Arthur Levitt Jr, SEC chairman, told Associated Press, 'I've been around our markets for most of my life and I can't understand much of what passes for disclosure.'

To help corporations comply, the SEC website offered an excellent free guide to writing plain language in financial documents, the *Plain English Handbook*. The foreword was by Warren Buffett, an investor with cult status in the US: 'When writing [my company's] annual report, I pretend that I'm talking to my sisters. I have no trouble picturing them: Though highly intelligent, they are not experts in accounting or finance. They will understand plain English, but jargon may puzzle them. My goal is simply to give them the information I would wish them to supply me if our positions were reversed. To succeed, I don't need to be Shakespeare; I must, though, have a sincere desire to inform.'

Bell Atlantic was among the first companies to comply with the new rules. It showed what could be done with a merger document, being happy to replace this:

> In the Merger, each share of NYNEX Common Stock issued and outstanding immediately before the Effective Time (excluding those held in the treasury of NYNEX and those owned by Bell Atlantic) without action on the part of the holder thereof, will be converted into the right to receive 0.768 of a share of Bell Atlantic Common Stock.

with this:

> If the merger is completed, Nynex stockholders will receive 0.768 of a share of Bell Atlantic common stock for each share of Nynex common stock that they own.

The value of thinking about an audience's needs and, ideally, testing the usability of public documents with them was evident in the muddle over the presidential elections in 2000. In Palm Beach County, the election supervisor decided that with ten names to fit on the ballot paper, two pages would be better than one—it would help the mainly elderly electorate. She got the design of the paper approved by all the parties and the authorities. Yet when the voters came to use it, the design so misled them that 19 000 people double-punched their papers, invalidating them, while many Democrats voted mistakenly for a right-wing candidate. From the ensuing mayhem, George W Bush emerged victorious. World history was to be significantly altered by the avoidable accident of a poor piece of document design.

United Kingdom developments There was a whiff of book-burning in 1979 as campaigners for plain English, in a protest I organized, shredded unclear government forms in Parliament Square. This persuaded the incoming Thatcher government to issue a policy statement ordering departments for the first time to count their forms, abolish unnecessary ones, clarify the rest, and report their progress annually to the prime minister. This meant something because Mrs Thatcher actually read the reports and held senior officials to account. By the end of the 1980s, under her onslaught, it was hard to find a truly dire central government form in the UK. Local government was also influenced. Some town halls have since set up groups of councillors and officials who vet forms and leaflets for clarity before they're printed. Even better, several housing associations use panels of residents for this purpose. Waverley Borough Council's housing leaflets bear a logo saying 'Tenant approved—Waverley Tenant Reading Group'.

Clarity accreditation schemes for documents and websites are also marketed commercially, two of the best known being run by Plain Language Commission (the Clear English Standard, from 1994) and Plain English Campaign Ltd (the Crystal Mark, from 1990). In each case, documents meeting the criteria may display the scheme logo, which further publicizes the accreditation and attracts new customers. Among those using the schemes are government bodies, utility firms, and insurers.

Often it's only when things go wrong that people look at the small print of their documents. After a House of Lords ruling in 2000 revealed a £1.5bn ($2bn) hole in the finances of the mutual insurer Equitable Life, customers rushed to their policies to see when they could extract their money on the most favourable terms. There they found a barrage of legalese with sentences of 125, 159, and even 218 words, and this relative minnow of 62 words:

> Notwithstanding anything hereinbefore contained no partial surrender may be effected unless both the sum payable on the partial surrender and the total after the surrender of the Participating Sum Assured and the Related Bonuses thereon and of all Further Participating Sums Assured and Related Bonuses thereon exceed a minimum sum which the Society shall determine at the time of the partial surrender.

A sentence need not be long for it to baffle people unused to high-level language. After a government agency wrote 'This charter is neither extensive nor exhaustive', an informal survey found that many of the target audience confused 'extensive' with 'expensive', and 'exhaustive' with 'exhausting', thus interpreting the sentence as 'This charter is neither costly nor tiring.' The text made better sense rewritten as 'This charter does not try to give you every detail.'

One bus driver in Derbyshire took matters into his own hands when confronted by a bemusing company textbook. He got national publicity in 2001 after translating its 183 rules into readable prose, much of which was adopted by the firm. Instead of 'Ensure the potential impact of non-routine factors and problems and other services are assessed and details notified promptly to an appropriate person', he wrote 'Inform the depot if you are stuck in traffic or involved in an accident.' Instead of 'Ensure machinery for issuing and endorsing tickets is confirmed as in working order and is set in accordance with approved procedure', he wrote 'Check the ticket machine is showing the correct date and price.'

Plain English has the best chance of flourishing when government opts for simplicity in its regulations and schemes. Housing benefit forms that seemed long at four or six pages in the 1980s are now routinely 16- and 24-page monsters. The questions may be reasonably clear, but there are hundreds of them. Similarly, the government's abolition in 1999 of personal equity plans and tax-exempt special savings accounts in favour of individual savings accounts spawned a new wave of incomprehension among consumers that persists to this day, despite supposed simplifications in 2008.

The words 'government' and 'simplification' rarely make good chums. In the UK, governments regularly promise to simplify the pensions and benefits systems but usually make them more complex. The Pensions Advisory Service annual report (2006) describes how complexity can cause trouble:

> Lack of understanding . . . lies at the heart of many of the enquiries we receive. Over a third of all calls to our helpline [that's over 20 000] involve people trying to understand their pension entitlements or rights. In many cases this reflects the complexity of pensions, but more often it reflects the incomprehensible language that faces them. Everyone must make a greater effort to ensure pensions communications are clear and intelligible. Also, they too often lack honesty, in that they aim to persuade employees that changes being made are in their best interests, when, in reality, the changes are for the employer's benefit.

Of course, some government bodies do well. One booklet, *Health and Safety at Motor Sports Events*, is a thing of beauty—lively writing, attractive page layouts, and good photos. Even if you dislike motor sport, this is a page-turner.

The 1974 Consumer Credit Act lays claim to the first use of the term 'plain English' in British law, requiring credit-reference agencies to give consumers, on request, the contents of their file 'in plain English'. So if companies were using code or some other abbreviated form, they had to convert the file into language that the ordinary person could readily understand.

European law has improved the clarity of consumer contracts. EC Council directive 93/13 requires unfair terms to be removed, and:

> In the case of contracts where all or certain terms offered to the consumer are in writing, these terms must always be drafted in plain, intelligible language. Where there is doubt about the meaning of a term, the interpretation most favourable to the consumer shall prevail.

The Office of Fair Trading (OFT) is one of the main enforcers of regulation 7 of the Unfair Terms in Consumer Contracts Regulations 1999, which, in line with the directive, requires that a 'seller shall [i.e. must] ensure that any written term of a contract is expressed in plain, intelligible language'. The OFT says: 'A term is open to challenge as unfair if it could put the consumer at a disadvantage because he or she is not clear about its meaning—even if its meaning could be worked out by a lawyer.' Even the core terms—those setting out the price or defining the product—must comply with the plain-language rule otherwise they can be subject to a test of fairness. The OFT says that 'jargon-free language is of no value to consumers unless it is in legible print', and has used its powers to ensure print is big enough to read. This affects, for example, car-hire contracts, which are often illegible without a magnifying glass. The OFT website publishes a quarterly bulletin of case reports on the contract terms it has ordered to be rewritten or deleted. Bulletins 23–25 (2003) condemn expressions like 'indemnify'; 'principals'; 'shall vest in the pupil'; 'tenants in common'; 'joint and several liability'; 'right of appropriation'; 'we shall lay blameless'; 'herein'; 'lien'; 'reversion'; 'long term reduced payment moratorium'; 'forthwith'; 'time is of the essence'; 'without prejudice'; '*mutatis mutandis*'; 'void or voidable'; 'successors in title'; 'demises'; 'undertake'; and 'condition precedent'.

Often an OFT challenge results in whole clauses being deleted because they're unnecessary, meaningless, or unlawful. This clause failed because it was too broad a general exclusion as well as being hard to understand:

> Neither we nor our servants or agents will be under any liability in respect of defects in goods delivered or for any injury, damage or loss resulting from such defects, whatsoever and however caused and whether such injury, loss or damage be by direct or consequential means and notwithstanding that the same may be due to the negligence act or omission of ourselves, our servants or agents, and our liability under this clause shall be in lieu of any warranty or

conditions implied by law as to the quality or fitness for any particular purpose of such goods.

In another case, a property business withdrew its entire tenancy agreement of 41 clauses and replaced it with model terms from a trade association, while Bradford and Bingley plc withdrew a 59-clause agreement after its clarity was challenged.

The language of the law itself needs clarifying. If there is deep complexity in law and policy, this will usually be reflected in guidance issued to the public. In 1994, Plain Language Commission tested my Clearer Timeshare Act (a law rewritten in plain English) with 90 senior law students. Nine out of ten preferred the plain version to the real Act. Performance also improved: on one key question, 94 per cent got the correct answer when working with the rewritten version, while only 48 per cent did so with the real Act. My pretend law was never meant to become the real thing, but it had an immediate effect. Two groups of tax and accountancy professionals were formed to persuade the government to translate tax laws into plainer English. I helped one of them convert a regulation from the original muddle agreed by Parliament. Surprisingly, the government's own law drafters did a similar thing, effectively rewriting a piece of their own work.

As a result, in 1995 the government set up the Tax Law Rewrite Project to transform tax law into plainer English. Chunks of the rewritten tax law are now in force, and there is also a new, clearer page layout for all laws. Some new laws read as if they have been heavily influenced by plain-language thinking. The Elections Act 2001, the Human Rights Act 1998, the Land Registration Act 2002, and the Arbitration Act 1996 all make good use of short sentences and well-constructed vertical lists. There is still much to do: one transposition of a European Commission (EC) directive into British law includes a 202-word sentence, even though the original EC text was fairly straightforward. This kind of complexity imposes a heavy cost on those who must comply.

Much depends on who is thought to be the audience for legislation. I believe legislators should regard their primary audience as interested private citizens, not lawyers. Laws may never be written in the plainest of plain language, but they should at least be understandable to reasonably literate, motivated people who are prepared to make an effort. It may be a pretty big effort, of course, especially in technical areas of law. Yet many non-lawyers must from time to time read laws in their raw state: police officers, local council officials, special interest groups, and that group of ordinary citizens who happen—usually without the benefit of any training in the law—to have been elected as members of the various UK parliaments. Focusing on their needs would help to clarify the law for all, including lawyers.

Less law should be made, too, and then people would have time to absorb it. From 1992 to 2005, a total of 39 000 pages of new primary law and 133 000 pages of secondary law (regulations) were passed. So people have had to swallow 172 000 new pages of law in fourteen years, an average of 12 200 pages. Inevitably, there has been indigestion, and the effect of new laws has been poorly communicated to the public. Even judges get lost in the labyrinth. In one case (R v William Chambers, 2008), three appeal court judges learned that an order they were about to make would be based on a regulation repealed seven years earlier. None of the highly paid lawyers in the case knew this. It was discovered by accident.

In 2008, one useful regulation did come into force. It said banks operating in Northern Ireland had to ensure that all their communications about personal current accounts were certified by an independent organization specializing in plain English or were otherwise tested with customers and found to be easily understandable. As most of these banks operate in Great Britain too, the regulation (Northern Ireland PCA Banking Market Investigation Order) has forced them to clear up much of their literature nationwide.

Anyone reading the daily papers in June 2006 might have thought plain English was about to become the language of the law. There was widespread coverage of the draft Coroner Reform Bill, which was said to be written in plain English. Indeed, a government news release stated this. Headed 'First Bill to be written in plain English', the release announced '[this] will ... be the first Bill that will be published in plain English – so that anyone can read it and know what changes it is making'. In *The Guardian*, the minister responsible wrote: 'So it's to help the public that my new bill which reforms the inquest system is drafted in—shock, horror—ordinary English. The "Plain English" coroner reform bill is accompanied by the usual legalese on the facing page.'

The real shock and horror, though, was that these claims were untrue. The Bill was written in the same style of most Bills ('the usual legalese'). The only innovation was that the explanatory notes that come with all Bills had been typeset opposite the proposed law, instead of being printed separately. There was, quite simply, no plain-English Bill of any kind. A false dawn.

Echoing the Palm Beach fiasco, in Scotland in 2007 a government changed hands because of baffling ballot papers. In this case, pre-testing and expert opinion predicted trouble but officials and politicians pressed on regardless. On election day, voters had to fill in two forms. On one, according to the small-print headings, they had to put a cross for a single candidate in each of two columns: the first column was for a proportional representation vote for a party list; the second was for a winner-takes-all constituency member of parliament. But many voters misread or didn't read the headings. They thought the two columns formed one continuous list, and put both their crosses in a single column, spoiling their papers. The second form, for the local council elections, used a different system—a single transferable vote. Voters had to put numbers alongside up to eight candidates in their chosen order. Naturally, many used the method they were familiar with and that they'd just used on the other form, marking a cross or sometimes several crosses in the boxes. This was wrong, too, so a total of 147 000 ballot papers (4 per cent) were spoiled and therefore rejected. In some constituencies, the number of spoiled papers outstripped the victor's majority. The governing party was defeated by a single seat. As the victorious SNP's platform includes independence for Scotland, a pair of unclear forms could well lead to the break-up of the UK. It proves again that when readers' behaviour is ignored, unintended consequences flow.

Work in other countries In Australia during the 1970s the first car insurance policy that could reasonably be called 'plain' was issued, and the example was widely copied and refined in that country and the UK. In 1984 the Australian government adopted a plain-language policy for its public documents and this has been extended to the language of the law itself. Law-writers in Canberra now take advice from their own *Plain English Manual*. In Queensland the Industrial Relations Reform Bill 1993 legislates for clarity—tribunal decisions must be 'expressed in plain English' and 'structured in a way that is as easy to understand as the subject matter allows'.

Advocates of plain Swedish have greatly influenced the language of new laws for many years. No government bill, including proposed acts of Parliament, can be printed without approval from the ministry of justice's 'division for legal and linguistic draft revision'. In 2001 it revised 1 306 acts and ordinances and 122 committee terms of reference. The website Klarspråk (clear language) and a *Plain Swedish Bulletin* spread news on good practice. The government runs a Plain Swedish Group, Klarspråksgruppen, which encourages Swedish authorities and agencies to do plain-language work.

In New Zealand, the Write Group runs the commercial WriteMark accreditation scheme for documents written in plain English. It sponsors an annual independently judged open competition for good documents, the WriteMark New Zealand Plain English Awards.

Internationally, two not-for-profit membership bodies promote plain language. Clarity publishes a regular newsletter (clarity-international. net) on plain legal English; and for professionals working in the field, Plain Language Association InterNational (PLAIN) provides an online discussion forum.

Does plain English work?

Research shows that documents carefully crafted in plain English can improve readers' comprehension. In an American study of instructions given by word of mouth to jurors, the plain versions improved comprehension by 14 percentage points, from 45 per cent to 59 per cent. In a further study the same instructions were given in both speech and writing. Jurors understood the plain versions 'almost fully', said the researchers. In a study to test understanding of medical consent forms in the US, readers of the original form could answer correctly only 2.36 questions out of 5. Using the plainer form they got 4.52 questions right, a 91 per cent improvement; they also took much less time to answer.

In 1999 the Social Security Administration wanted to issue an annual benefit statement to every working American over 25 years old, some 125 million people. Plain-language experts at the Center for Clear Communication, Inc. tested the previous six-page form and found it poorly structured and presented, with some important details buried. So they wrote, designed, and pilot-tested four prototypes of a new form.

These versions had a clear title, good organization, and a design that reduced production and handling costs. They were consumer-tested through a national mail survey of 16 000 people. A Gallup survey in 2000 reported that '... the results to date are glowing. The new social security statements have played a significant role in increasing Americans' understanding of social security'.

Much of the most convincing research on the benefits of plain English relates to legal documents. And the most telling point of all is that no company that has issued a plain-English insurance policy, pension contract, or bank guarantee has ever reverted to a traditional, legalistic style of wording.

A short history of plain English

Pleas for plain English have been around a long time. In the 14th century Chaucer had one of his characters demand:

**Speketh so pleyne at this time, I yow preye
That we may understonde what ye seye.**

When William Tyndale translated the Bible into English from Latin in 1525, he could have used an ornate, high-level style. Instead he chose the direct and pungent voice of the common people of his day, and was executed for his trouble. Tyndale seems to have been keen on the modern plain-English principle of keeping the readers in mind, if his growl to one opponent is anything to go by: 'If God spare my life, ere many years I will cause a boy that driveth the plough shall know more of the scripture than thou dost.'

In 1550, after only three years on the throne of England, Edward VI had become so exasperated with the law that he remarked:

I would wish that the superfluous and tedious statutes were made more plain and short, to the intent that men might better understand them.

In the same century some writers wanted to halt the influx of what they called inkhorn terms such as 'revoluting', 'ingent affabilitie', and 'magnifical dexteritie', which were meant to broaden what could be said in

English and make it sound more grand. Some inkhorn terms like 'defunct' and 'inflate' survive to this day.

In 1604 Robert Cawdrey's first-ever English-to-English dictionary sought to explain:

> **hard vsuall English wordes, borrowed from the Hebrew, Greeke, Latine, or French. &c. With the interpretation thereof by plaine English words, gathered for the benefit & helpe of Ladies, Gentlewomen, or any other vnskilfull persons.**

Patronizing though that seems today, this dictionary of about 2 000 entries was meant to help people whose lack of access to private tutors and grammar schools left them unable to understand the heavily latinized English that was then so fashionable among the high and powerful.

From the 17th century, Protestants, especially Quakers, tended to favour a simple style in their writing and speaking. They called it plain language. In 19th-century England, others sought a weird kind of linguistic purity by trying to replace Latin-derived words with those of a Saxon look. William Barnes, for example, preferred 'leechcraft' to 'medicine', 'speechlore' to 'grammar', and 'swanling' to 'cygnet'. His terms 'foreword' (instead of 'preface') and 'handbook' (instead of 'manual') are today as popular as their alternatives. The English barrister George Coode began trying to get legal sentences written more clearly. He said, rather too optimistically:

> **Nothing more is required than that instead of an accidental and incongruous style, the common popular structure of plain English be resorted to.**

The philosopher Jeremy Bentham called for laws to be divided into sections (this was happening in France), demanded shorter sentences (one law included a 13-page sentence), and suggested that lawyers should 'speak intelligibly to whom you speak'.

In England in the 1920s, C K Ogden and I A Richards devised Basic English. Its core was a vocabulary of 850 words which, in various combinations and using a narrow range of sentence structures, could, they believed, say everything that needed to be said. Their three aims were that Basic should be an international language, an introduction to full standard English for foreigners, and a kind of plain language for use in science, commerce, and government. Basic was supported by Winston

Churchill, the prime minister, and Franklin Roosevelt, the US president. Though influential to this day in the teaching of English as a foreign language, Basic became bogged down in academic controversy and eventually fizzled out as a force for plain language in the 1950s. Its main legacy is in the restricted vocabulary and grammar of Simplified Technical English, which is widely used internationally in aerospace and military manuals.

In the late 1940s a landmark for plain English was erected when the British government's Treasury commissioned Ernest Gowers, a top civil servant, to write a book encouraging clear writing in the civil service and elsewhere. This eventually became *The Complete Plain Words*, still widely read in updated editions. Unfortunately the book continues to exempt many forms of legal drafting from its advice, a loophole that some lawyers have pleaded in mitigation of their often wayward writing habits.

Summary of guidelines

Most of the chapters begin with a guideline that is then expanded and discussed. The 25 guidelines are set out below. Numbers correspond to chapter numbers.

Style and grammar

1 Over the whole document, make the average sentence length 15–20 words.
2 Use words your readers are likely to understand.
3 Use only as many words as you really need.
4 Prefer the active voice unless there's a good reason for using the passive.
5 Use clear, crisp, lively verbs to express the actions in your document, and avoid using noun strings.
6 Use vertical lists to break up complicated text.
7 Put your points positively when you can.
8 Reduce cross-references to a minimum.
9 Put accurate punctuation at the heart of your writing.
10 Remember the average reading age of the population: about 13 years.
11 Avoid being enslaved by writing myths.
12 Try to avoid sexist language.
13 Use good grammar even if you don't know hundreds of grammatical terms.
14 In letters and emails, avoid fusty first sentences and formula finishes.

Preparing and planning

15 Plan before you write.

Organizing the information

16 Organize your material so that readers can grasp the important information early and navigate through the document easily.
17 Consider different ways of setting out your information.

Management of writing

18 Manage colleagues' writing carefully and considerately to boost their morale and effectiveness.

Plain English for specific purposes: emails, instructions, the Web, legal documents, and low-literacy readers

19 Take as much care with email as you would with the rest of your writing.
20 Devote special effort to producing lucid and well-organized instructions.
21 Don't waffle on the Web—put the big news early and make the style and structure punchy.
22 Apply plain-English techniques to legal documents such as insurance policies, car-hire agreements, laws, and wills.
23 For people with low literacy, cut out the fine detail, be brief, and test your documents with the real experts—the readers.

Layout

24 Use clear layout to present your plain words in an easily accessible way.

Proofreading

25 Check your stuff before the readers do.

1 Writing shorter sentences ... or chopping up snakes

Guideline: *Over the whole document, make the average sentence length 15–20 words.*

More people fear snakes than full stops, so they recoil when a long sentence comes hissing across the page. Here's one from an accountant's letter to his self-employed client:

> Our annual bill for services (which unfortunately from your viewpoint has to increase to some degree in line with the rapid expansion of your business activities) in preparing the accounts and dealing with tax (please note there will be higher-rate tax assessments for us to deal with on this level of profit, which is the most advantageous time to invest in your personal pension fund, unless of course changes are made in the Chancellor's Budget Statement) and general matters arising, is enclosed herewith for your kind attention.

At one level, the sentence is easy to read—all the words are simple for a literate client. What makes it hard work is its length and muddle, with asides and additions attached as they sprang into the writer's mind.

Muddle is more likely in a long sentence unless the construction is straightforward. Instead of making one main point—and perhaps one related subsidiary point—a long sentence force-feeds the reader with numerous points. This demands more effort and short-term memory, leading to overload if the topic is complicated. If you want to get your recommendation agreed by a board of directors, it's unwise to waste their time disentangling a 68-word sentence like this:

> Although Mr Smith's requested increase in borrowing facility is substantial and the Smith Group has not yet returned to acceptable profitability, in fact because of dividends paid there was a deficit of £10 million transferred to revenue reserves, profits at the trading level have increased with considerable opportunity to advance further as the recession eases and consumer confidence improves, therefore an increased limit to £12.5 million is recommended.

But what length of sentence is too long? Ignore advice that prescribes an upper limit, though if you regularly exceed 40 words you will certainly weary and deter your readers. Better to aim for an average of 15-20 words throughout. The key word is *average*, so not all sentences need to be in this range; there should be plenty of variety. While an occasional short sentence will punch home an important point effectively, too many will make your writing staccato and noisy, like a misfiring engine. There is no lower limit: a sentence could be just one word, such as 'Why?', or two words, such as 'I disagree' or 'Not so'. These very short sentences can help your writing seem poised, confident, and controlled.

One reason for keeping to a 15-20 word average is that people are used to it. In the mid 1960s, a million words of published US writing were analysed. The average sentence length was 19 words. These were the scores for particular types of document:

- Miscellaneous: government   25
- Learned and scientific   24
- Press: reports   21
- Humour   18
- Fiction: romance/love   14
- Fiction: science/detective   13

It's notable that government documents, perhaps the only material that could be classed as essential information, came top.

If you find yourself writing long sentences or having to edit them for other people, there are six main ways of clarifying them:

- Split and disconnect.
- Split and connect.
- Say less.
- Use a list.
- Cut verbiage.
- Bin the sentence and start again.

Let's examine each of these.

Split and disconnect

Full stops enable readers to digest your latest point and prepare for the next. This sentence from a local government report makes good sense but, at 58 words, is too long for busy people to grasp at first reading:

> I understand that some doctors making night calls have been attacked in recent months on the expectation that they were carrying drugs and their caution when visiting certain areas in the south of the city has been very exacting and has even included telephoning the address to be visited from their car when they arrive outside the house.

Look for the main break in the sense. It comes in the second line after 'drugs', where the writer starts talking about caution. So you could split it there, delete 'and', and produce this:

> I understand that some doctors making night calls have been attacked in recent months on the expectation that they were carrying drugs. Their caution when visiting certain areas in the south of the city has been very exacting and has even included telephoning the address to be visited from their car when they arrive outside the house.

That may be enough. But you could go further and split it again after 'exacting', producing this:

> I understand that some doctors making night calls have been attacked in recent months on the expectation that they were carrying drugs. Their caution when visiting certain areas in the south of the city has been very exacting. It has even included telephoning the address to be visited from their car when they arrive outside the house.

Now the paragraph can be readily grasped at first reading, though you could go further and express the ideas more smoothly:

> Recently, some doctors making night calls have been attacked because they were thought to be carrying drugs. So they have started to take strict precautions when visiting the south of the city. These have even included phoning the patient's home from their car on arrival.

Split and connect

This means putting in a full stop and restarting the sentence with a connecting word like 'however', 'but', 'so', 'also', 'yet', or 'further'. The technique would be helpful in this example from a lawyer's letter:

> Whilst it is expected by the donor's family that the present arrangement for caring for the donor will continue for the rest of her life, should it at any stage become necessary to transfer the donor once more into a nursing institution, the donor's family envisages that the second-floor flat will be sold and the

donor's share in the proceeds used to provide any additional income necessary to ensure her continued well-being.

That's a 73-word sentence—nearly four times the US average from the 1960s—and certainly a candidate for splitting. The obvious break point is after 'life' in the second line:

Whilst it is expected by the donor's family that the present arrangement for caring for the donor will continue for the rest of her life.

But this fails, because the sentence is unfinished—nothing complete has yet been said. Striking out 'Whilst', however, creates a complete sentence and the next can begin with 'but' (see chapter 11 if that worries you):

W̶h̶i̶l̶s̶t̶ It is expected by the donor's family that the present arrangement for caring for the donor will continue for the rest of her life. But should it at any stage become necessary to transfer the donor once more into a nursing institution, the donor's family envisages that the second-floor flat will be sold and the donor's share in the proceeds used to provide any additional income necessary to ensure her continued well-being.

Other improvements are possible. At the start, it would be simpler to say 'The donor's family expects…'. The second sentence could end at 'sold', and a new sentence could begin 'The donor's share in the proceeds would then be used…'. The word 'institution' could become 'home' and so on.

Say less

Sometimes a sentence is lengthened by needless repetition, as at the start of this lawyer's letter:

Dear Sirs
Trial of John Smith and James Jackson
Trade Descriptions Act 1968, Manchester Crown Court, 10.30 am, Tuesday 7 June 2000
The above defendants are to be tried at the Manchester Crown Court on Tuesday 7 June 2000 at 10.30 am for several offences under the Trade Descriptions Act 1968 concerning the supply of motor vehicles to which false trade descriptions had been applied.

As the first sentence repeats most of the heading—a common practice—it could say merely:

The above defendants are to be tried for several offences concerning the supply of motor vehicles to which false trade descriptions had been applied.

That saves 19 words and preserves the meaning. It also lets the heading do its job.

Use a list

Vertical lists break long sentences into manageable chunks. They are particularly useful when describing a procedure, as in this safety message to hospital staff about a machine for keeping babies warm:

The attachment of the warmer support-bearing assembly system must be checked to ensure that it is adequately lubricated, its securing screws are tight and that the warmer head can be easily repositioned without the support bearing sticking.

Not a hard sentence for people in the trade—though it's 37 words long—but easier for busy people to grasp quickly if it's split into a vertical list with 'you' at the start to make it more direct:

You must check the attachment of the warmer support-bearing assembly system to ensure that:

(a) it is adequately lubricated,

(b) its securing screws are tight, and

(c) the warmer head can be easily repositioned without the support bearing sticking.

There's more on lists in chapter 6.

Cut verbiage

Sometimes the key ideas in a long sentence are buried beneath verbiage:

The organizers of the event should try to achieve greater safety both from the point of view of ensuring that the bonfire itself does not contain any unacceptably dangerous materials such as aerosol cans or discarded foam furniture and from the point of view of ensuring the letting-off of fireworks in the designated area, with easily identifiable wardens to be available during the event to prevent people indiscriminately letting off fireworks, to the possible danger of people attending the event.

The redundant words include 'from the point of view of' (twice), 'itself', 'unacceptably' (what would 'acceptably' dangerous materials be?), 'discarded' (they wouldn't be on the bonfire otherwise), 'during the event', and 'to the possible danger of people attending the event' (redundant because crowd safety is what the whole sentence is about). With verbiage crossed through and insertions underlined, the sentence could be:

> The organizers of the event should try to achieve greater safety ~~both~~ by ~~from the point of view of~~ ensuring that the bonfire itself does not contain any ~~unacceptably~~ dangerous materials such as aerosol cans or ~~discarded~~ foam furniture and ~~from the point of view of~~ by ensuring the letting-off of fireworks in the designated area, with easily identifiable wardens to be available ~~during the event~~ to prevent people indiscriminately letting off fireworks~~, to the possible danger of people attending the event~~.

Then, with a few minor modifications and a full stop after 'area', the sentence becomes:

> The organizers of the event should try to achieve greater safety by ensuring that the bonfire does not contain any dangerous materials such as aerosol cans or foam furniture, and that fireworks are let off only in the designated area. Easily identifiable wardens should be present to prevent people letting off fireworks indiscriminately.

And it could also be converted into a list, using the first 'that' as a pivot and deleting the second 'that':

> The organizers of the event should try to achieve greater safety by ensuring that:
>
> - the bonfire does not contain any dangerous materials such as aerosol cans or foam furniture
> - fireworks are let off only in the designated area, and
> - easily identifiable wardens are present to stop people letting off their own fireworks.

There's more on cutting verbiage in chapter 3.

Bin the sentence and start again

When there's no hope of untangling a sentence by other means, all you can do is discard it and rewrite. Here is that accountant's sentence from the top of the chapter, sadly unimproved since we left it:

1/ Our annual bill for services (which unfortunately from your viewpoint has to increase to some degree in line with the rapid expansion of your business activities) in preparing the accounts and dealing with tax (please note there will be higher-rate tax assessments for us to deal with on this level of profit, which is the most advantageous time to invest in your personal pension fund, unless of course changes are made in the Chancellor's Budget Statement) and general matters arising, is enclosed herewith for your kind attention.

It's no good just inserting full stops because the new sentences won't make any sense, and using a vertical list doesn't seem feasible. Nor does it help to make fewer points—it's all useful detail, though verbiage like 'from your viewpoint', 'general matters arising', 'herewith', and 'kind' could all be cut. So we need to start again and plan out the main points, which are:

(a) Here is our annual bill for services.
(b) We're charging more than last year for two reasons: your business has grown rapidly, and we'll have to work out a higher-rate tax assessment as you've made a lot more profit.
(c) Now is a good time to pay into your pension fund as you'll get higher-rate tax relief on your contributions, unless the rules alter in the Chancellor's budget.

This isn't the best sequence of points—the good news ought to come first. So, with the points in c-a-b order and written as sentences, the result could be:

2/ Now is a good time for you to pay into your pension fund as you will get higher-rate tax relief on your contributions—unless the Chancellor's budget changes the rules.
I have enclosed our annual bill for services. Unfortunately it is higher than last year. This is because your business has grown rapidly and, since your profits are much greater, I will need to calculate a higher-rate tax assessment.

Four sentences—and readily understood at first reading. If you prefer a more informal style, you could use contractions like *I've*, *you'll*, and *I'll*:

3/ Now is a good time for you to pay into your pension fund as you'll get higher-rate tax relief on your contributions—unless the Chancellor's budget changes the rules.
I've enclosed our annual bill for services. Unfortunately it's higher than last year. This is because your business has grown rapidly and, since your profits are much greater, I'll need to calculate a higher-rate tax assessment.

The last paragraph could also be written as a vertical list:

4/ Now is a good time for you to pay into your pension fund as you'll get higher-rate tax relief on your contributions—unless the Chancellor's budget changes the rules.

I have enclosed our annual bill for services. Unfortunately it is higher than last year. This is because:

- **your business has grown rapidly; and**
- **I will have to work out a higher-rate tax assessment as your profits are much greater.**

A 35-strong focus group (see page xii) assessed three of the four versions for clarity. They rated Version 4 the clearest, with an average score of 18 points from a possible 20. It was the first preference of 26 people. Version 2 got an average score of 14 but only three first preferences. Version 1, the original, scored only 5 points—seven respondents gave it no points at all. These results suggest that sentence length and layout significantly affect readers' perception of clarity.

Why bother?

Few people would think any less of accountants who occasionally write a bad sentence; after all, they're mainly in the figures business. But as the focus group showed, people do notice the difference between an accountant who writes considerately and one who doesn't. Most professionals want to be held in high esteem by their customers. So, if only for commercial reasons, it is important to control sentence length carefully. Fortunately this is easily done, and the full stop then becomes the commonest punctuation mark on the page.

2 Preferring plain words

Guideline: *Use words your readers are likely to understand.*
Here is a US Secretary of State refusing an assistant's request for a pay rise:

> Because of the fluctuational predisposition of your position's productive capacity as juxtaposed to government standards, it would be momentarily injudicious to advocate an increment.

And here is a local government official in England being obstructive to citizens who wish to display posters in a public library:

> Your request raises a question as to the provenance and veraciousness of the material, and I must consider individually all posters of a polemic or disputatious nature.

Both sentences overdress simple ideas in phrases designed to impress not inform. In forelock-tugging times, people might have been impressed. Now they smell pomposity, and dislike being forced to translate.

For business writers this may be costly. An accountancy firm wrote a business proposal in this kind of language:

> At present the recessionary cycle is aggravating volumes through your modern manufacturing and order processing environments which provide restricted opportunities for cost reduction through labour adjustments and will remain a key issue.

What they probably meant was:

> Output and orders have fallen because of the recession. But there is little scope for cutting costs by reorganizing the way staff work.

Whatever they meant, they baffled their audience and didn't win the business.

A selling point obscured by waffle is likely to be missed by the readers. An aeronautics firm wrote to a prospective customer:

> We would anticipate being able to optimize the engine design from an emissions point of view.

In such a haystack of verbiage, the needle of meaning was lost:

We can improve the engine design to reduce emissions.

The BBC, which is in the clear communications business if anyone is, operated under a royal charter of such baffling complexity that it won Plain Language Commission's 'Golden Rhubarb' trophy in 1996. Amid sentences of 141 and 210 words, the vocabulary was strange and obscure: *mutatis mutandis*; conveyance of signals serving for the impartation of any matter; whereas on divers dates; subject as here-inafter provided; the aggregate of moneys; residual part thereof; aforesaid objects; requisite for the proper performance and obser-vance of its functions; the concurrence of the Council; deemed to vitiate any proceedings; exemplification thereof; determination of the said term; and anywise notwithstanding. Responding to my com-plaint about the charter's lack of clarity, the minister for media and heritage said in 2004: 'Although the wording of the beginning and end of the Royal Charter is fixed, the only requirement for the text of the body is that it is legally sound. Within that framework, I will make sure that the points you raise—which I agree with—are taken into account when any new Charter and Agreement are being drafted.' He kept his promise to some extent, and the 2006 royal charter has lost most of its archaic phrasing. One section even begins: 'To enable this Charter to be drafted in language which is not too cumbersome or complex ...', which suggests at least some interest in clarity. The English is generally modern, though there are unusual words like 'peripheral', 'ancillary', and 'overarching', and one sen-tence stretches to 85 words. The original version, according to read-ability tests (see chapter 10), was understandable only by people with high-level legal training. Now, the tests show, it can be read by those with graduate-level reading ability. Not exactly a triumph, but pro-gress.

In 1995 the British government issued a booklet to every household in Northern Ireland on its ideas for peace in the province. Four times the prime minister's foreword said that people should read, understand, and comment on it as part of a public debate. Yet the booklet was largely incomprehensible, with an average sentence length of 35 words and vocabulary that included strange terms like unicameral; *ultra vires*; *inter alia*; cognizant of either option and open to its democratic realization; embrace the totality of rela-tionships; instrument for an intensification; designated functions;

appropriate new provisions entrenched by Agreement; comprehensive political accommodation; weighted majority; adumbrated; prejudicing workability; interlocking and mutually supportive institutions; and quantum of public expenditure. There was no glossary to explain 'unicameral' and 'weighted majority', which were fundamental to the proposals. A local TV company took soundings in Belfast's markets area and found only mystification. One shopper said, 'I would like somebody to explain it to us all in words that we can understand. I want plain English. I want it set down in front of me so that I can understand it and I can go to my children and say, this is what's happening.'

Especially outmoded is the ceremonial language found in town-twinning proclamations—written by normally down-to-earth city governments—and in royal pronouncements such as this citation on the Queen's Award for Export Achievement:

> **XYZ Company Limited: Greetings! We being cognizant of the outstanding achievement of the said body as manifested in the furtherance and increase of the Export Trade of our United Kingdom of Great Britain and Northern Ireland, our Channel Islands and our Isle of Man and being desirous of showing Our Royal Favour do hereby confer upon it the Queen's Award for Export Achievement.**

Monarchs, like captains of any great corporation, should demand that their staff put clear, if dignified, language into their mouths—to be eloquent without being grandiose and absurd. Plain English needs to become the Queen's English.

As English-speaking countries become more informal, many official bodies have made public promises to use plain language in their dealings with citizens. Sir Ernest Gowers' motto in *The Complete Plain Words*, 'Be short, be simple, be human', has gained a foothold.

Is there no place for unusual words?

The chief reason for workplace writing is to give information in a way that's readily understood—to bridge the gap between what you know and what the reader knows. Generally, plain words do this best. If you wanted to say:

Local Government
OMBUDSMAN
ADVICE TEAM 0845 602 1983

What we can't do

We cannot usually question what a council has done simply because you do not agree with it. There must be some fault by the council. But even then we may not investigate your complaint if you're only slightly affected by what has gone wrong.

There are some things we may not investigate because there is a more appropriate body to deal with your complaint, or because we don't have the legal power to do so. If we can't help, we will tell you about other organisations that may be able to help.

When to complain

If you have a complaint, the first thing to do is complain to the council. You can find out how to complain from the council, or you can ask a councillor to help. In most cases, the council must have a chance to sort out the complaint before we can consider it.

If you are not satisfied with the council's answer, or if it does not give you an answer within a reasonable time, you can complain to us. We think up to 12 weeks is a reasonable time for the council to investigate your complaint and reply to you.

But where the complaint is urgent, for example, because it is about a school place for next term or because you are particularly at risk, we may be able to deal with it straight away.

You should normally complain to us within 12 months of when you first knew about the problem you are complaining about. If you leave it any later, we may not be able to help.

This page from the Local Government Ombudsman's leaflet *Complained to the council? Still not satisfied?* uses clear and homely language to explain a procedure. Notice the use of personal pronouns (31 uses of *we*, *us*, *you*, and *your* in 268 words), short sentences (average 20 words), and everyday English. Two sentences start with 'But'—see chapter 11. The Flesch Grade Level (see chapter 10) is 8.4 (UK reading age 13.4). The two-column layout is open and easy on the eye, with headings in sentence case, ample white space between paragraphs, and unjustified type without line-end hyphenation—see chapter 24. (Size reduced. Second colour shows as greyscale. By permission of the Local Government Ombudsman.)

To keep our street trees safe and attractive, we'll be spending more money on pruning and maintaining them.

those are the everyday words you would use. You wouldn't make people battle through the fog of planning-speak that was, in fact, issued:

We will implement additional expenditure on arboricultural pruning and maintenance to enhance the safety and visual amenity of street trees.

Not that there's anything wrong with long or unusual words in the right place and for the right audience (and many long words aren't unusual—think of 'immediately' or 'disappointment'). Sometimes an unusual word is perfect for the job, expressing just what you want to say. Then you should use it and either give an explanation or trust the context to explain. A more distant hope is that busy readers will be willing to consult a dictionary, though online dictionaries have increased that possibility. In a technical document, there is a place for technical words, which will be plain enough to technical people. But while doctors might readily understand 'cardiac atheroma' and 'pulmonary oedema', a mass audience will get a clearer sense of the ailments if explanations are added—'furring-up of the heart's arteries' and 'fluid in the lungs'. It is pointless to say that someone is exhibiting xanthochromia and diaphoresis if you can say he is yellow and sweating. Generally, therefore, the place for unusual words is in technical contexts or in literature and journalism, where readers are prepared to travel further with a writer's flight of fancy because the topic is interesting or the story pulls them along.

Sometimes highly educated writers are surprised that words they regard as ordinary are unknown to the person sitting next to them on the train. Take that example about displaying posters in the library:

Your request raises a question as to the provenance and veraciousness of the material, and I must consider individually all posters of a polemic or disputatious nature.

Of the hundreds of educated people I've shown it to during writing-skills courses, only a handful have known that 'provenance' means 'origin' or 'source'. That may be regrettable but it sends a message to anyone with a wide vocabulary: don't assume that others know all the words you do. A paediatrician in the UK who stated her profession on a plaque outside her house found that her doors and windows were daubed with anti-paedophile graffiti. The vandal clearly didn't know what a paediatrician was, and hadn't stopped to wonder why a paedophile would advertise the fact on her house. Similarly, *Personnel Today* reported that when a communications director said in an office memo that he favoured a 'pedagogic' approach during training programmes, he was told to be out of the building by lunchtime as the company did not tolerate 'paedophilic perverts'. After he successfully pleaded a defence based on the *Concise Oxford Dictionary*, a directive was sent to the entire staff saying that only words to be found in the local newspaper would be allowed in future memos—a solution that owed more to face-saving than common sense.

In the queue at a bank cashpoint I eavesdropped as a young man tried to decide from his balance slip whether his account held enough money to permit a withdrawal. He read it out to his friend: '£50.23 CR', but neither of them could tell whether CR (short for 'credit') meant he owed money to the bank or vice versa. In the end, they decided he was in debt and left without withdrawing any cash. Wrong decision, of course, but understandable since if you get credit you are putting yourself in debt. Some UK banks now speak of payments and receipts, not debits and credits, and the columns on bank statements may be headed 'Money in' and 'Money out' or 'Paid in' and Paid out' instead of the more traditional 'Deposits' and 'Withdrawals'. It can't be long before the columns have the even more basic headings 'In' and 'Out'. Writers who want to be readily understood by a mass audience have a very tough job: they have to guess what words or symbols the average reader is likely to know, and write accordingly.

A similar problem arises with a word favoured by lawyers: 'notwithstanding'. When testing people's comprehension of legal documents, I've found that few non-lawyers can explain it—even in context. Alternative plain words are available: 'despite', 'in spite of', 'however', or 'but' can all do the same job. 'Notwithstanding', like 'forsooth', 'peradventure', 'thrice', and 'verily', has virtually disappeared from everyday speech and writing. Removing it and other oddities from legal documents will aid understanding, not promote illiteracy by reducing people's exposure to unusual words. On a clear-writing course in a law firm in 2008, one of the young lawyers—a bright, savvy graduate—expressed surprise at seeing 'criterion', the singular of 'criteria'. She'd never seen the word before and thought 'criteria' was the only form. When this happens among educated users, it may be just a matter of time before dictionaries—which like to say they reflect popular usage rather than prescribe it—start to record 'criteria' as a feasible singular.

We shouldn't worry if words fall into disuse and become archaic unless they take useful distinctions of meaning with them. If people no longer understand a word, or if it's not doing a useful job, its day is done and other words will move in or be invented to fill any gap. This has happened throughout history. Once, it was thought correct to use 'ye' in such constructions as 'ye said' and 'gather ye rosebuds while ye may'. But 'you' has ousted its rival and we seem to be none the worse. It is dismaying, though, when so many authors and speakers use 'refute' to mean merely 'deny', because this endangers the special meaning of refute (disprove by giving good evidence) and leaves readers or listeners wondering what meaning was intended.

In English the scope for using simple vocabulary—and the opposite—is wide because so many words have the same or similar meanings ('synonyms'). For example, the cauldron that bubbled for centuries with bits of Latin, French, Old Norse, and Old English threw up several synonyms for 'start'—'begin', 'commence', 'initiate', 'institute', and 'originate'. There is room for all these words, but only 'start' and 'begin' are first choices in today's plain-English lexicon.

Let's look at two main ways of removing officialese and pompous language:

- Use simpler alternatives.
- Reorganize the sentence.

Use simpler alternatives

In this section, for the sake of clarity, the officialese and the equivalent plain English are underlined.

A local government department is writing to a tenant who has fallen behind with her rent. In law, the authority doesn't have to rehouse tenants it regards as deliberately homeless:

> In the event of your being evicted from your dwelling as a result of wilfully failing to pay your rent, the council may take the view that you have rendered yourself intentionally homeless and as such it would not be obliged to offer you alternative permanent housing.

Using plain words and splitting the sentence, this could become:

> If you are evicted from your home because you deliberately fail to pay your rent, the council may decide that you have made yourself intentionally homeless. If this happens, the council does not need to offer you alternative permanent housing.

Our focus group found this version far clearer, with 31 out of 35 preferring it. They gave it an average clarity mark of 17 out of 20, as against 12 for the original (a remarkable show of tolerance).

A hospital wants to resolve the chaos in its car parks by charging parking fees:

> If my proposals are accepted, the income from fees would ensure that car parking control could be effected without utilising monies that should be expended on health care.

This becomes:

> If my proposals are accepted, the income from fees would ensure that car parking could be controlled without using money that should be spent on health care.

An official is writing to a citizen about a claim for housing benefit:

> I am in receipt of information from the citizens advice bureau, which I believe is acting on your behalf, with regard to matters appertaining to your benefit claim. Will you please furnish the bureau with particulars of your savings.

This becomes:

> I have received information from the citizens advice bureau, which I believe is acting on your behalf, about your benefit claim. Will you please give the bureau details of your savings.

A firm's conditions of service say:

> Holidays will be taken by mutual agreement after the exigencies of the service have been considered.

This becomes:

> **Holidays will be taken by mutual agreement after the <u>needs</u> of the service have been considered.**

Reorganize the sentence

The technique is to spot the unusual word or phrase and use its plain meaning as an aid in revising the sentence.

A trade union writes to its members:

> **It behoves management to give details of the planned redundancies, and it is incumbent on all members to participate fully in this dispute.**

Deleting the unusual words, this becomes:

> **Management should [or 'has a duty to' or 'must'] give details of the planned redundancies, and all members should [or 'must'] participate fully in this dispute.**

A treasurer's report explains how many errors are being made when handling payments:

> **An approximate frequency for the mistakes was given by Mrs Jones as ten a month.**

This becomes:

> **Mrs Jones said there were about ten mistakes a month.**

J Edgar Hoover, when head of the US Federal Bureau of Investigation, was worried about Picasso visiting the country (he was said to have left-wing leanings). Hoover wrote to a special agent in Paris:

> **In the event information concerning Picasso comes to your attention, it should be furnished to the Bureau in view of the possibility that he may attempt to come to the United States.**

He might have said:

> **If you get any information about Picasso, please tell the Bureau in case he tries to visit the US.**

A company training officer is explaining a trend towards computer-based training:

> **The ready availability of computer-based tutorials associated with applications software has become prevalent since the development of Microsoft Windows.**

To a fellow professional, none of these words would be hard to understand. But look closely at what is being said: 'The ready availability ... has become prevalent'. Since 'ready availability' and 'prevalence' are so similar in meaning, the writer was probably trying to say:

> **Computer-based software tutorials have become readily available since Windows was developed.**

Now the meaning is clear and the sentence brief.

An example of good plain words

Writing is harder when you lack the freedom to tackle interesting topics like music, marine life, and football. Your writing day could be occupied by matters so humdrum they would make a great novelist weep: the rent for a piece of waste land; inefficient plumbing in the office toilets; a small rise in the price of custard.

Faced with a dull topic, there's great skill in creating a clear document that rises above the bland and boring. The following letter from an official to an anxious elderly couple is a model of simplicity. It doesn't give them everything they want—that would be an easy letter to write—but it does explain things reassuringly and fully. No doubt it could still be improved, but here it is, untouched:

> **Dear Mr and Mrs France**
> **I write concerning an enquiry on your behalf by Councillor Jameson on several matters relating to your home. One of my colleagues will be writing to you about the bath, as I understand you are now having some difficulty with this. As to the decoration of a further bedroom, I am arranging for the foreman painter to call and measure up in order to do the work.**
> **I would expect this to be early in the new year so that the work can be done before the end of March.**
> **At present there are no plans to install central heating in Jasmine Row. None of the properties in Jasmine Row were included in this year's programme. The programme of installations for next year and future years has not yet been drawn up and I cannot say at this stage whether Jasmine Row will be included in it.**

It is our policy to install central heating in all our properties in the next few years, and we are steadily working towards this goal. As soon as I have any definite information I will write to you setting out our proposals.

If I can help further, please contact me.

Adjusting the style to the audience

Prominently placed in a hospital leaflet about healthy eating is a sentence taken from a UK Department of Health report, *Weaning and the Weaning Diet* (1994):

The provision of adequate dietary energy to ensure normal growth and development should be a principal determinant of the diets of children under five years of age.

This may be well understood by an audience of health professionals, but what if they want to get the same ideas across to a mass audience? Terms like 'principal determinant' and 'dietary energy' will be puzzling. According to the Department of Health, the latter just means 'calories', a technical term that will probably be better understood by lay people who know it from diet guides. So the sentence holds an important message for parents of under-fives, namely, 'Give them plenty of calories, not muesli and skimmed milk, otherwise they could die of malnutrition'—which has indeed happened. One reason the sentence doesn't get this point across is that the verbs are feeble—'should be' and the infinitive 'to ensure'. Better verbs will bring new life. For example, you could say:

To ensure that children under five grow and develop normally, one of the main things they need is calorie-rich food.

You would then continue by saying what else was needed, as you would if you were trying to get these points across to an individual parent:

While Helen is under five, she needs food that has plenty of calories. This means things like a, b, and c. These foods will help her to grow and develop normally. She also needs some x, y, and z for taste and variety.

So while the original is in good English, it needs rewriting in plain English to meet the needs of a different audience. By doing this, an apparently complex idea can be communicated clearly in a way that will not short-change any of the audiences. This is not 'dumbing down'—a criticism often levelled at advocates of plain English—but clearing up. It's writing as if readers matter.

What are regarded as common words may sometimes be misunderstood. A survey of 700 patients in an inner-city accident and emergency department found that half thought 'unconscious' people would still be able to hear; 41 per cent believed their eyes could not remain open after losing consciousness; 15 per cent thought they could still talk; and 15 per cent thought they could remain standing. The study, reported in the *Journal of Accident and Emergency Medicine*, has implications for anyone designing public health information including the scripts that emergency services use when responding to phone calls. In a leaflet, the signs of unconsciousness would have to be stated; in a call script, questions designed to test for unconsciousness would have to be included.

At Liverpool's Alder Hey children's hospital during the 1980s and 1990s, parents signed consent forms saying 'I hereby consent to a post mortem examination and to the removal of tissue (other than for the purpose of transplantation) at the time of this examination...'. They were unaware that this allowed doctors to harvest and store body parts and whole organ systems. Using similar consents, various hospitals are thought to have stored 150 000 organs. The word 'tissue', taken direct from the Human Tissue Act, wasn't apparently difficult. But its legal meaning differed from its everyday meaning and should have been explained. Parental grief arising from this led to a government inquiry and fierce legal disputes.

The need to consider the audience is even more obvious in cross-cultural messages. This spam email from the US blithely uses the phrase 'pledging a sorority', which is just as strange to British ears as medieval expressions like 'plighting my troth':

> **Hey there! My name is Michelle and I'm currently a freshman in college. I've been a little busy lately cause I'm pledging a sorority but I still find time to do stuff online.**

Conquering fear

The main cause of bloated, show-off writing is fear. First there's fear that being clear means being definite and that being definite leaves no room for wriggling. Yet if you want to hedge, a plain-English style lets you. You can evoke a full range of doubt and uncertainty—and even the possibility of being just plain wrong—with such words as 'may', 'might', 'could', 'should', 'perhaps', 'normally', and 'generally'. Plain English need not mean being unsubtle.

Then there's the fear that if you write simply you won't be thought eminent, scientific, or literary enough. This fear was examined in a research study in 1978. Over 1 500 scientists from industry and the academic world were asked their opinion of two short pieces of scientific writing. Both gave exactly the same facts in the same sequence of points, and used the same five technical terms. The only difference was in the style of the non-technical language. The first version used everyday words and short, simply constructed sentences. The second did the opposite, though without going to extremes. Nearly 70 per cent of the scientists preferred the plain version; they also found it 'more stimulating' and 'more interesting'. Three-quarters judged the writer to be more competent as a scientist and to have a better-organized mind.

So don't be afraid of plain English. Carefully used, it will reveal your competence far better than the wooden style of so many academic and technical journals.

Plain English word list

If you overuse the words in the left-hand column of the table, your writing could be perceived as pompous, officious, and long-winded. Not that anyone should forbid you from ever using them, but judicious use of the alternatives will help you to be shorter, simpler, and more conversational. The alternatives aren't always synonyms, so use them with a proper care for meaning and for the job they have to do in the sentence. In some contexts, words like 'remuneration', 'domicile', and 'residence' have technical meanings and can't be replaced by plainer alternatives.

Instead of	*Consider using*
accede	agree, grant, allow
accordingly	so
accustomed to	used to
acquaint yourself	find out, read
additional	more, extra
address (sense 'consider')	tackle, deal with, consider
advices	information, instructions
advise (sense 'inform')	inform, tell, let [me] know
aforementioned, aforesaid	[omit or be specific]
aggregate (noun)	total
alleviate	ease, reduce, lessen
apprise	inform, tell, let [me] know
as a consequence of	because
ascertain	find out
assist, assistance	help
attain	reach
attribute (verb)	earmark
category	group
cease	stop, end
cognizant of	aware of, know about
commence	start, begin
commensurate with	consistent with
component	part
concept	idea
concerning	about
consequently	so
constitute	make up, form

Instead of	Consider using
construe	interpret
corroboration	evidence, proof, support
deduct	take away, take off, subtract
deem	treat as, consider
defer	put off, postpone
desist	stop
despatch	send
despite the fact that	although, despite
determine	decide
determine (legal sense)	end, terminate
disburse	pay
discharge (verb)	pay off, settle
disconnect	cut off
discontinue	stop, end
due to the fact that	as, because
dwelling, domicile	home, property
elect, election	choose, choice
emanate from	come from, stem from
endeavour	try, attempt
entitlement	right
envisage	expect, imagine, forecast, think
equitable	fair
erroneous	wrong, mistaken
establish	set up, create, form
eventuate	result, occur, happen
expedite	hasten, speed up
expenditure	spending
expiration	end

Instead of	*Consider using*
facilitate	help
failure to	if you do not
for the duration of	during, while
for the purpose of	to
forward (verb)	send, give
furnish	give, provide
henceforth	from now on
heretofore	until now
herewith	with this
hitherto	until now
hypothecate	earmark
if this is not the case	if not
if this is the case	if so
impart	give, pass on, tell, inform
implement (verb)	carry out, do
in accordance with	in line with
inasmuch as	because, in that
incidence	rate of occurrence, how often
in conjunction with	with
increment	step, increase
indebtedness	debt
initiate	begin, start
in lieu of	instead of
in order to	to
in receipt of	get, have, receive, receiving
in regard to	about, concerning, on
insofar as	as far as
institute (verb)	begin, start

Instead of	Consider using
interim (noun)	meantime, for the time being
in the event of	if, when
in the eventuality of	if, when
in view of the fact that	as, because
manner	way
monies	money, amounts of money
necessitate	need, have to, require
nevertheless	even so, however, yet
nonetheless	even so, however, yet
not less than [ten]	at least [ten]
not more than [ten]	[ten] or less, [ten] or fewer
notwithstanding	even if, despite, still, yet, but
obtain	get, receive
other than	except
particulars	details, facts
persons	people
peruse	read or study carefully, examine
polemical	controversial
principal (adjective)	main, chief
prioritize	rank
prior to	before
provenance	source, origin
provisions [of a law, policy]	the law, the policy
purchase	buy
purport (verb)	pretend, claim, profess
pursuant to	under
reduction	cut
regarding	about

Instead of	*Consider using*
reimburse	repay
remittance	payment
remuneration	pay, wages, salary
remunerative employment	paid work
render	send, make, give
representations	comments
reside	live
residence	home, property, address
save (coordinator)	except
shall (legal obligation)	must
stipulate	state, set, lay down
sufficient	enough
supplementary	extra, more
terminate	end, stop
the law provides that	the law says
thereafter	then, afterwards
timeously	in good time
tranche	slice, portion, share, chunk
utilize	use
verify	check, prove
whensoever	when, whenever
whereby	by which, because of which
whilst	while
wilfully	deliberately
with reference to	about, concerning
with regard to	about, concerning
with respect to	about, for, concerning

Frequency count

It makes sense to use plain words in essential information because people are already familiar with them from other texts, as shown by their frequency in a set of 200 million words of contemporary British and American English collected by Oxford University Press. The figures below show frequency per million words.

Instead of	Consider using
accordingly 23	so 2 021
advices 0.1	information 496, instructions 38
attain 18	reach 236
category 81	group 514
cease 25	stop 220
commence 13	begin 454
concept 115	idea 324
entitlement 6.51	right 388
forward (verb) 6.55	send 226
initiate 24	begin 454
in the event of 8.12	if 2 461
monies 2.89	money 320
notwithstanding 7.53	despite 150
particulars 4.29	details 107
persons 43	people 1 175
prior to 26	before 860
purchase 62	buy 235
regarding 44	about 1 943
shall 162	must 667
terminate 12	end 151
utilise/utilize 24	use 1 424
whilst 45	while 667

The figures don't fully compare like with like because it wasn't possible to examine the senses in which the words were used. However, they do include the plurals of all the nouns, and all forms of the verbs.

The *Collins Cobuild English Dictionary* is a good source on word frequency. It also gives information about the grammatical framework that particular words tend to inhabit, and with which other words they usually combine. This can be helpful in creating sentence structures that readers will be familiar with.

Another useful source, covering 1 200 words often seen in official, business, and legal documents, is the *Plain English Lexicon* (www.clearest.co.uk). This draws on the findings of the *Living Word Vocabulary* (LWV) by Edgar Dale and Joseph O'Rourke, who in a 25-year project tested the level of schooling needed to understand particular words. The lexicon states the US grade level at which the word was understood by at least 67 per cent of those tested, the percentage of students who understood it at that level, the UK reading-age equivalent of the US grade level, and the number of times the word appears in the British National Corpus, a 100 million-word collection of late 20th-century English (90 per cent written, 10 per cent spoken). There's also a commentary on whether authors should use an alternative to many of the words.

A word on some troublesome words

absolutely This is sometimes printed as the emphatic answer to question-headings like 'Do pensioners qualify for this discount?' But 'Yes' does the job perfectly well. In the BBC's adaptation of Charles Dickens' *Little Dorrit* (2008), 'absolutely' was the preferred affirmative of Sparkler, dimwitted jobsworth of the Circumlocution Office.

address 'We are addressing the issue and will let you have a reply soon.' Occasionally ambiguity arises from the use of 'address' in this way: 'The minister has been addressing the letter he received from Mr Smith.' Cynics also say the verb is used as a cover for inaction. More precise verbs are usually available, such as 'consider' and 'tackle'.

advices Still a favourite pomposity among lawyers: 'I await your advices in respect of this matter.' Better to be precise and use 'instructions', 'suggestions', or 'comments'.

advise Near-universal business English for 'inform', 'tell', or 'let me know', but to avoid ambiguity it's better to use one of these and keep 'advise' for 'give advice to'. This avoids such officialese as 'please be advised that your cheque is in the post' which, apart from usually being untrue, begins with four redundant words.

and/or The oblique puts the reader to the trouble of creating three possible meanings. Instead of writing 'We will bring horses and/or donkeys', prefer 'We will bring horses or donkeys or both.' When used in legal documents, 'and/or' has caused much litigation. If you can avoid it, do so.

anticipate Often used as a posh word for 'expect'. Their different meanings should not be allowed to merge, say careful users. 'Anticipate' means to take some action to forestall, or benefit from, a future event:

Customers anticipated the rise in interest rates by choosing fixed-rate loans.

apropos or **à propos** Prefer 'about', 'concerning', or 'with reference to'.

as and when This never seems to mean anything more than 'when' or 'if':

As and when the go-ahead is given, the project will involve the construction of a new underground station as well as rail tunnels.

—which probably means:

As soon as we get the go-ahead for the project, we'll start building a new underground station and rail tunnels.

as at 'The value of your shares as at 5 April was £324.' Normally 'on' or 'at' will do.

as per 'I enclose the form as per our conversation.' It's better, if not always possible, to avoid mixing English and Latin in the same phrase. Prefer 'I enclose the form as discussed.' Alternatively, 'in accordance with' will often do the job. 'As per usual', instead of 'as usual', is especially cringe-making.

at the end of the day This is waffle for 'ultimately', 'eventually', or 'in the end'. The only thing that really occurs 'at the end of the day' is nightfall.

avail yourself 'If you fail to avail yourself of the facilities above, your electricity supply could be cut off without further notice.' Avoid such woolly, pseudo-genteel expressions. Prefer 'If you do not use [or 'take up' or 'make use of'] one of the repayment methods shown above ...'.

brainchild This is journalese for 'idea'. If you have several ideas, please don't call them brainchildren.

can Careful users are very careful with 'can' and 'may'. The first means 'is able to' as in 'Helen can take solid food now that her jaw is mended.' The second means 'is permitted to', as in 'Helen may take solid food because the doctor says it's safe to do so.' The second meaning is common in legal documents:

> **The secretary of state may make rules requiring a patents register to be kept. The rules may delegate the keeping of the register to another person.**

Concern that 'may' will not be understood correctly has led to at least one credit-card company trying to explain it in its terms and conditions:

> **If we agree with another person or business (the transferee) for it to take over all our rights and obligations under this agreement, we may (but do not have to) give you at least 30 days' notice beforehand.**

This is odd because the rest of the document uses 'may' freely without a similar explanation (e.g. 'We may introduce and vary charges in the future'). A court might decide that the two forms of 'may' were meant to have different meanings because one was explained.

'May' can also imply a positive possibility:

> **You should show this letter to other joint shareholders as they may receive different information from elsewhere.**

whereas 'might' in that position would suggest that the possibility was more remote. In practice most people use 'may' and 'might' interchangeably in such situations. This makes sticklers furious because 'might' is the past tense of 'may'.

consult with In phrases like 'We consulted with the public', just omit 'with'. It's redundant.

determine/determination In the legal sense, this means 'terminate' (e.g. 'This agreement shall forthwith determine') but most people won't understand it in this sense and the same goes for 'determination'. If variations on 'end', 'stop', 'finish', or 'cease' won't work, then 'terminate' and 'termination' are likely to be clearer than 'determine' and 'determination'.

die Don't be afraid of this word. It's preferable to euphemisms like 'passed away' and 'is deceased'.

disconnect 'We regret that your supply could be disconnected unless you make a satisfactory arrangement to pay the arrears.' It used to be impossible to persuade electricity and gas suppliers to use the plainer 'cut off'—it was thought to be aggressive or too basic. Now it's widespread.

discriminate/discrimination Without discrimination, nobody would choose anything or anybody, because the word merely means making a choice between things or people. So when organizations proudly proclaim that they won't discriminate against anyone, they aren't quite telling the full story. What they mean is they won't discriminate against anyone unfairly or unlawfully on particular grounds, such as age, sex, religion, sexual preference, and disability.

documentation 'We will let you have the documentation in the next ten days.' This is pompous: 'documents' will nearly always do.

duly If this means anything, it means 'in the correct manner'. A company's share-offer letter includes a rash of 'dulys':

I am pleased to tell you that ... as a qualifying shareholder, an application for shares duly made by you ... will receive special treatment ... This means that, if you duly apply in the offer ... If you duly apply on this application form ...

The company could have avoided the word by saying on the application form that only correctly completed forms would qualify for the offer.

etc. (Latin: *et cetera*, meaning 'and the rest'.) This is perhaps the best understood Latin abbreviation and, though sometimes labelled '*e*xtreme *t*hought *c*ollapse', is harmless if used in moderation and if precision is not required:

The burglar stole televisions, videos, etc.

If a list is introduced by a word like 'such as' or 'includes', 'etc.' is unnecessary because the reader knows the list is incomplete:

The stolen goods included televisions, videos, and stereos.

general consensus of opinion 'Consensus' covers it, in a word. And it needs three *s*'s.

get, got Primary-school teachers' exasperation at the overuse of these words has left many people afraid to use them at all in formal writing. The alternatives 'receive' and 'obtain' are plain enough but there's no harm in 'get' and 'got' (words with a thousand years of common use behind them) when you feel that their simplicity and informality are helpful:

I got your letter yesterday. Thanks for keeping me informed. I'll send someone around to fix the problem.

If your managers forbid the words, you could do worse than quote the text that adorns the dome of Manchester's central library (from Proverbs in the Bible):

Wisdom is the principal thing therefore get wisdom and with all thy getting get understanding.

which doubles as a counterblast to people who say you shouldn't repeat the same word in a sentence or paragraph.

going forward(s) This space-filling, falsely dynamic phrase has become one of the verbal weeds of the 21st century, spread on the airwaves by business commentators and politicians. It's now being written, too, e.g. 'The department would like you to attend a workshop designed to debate specific issues in depth and identify potential recommendations going forward.' The phrase is usually redundant because the context implies a future sense.

having said that or **that having been said** A waffling way of writing 'but', 'however', or 'even so'. Addicts can withdraw slowly with 'that said'.

head up In 'Mrs Smith heads up the team', omit 'up'.

heads-up It's hard to dislike this informal alternative for 'notice' or 'warning', as in 'Mr Jones gave us the heads-up that changes were on the way', but often a more exact verb will do, e.g. 'Mr Jones alerted/warned/told us …'.

hence A useful but regrettably uncommon word. It can mean 'as a result' ('hence the election will take place next week') or 'from now' ('The election will take place two weeks hence'). Use the word regularly or it will disappear.

herewith, hereby, hereof, heretofore, hereinbefore, hereto, herein These smell of old law books; they are not plain words. 'I hereby declare' just means 'I declare'. 'The document attached hereto' just means 'the document attached' or 'the document attached to this'. Happily, these words are slowly disappearing from business and legal use, which should cause no one to fear the imminent death of the language. Do we miss, for example, a range of once-common words beginning with the 'wan-' prefix: 'wanthrift' (extravagance), 'wan-hap' (misfortune), 'wantruth' (falsehood), and 'wanchance' (ill luck)? Only 'wanton' (undisciplined) remains in fairly common use.

however As this is often used as a more leisurely alternative to 'but', it is usually preceded and followed by a comma:

It seems clear that your opponent lied in court. We do not believe, however, that she is likely to be convicted of perjury.

If 'however' begins a sentence—often the best position, since it tells the reader immediately what sort of point is coming up—a comma will normally follow:

However, we do not believe that she is likely to be convicted of perjury.

The next sentence shows a common mistake with 'however':

You have told us that the ring was stolen while the back door was left open, however, the policy only covers theft from your home if force is used to enter or leave.

Because 'however' seems to lengthen the pause that precedes it, effectively creating a second sentence, a comma is not enough. A semicolon or full stop (see also chapter 9) would be better:

You have told us that the ring was stolen while the back door was left open. However, the policy covers only theft from your home if force is used to enter or leave.

Or you could use 'but' and save some of the punctuation:

You have told us that the ring was stolen while the back door was left open, but the policy covers only theft from your home if force was used to enter or leave.

Obviously there is no need for a comma after 'however' in such sentences as 'However likeable he was, he had a vicious streak.'

impact on/with 'The defeat will impact on us badly.' Use 'affect'— 'The defeat will affect us badly.' It saves a word, shows you can tell your affects from your effects, and enables you to be more precise. This example from *The Times* shows how woolly the phrase can be: '[The professor] has been studying the long-term effects of structured play and the way it has impacted at university level.' The author might have written: 'The professor has been studying the long-term effects of structured play and how it leads children to become timid and dependent university students.'

I write or **I am writing** Many writers are told not to begin letters with these phrases because it's obvious they are writing. But 'I write to explain the department's policy on …' is quite harmless—you could not start with 'I explain …'. On the other hand 'I write to inform you that' may as well be deleted, as nothing useful has been said.

meet up with In British English, it is usually neat to use only 'meet'. The longer form may suggest a more complicated rendezvous, like 'we'll try to meet up with each other in Kathmandu'.

methodology This means a body of methods or the study of method and its application in a particular field. It is often misused as a posh word for 'method'.

Ms This, pronounced 'miz', is the chosen courtesy title of women who do not wish their marital status to be disclosed by 'Miss' or 'Mrs'. Use it unless the woman has asked to be addressed by a different title. If a woman signs her letters 'Susan Hopkins' without indicating a preferred title, there's no harm in writing to her as 'Dear Susan Hopkins' or 'Dear Ms Hopkins'.

null and void 'Null' means 'void' (of no effect), so there's no need for both words in a phrase like 'the agreement is null and void'. Simplest is 'void' or 'worthless'.

opine 'The barrister opined that the case would fail in court.' This unusual verb smells of pomposity in British English and is best avoided. This is a pity as it leads to wordiness like 'It is the opinion of the barrister that …'. Alternative verbs include 'believe', 'consider', and 'say'.

prior to This pompous way of saying 'before' tends to produce clumsy, verbless constructions: 'Prior to the abandonment of the mine by the company …' instead of 'Before the company abandoned the mine …'. It's better to keep 'prior' as an adjective— 'prior approval', 'prior discussion'—or as a noun for people in charge of monasteries.

re 'Re: Claim for housing benefit.' A Latin remnant from the word *res* ('a thing'), this is not a short form of 'reference' or 'regarding'. The word should be struck out of all headings to letters and emails—let them stand on their own. In text, prefer 'about', 'concerning', or 'on'. When referring to cases, lawyers often use 're' to mean 'in the matter of': 'Re [or even *In re*] Casaubon 1992'. Better is 'In Casaubon 1992'.

revert In phrases like 'I'll revert to you soon', lawyers use this as an alternative to 'I'll get back to you soon' or 'I'll contact you soon'. It's not in popular use yet but it's neat and concise.

shall The old rule was that when writing of future events you would say 'I *shall*; you will; he/she/it will; we *shall*; you (plural) will; they will' but that when writing of promises, obligations, or commands, the *wills* and *shalls* would change places. This is why the British coronation oath goes:

> **Archbishop: Will you to your power cause law and justice, with mercy, to be executed in all your judgments?**
> **Sovereign: I will.**

And it's why Binyon's poem of 1914, often quoted in memory of the war dead, says:

> **They shall grow not old, as we that are left grow old,**
> **Age shall not weary them, nor the years condemn.**
> **At the going down of the sun and in the morning**
> **We will remember them.**

But only one person in a million now understands these distinctions, so there is confusion when legal documents use 'shall' in an effort to impose an obligation. 'Must' is clearer for this purpose: 'The tenant must pay the rent on time.' Conveniently for people who take this view, the Old English root of 'shall' is *sceal*, meaning 'I must' or 'I owe'. The Oxford University Press figures referred to earlier in this chapter show 162 uses of 'shall', so it is still common, but 667 of 'must'. For legal prohibitions, 'may not' and 'must not' are widely used, though the latter has been condemned as barbarous by at least one judge.

should Traditionally this was the correct form of the conditional tense in the first person singular and plural. Or, in plain English, it was right to say 'I *should*; you would; he/she/it would; we *should*; you would; they would'. This is why many still prefer to write: 'I should be grateful if you would …' not 'I would be grateful if you could …' or 'I would be grateful if you would …'. A neat sidestep is to write 'I'd be grateful if you would …' or 'Would you please …'.

to hand 'I have to hand your letter of 15 January.' This is the kind of snooty language that gets bureaucrats a bad name. Avoid it with 'thank you' or 'I refer to'. If you want to say 'please have the documents to hand when I call', you could use 'ready' instead.

transportation Though terms like 'department of transportation' are common in the US, 'transport' is still the plainer term in British English except when referring to a form of punishment once meted out to sheep-stealers and the like.

unless and until 'Unless and until the conditions are met, the deal is off.' This usage smells of officialdom. Either 'unless' or 'until' will do.

whilst This is becoming unusual (especially in American English). Its job has been usurped by 'while', with which it is interchangeable in standard English.

within In phrases like 'If you look within the box …', the more concise 'in' works well instead. This seemingly trivial change will often save a line of type.

with regards to The traditional expressions are 'with regard to', 'in regard to', and 'as regards'. The bastard phrase 'with regards to', which marries 'with regard to' and 'give my regards to Broadway', is displacing the first two of these in popular use. Sticklers will cleave to 'with regard to'.

Words often confused

Your documents will seem unprofessional if you muddle up similar-sounding words, like these:

- *affect* (verb) means to alter or change ('Damage to the rudder affected the steering') or pretend ('They affected not to listen').
  effect (verb) means to do, make, implement, bring about, accomplish.
  affect (noun) means an emotion, feeling, or desire.
  effect (noun) means a result.

- *criteria* is the plural of *criterion*.

- *desserts* are puddings, only.
  deserts are what you deserve (e.g. 'just deserts'), or wastelands.

- *defused* means that a fuse has been taken out or, figuratively, that tension has been lessened ('The row was defused by immediate action').
  diffuse (verb) means to spread widely ('Light diffused throughout the cellar').

- *discreet* means tactful, secretive, trustworthy, circumspect.
  discrete means separate, individually distinct.

- *flaunt* means to act in a showy or brazen way.
  flout means to disobey or show contempt for.

- *hone* means to polish, refine, sharpen ('They honed their blades and waited').
  home means to move in on or focus ('He homed in on this bright idea').

- *imply* means to suggest or indicate ('She implied she had never married').
  infer means deduce, draw an inference from ('The pathologist inferred she had had several children').

- *incidence* means rate of occurrence, and is singular ('The incidence of HIV/AIDS is rising in the Baltic states').
  incident is an event.
  instance is an occasion or occurrence ('There have been several recent instances of needle-stick injuries').

- *mitigate* means to excuse or lessen the severity ('His guilty plea mitigated the sentence').
  militate against means to operate powerfully against.

- *minuscule* means tiny (and is a technical word for lower-case lettering) while *miniscule* doesn't exist, according to most dictionaries.

- *moot* means to put forward or float an idea.
  mute means silent or to silence.

- *phenomena* is the plural of phenomenon.

- *principle* is a rule of conduct ('He lived according to his principles').
  principal means main, chief ('Our principal aim is world domination'), or a sum of money on which interest is payable.

- *refute* and *rebut* mean to disprove by argument or evidence. The words they are often confused with, *deny*, *reject*, and *repudiate*, mean to dispute a statement without using argument or evidence.

- *restaurateur* is someone who runs a restaurant, while *restauranteur* doesn't exist—or may perhaps be a waiter doing a Gordon Ramsay-style rant.

Foreign words

English is certainly the richer for its contact with foreign words, with hundreds of direct borrowings like 'caravan', 'trek', 'graffiti', 'bastard', 'clan', 'crag', 'criterion', 'phenomenon', 'slogan', 'corgi', 'garage', and 'armada'. Then there are thousands of foreign-derived words such as 'plant', 'fantasy', 'custom', 'interest', 'jury', 'mutton', and 'tea'. (Any large single-volume dictionary will show the foreign derivation of thousands of words, with perhaps 70 per cent of all English words having Latin or Greek roots.)

It's not always easy to judge which foreign words have gained enough currency to be well understood. 'Ad hoc', in such phrases as 'ad hoc group' and 'ad hoc committee', usefully fills a gap. The terms 'i.e.' and 'e.g.' are concise but fewer people can now distinguish between them as most schools have stopped teaching Latin. For a mass audience the English equivalents are safer. Times have certainly changed. In 1939 a famous book on punctuation began:

> **In writing this book I have had more especially in mind three classes of readers: those who, professionally or otherwise, are faced with the task of reading proofs; those who at school are learning to write English correctly (and perhaps a few of their teachers, *quorum pars parva fui*); and those ordinary folk—I have met plenty—who remark somewhat vaguely 'I know nothing about punctuation' ...**

Most authors today would feel obliged to give a translation of the Latin phrase (it means 'of which I was once one'). In 1999, the BBC dropped its award-winning science series *QED* because few viewers knew what the title meant or that it had any connection with science. The BBC's head of science told the *Daily Record*: 'It's not surprising that the audience didn't have the faintest idea what it meant.' The series was reinvented as *Living Proof*, but its disappearance soon after suggests that the allegedly obscure title may not have been its only shortcoming. Using uncommon foreign-language terms may look like showing off, so unless you're sure of your audience it's best to avoid those words so often seen in the literary review pages like 'oeuvre', 'Bildungsroman', and 'auteur'. If you want your staff to provide a guide or a briefing note, don't ask them for a 'vade mecum'. Writing in the *Johns Hopkins Magazine* in 1991, the academics R Wallers and T H Kern tell students: 'Avoid using the Latin terms *ibid.*, *op cit.*, and *loc cit.* Odds are, you don't know what they really mean, and neither do most professors.'

Some terms haven't entirely lost their strangeness but have made the transition into plain English. In this group are 'vice versa', which saves the writer many words of explanation (though 'the other way round' or 'on the contrary' are sometimes good enough), 'per cent', and 'etc.'. 'Curriculum vitae' seems likely to endure, shortened to 'CV'. The best alternative that American English can come up with is French—résumé—while in south-east Asia the pleasing 'biodata' is widespread.

Latin still fights a rearguard action on the British pound coin, where it is more heavily represented than English or Welsh with phrases like *Nemo me impune lacessit* ('No one harms me and gets away with it') and *Decus et tutamen* ('Glory and protection'). Latin's conciseness undoubtedly helps when space is tight, but its use on the currency suggests that the plain languages of the UK are not thought good enough for some ceremonial purposes. Tendring District Council's official crest artfully hedges its bets by offering the Latin and English together: *'Pro bono omnium'* and 'For the good of all'.

Term of Latin or French [F] origin	*Meaning or alternative term*
ad hoc	for this purpose or occasion
carte blanche [F]	a free hand, freedom
cause célèbre [F]	controversial cause
ceteris paribus	other things being equal
cf. (*confer*, Latin imperative of *conferre*)	compare
circa	about
de minimis	trivialities, small amounts
e.g. (*exempli gratia*)	such as, for example
en bloc [F]	as a whole, together
en suite [F]	bathroom in, or adjoining, a bedroom
etc. (*et cetera*)	and so on, and the rest
ex officio	by virtue of the office held
ibid. (*ibidem*)	in the same place, book, etc.; same source

Term of Latin or French [F] origin	*Meaning or alternative term*
i.e. (*id est*)	that is
inter alia/alios	among other things/people
loc. cit. (*loco citato*)	in the passage cited above
modus operandi	way of working, method
mutatis mutandis	with the necessary changes
op. cit. (*opus citatum*)	the work quoted
per annum	per year, a year, annually
per capita	per head, per person, each
per diem	per day, a day, daily
per se	as such, by or in itself, essentially
pp (*per procurationem*)	on behalf of, by the agency of
pro forma	a form
QED	proved as required
q.v. (*quod vide*)	see
seriatim	one at a time, in the same order
sic	thus! (drawing notice to an error)
sine die	indefinitely
vis-à-vis [F]	as regards, regarding, on, about
viz. (*videlicet*)	namely
vs (*versus*)	v, versus, against
v.s. (*vide supra*)	see above

3 Writing tight

Guideline: *Use only as many words as you really need.*

Flab. Writing is full of it. These 95 words from a loan company tell borrowers they have fallen behind with their repayments:

> Arrears at present subsist on your mortgage account in the sum of £1 032, with a further payment becoming due on the 11th April. In view of the account being a mortgage account, we are not in a position to stop interest being debited each month and in order to prevent the account situation from deteriorating, it is necessary that payments are received each month which represent the interest debit. At present this amount is £242 and therefore it is regretted your offer to make payments in the sum of £80 a month is not sufficient.

You may like to blue-pencil it yourself, but at the end of the chapter we'll see how more than a third of the words can be cut without losing any meaning.

Part of writing well is writing tight, ruthlessly cutting dross. Most readers are busy people who want to know the main points of your message, and fast. Making them read excess words is an unfriendly act, especially in business where a deluge of unwanted paper and emails falls on everyone at every level.

Not that shorter is always better: sometimes you need more words to make a point clear. Plain, certainly. Tight, certainly. But not so plain or tight that you miss out essential points or seem blunt and rude. Being ruthless with words needn't mean being graceless with people.

Cutting dross enables your information to shine more clearly. In the early 1900s, Professor William Strunk used to tell his students: 'Omit needless words, omit needless words, omit needless words.' (Once should have been enough, but he was keen.) He believed that just as drawings should have no unnecessary lines and machines no unnecessary parts, so sentences should have no unnecessary words.

Easy to agree with, perhaps, but hard to do. The key is to let the first draft stand as long as possible, then return and revise it. Then revise it again. And probably again. In business, of course, time is against you: that letter or report must go out tonight. And useless words aren't always obvious—they have to be hunted. So let's examine the three main techniques for dealing with them:

1 Striking out useless words.
2 Pruning the dead wood, grafting on the vigorous.
3 Rewriting completely.

Striking out useless words

The most obviously useless words are straight repetition:

The cheque that was received from Classic Assurance was received on 13 January.

'Was received' occurs twice, so the sentence could say:

The cheque ~~that was received~~ from Classic Assurance was received on 13 January.

or

The cheque ~~that was received~~ from Classic Assurance ~~was received~~ came on 13 January.

Spotting this kind of thing becomes harder as the distance between repetitions increases:

The standard of traffic management on the A57, A59, and A623 is of a lower standard than on other major roads in the region.

It doesn't make sense that a 'standard . . . is of a lower standard', so the rewrite would be:

The standard of traffic management on the A57, A59, and A623 is ~~of a~~ lower ~~standard~~ than on other major roads in the region.

Then there are words that repeat an idea:

We attach herewith a financial statement.

If the statement is attached—or enclosed—it must be 'herewith', so the word can disappear.

Journalists occasionally succumb, too. 'In a strongly worded blistering attack at the HFEA's conference, Ms Leather will accuse Prof Zanos of "breathtaking hubris".' If the attack is to be blistering, it will doubt-less be strongly worded, so those words can be omitted. (And since at least half the audience won't understand 'hubris', she might as well say 'arrogance'.)

Wordiness often comes from trying to make a simple procedure sound impressive:

A new bank account is in the process of being set up for you.

Delete four words and this becomes:

A new bank account is ~~in the process of~~ being set up for you.

The verb 'carry out' (like 'undertake' and 'perform') always merits suspicion; often a more vigorous expression will make the same point more economically. For example, it can simply be deleted:

Work is required to be carried out on the flue and funnels.

becomes

Work is required ~~to be carried out~~ on the flue and funnels.

Or 'carry out' can be cut by strengthening the verb it supports:

The firm does not intend to remove the lime trees but it is necessary to carry out pruning to the trees to keep them healthy.

This becomes:

The firm does not intend to remove the lime trees but it is necessary to ~~carry out pruning to~~ <u>prune</u> the trees to keep them healthy.

or

The firm does not intend to remove the lime trees but pruning will keep them healthy.

It's not always so easy to see redundancy. Take this sentence:

For the benefit of new members, the secretary described the rules of the committee and the remit that had been given to it.

Since 'remit' means the committee's terms of reference and a remit must, by its nature, be 'given', the last six words are redundant:

For the benefit of new members, the secretary described the rules of the committee and ~~the~~ <u>its</u> remit ~~that had been given to it~~.

You can safely cut out useless phrases like 'it should be pointed out that', 'it must be noted that', 'I should mention that', 'I would inform you that', and 'I would stress that'. Better just to point it out, note it, mention it, or stress it. In the following examples, the useless words are underlined; what remains makes perfectly good sense on its own:

> <u>I must point out that</u> I am legally obliged to charge rates on the property's current value.
>
> <u>I would like to take this opportunity to</u> apologize for the delay in replying to your complaint.
>
> <u>It should be appreciated that</u> there is always an element of under-reporting of accidents, particularly if no one is injured. <u>It should</u> also <u>be noted that</u> our accident figures exclude occurrences where the system for explosion relief operated effectively.
>
> <u>It is only fair for me to point out at this point that</u> the committee showed great concern about your case at its last meeting.
>
> <u>This letter is to advise you that</u>, following our successful seminar last year for suppliers, we plan to hold another on 13 October.

Pruning the dead wood, grafting on the vigorous

Dead wood often looks alive, so a keen eye is needed. In this example, ten unnecessary words could be replaced by one:

> May I draw your attention to the final account dated 28 June from which I note that six payments of £18 were credited to your account from 28 March to 25 August, totalling £108.

The first six words are courteous but they delay the main message unduly and could go. Then, 'from which I note' is pompous—what matters is not what the writer notes but what the final account shows. Using the vigorous verb 'shows', the sentence becomes:

> ~~May I draw your attention to~~ the final account dated 28 June ~~from which I note~~ shows that six payments of £18 were credited to your account from 28 March to 25 August, totalling £108.

Certain words are prime candidates for pruning. They include 'situation', 'aspect', 'facility', 'issue', 'element', 'factor', 'matter', and 'concept'. All are occasionally useful but they tend to be overworked at the expense of more concrete words:

> The company has one engineer on call at all times, giving excellent speed of response in emergency situations.

'Emergency situations' are nothing more than emergencies, which is the only word needed.

Another phrase often accompanied by verbiage is 'the fact'. There is 'given the fact that' and 'in the light of the fact that' (which just mean 'as' or 'since'); 'despite the fact that' (which means 'although'); and a wordy phrase favoured by politicians, 'the fact of the matter is' (which, if it means anything, means 'the fact is'). Here, the six deleted words could simply be replaced by 'As':

> ~~In view of the fact that~~ the central heating was fitted by Union Gas, they have cancelled the bill in the interests of good customer relations.

By removing padding, the weakness of the text often becomes evident. In this example:

> We want to improve the physical condition of our leisure facilities.

it's clear that 'physical' adds nothing as the facilities don't have a mental dimension, and 'condition' is probably redundant too because improving the facilities will mean improving their condition. This leaves us with:

> We want to improve our leisure facilities.

but this says so little that the author needs to add some detail about how the facilities will be improved.

Rewriting completely

When there are far too many words for the message but neither of the first two methods will work, a total rewrite is the only alternative. Various signals may alert you to this need:

- The meaning isn't clear.
- The sentence is long and the verbs are few.
- The verbs are feeble—for example, they are smothered by nouns (see chapter 5), they are in the passive voice (see chapter 4), or they are derived from 'to be' or 'to have' (see chapter 4).

For example, an engineer is writing about the cost of materials for a road scheme:

> Over-estimating on one type of material could have a detrimental cost effect for the clients, depending on the prices in the Bill of Quantities.

Alarm bells ring at 'have a detrimental cost effect'. First because 'have' seems feeble as the solitary verb in the sentence, and second because 'detrimental cost effect' is a showy way of expressing the simple idea that the clients may have to pay more. So the whole sentence could say:

Over-estimating on one type of material could cost the clients more, depending on the prices in the Bill of Quantities.

While this saves only four words, there is now a powerful verb, 'cost', and the message is clearer.

Local councils publish numerous booklets, most of them too wordy, explaining their policies and practices to residents. Here's a paragraph explaining the main reason why one council has chosen a group of five associations to take over its housing stock:

Between them the group members own the majority of Housing Association owned properties throughout Blackshaw. There are around 5,000 properties that are owned by Housing Associations throughout Blackshaw. The five Associations that are in the Blackshaw Housing Partnership own approximately 4,450 of these properties (89%).

Whenever authors find themselves wading in treacle like this, they need to stop and drain some of it away. Here, there's repetition of 'association', 'housing', 'owned', and 'properties'. There are also several references to quantities of homes, yet few readers will care whether the partnership owns 89 per cent or 96.5 per cent—the exact figure doesn't matter in this context. So, instead of 44 words, all that's needed are the following fourteen:

Between them, group members own 4 450 of the 5 000 housing association properties in Blackshaw.

An insurance firm is thinking of publishing a guidance booklet for managers of company car fleets. Its internal report on the idea begins:

AIM OF PROPOSED CAR FLEET MANAGEMENT GUIDE
This guide would have the objective of highlighting to car fleet managers the best way to achieve, and the benefits of adopting, a professional approach vis-à-vis managing a car fleet.
There are only a few publications at present covering the subject of car fleet management and with no current insurance company involvement there would appear to be a definite market niche for us to explore.

This makes sense but is far too flabby:

- 'Would have the objective of highlighting' is a wordy way of saying 'aims' or 'seeks'.
- In plain words, 'vis-à-vis' means 'towards' or 'to'.
- Sentences beginning 'there are', 'there is', and 'there were' are often wordy and reduce the strength of any remaining verbs. Two 'there' verbs are present here.
- In 'the subject of car fleet management', the first three words are redundant because readers know from the heading that 'car fleet management' is a subject.
- 'No current insurance company involvement' smothers the verb 'involve' (see chapter 5). In any case, a more expressive verb would be 'publish' or 'produce'.
- 'Insurance company' could be reduced to 'insurer'.

So a first redraft might say:

AIM OF PROPOSED CAR FLEET MANAGEMENT GUIDE
This guide would show car fleet managers how they could best achieve a professional approach to managing a car fleet and the benefits of doing so.
At present, only a few publications cover car fleet management. None of them is produced by insurers so there is a definite market niche for us to explore.

A second redraft would go a little further:

AIM OF PROPOSED CAR-FLEET MANAGEMENT GUIDE
This guide would show car-fleet managers how to do their work more professionally and why this would benefit them.
Few publications cover car-fleet management, none of them from insurers. So there is a market niche for us to exploit.

The original had 72 words, this has 48—a cut of one third. What remains is tight and doesn't waste the reader's time.

Resist the temptation to deluge your readers with verbal diarrhoea merely because your need is great and your cause is just. Here is a charity-shop manager trying to communicate a simple message to his boss, namely, 'Please arrange for the planned electrical tests to be postponed for two weeks as we're really busy just now':

Due to the stock overload, the start of the new academic year, and personal study pressure, I'd appreciate the shop not having the electricals tested until after 16 October.

Problems are caused by the shop's counter-cyclic relationship between customers and volunteers (demand is highest when courses start) and donations and volunteers (donations are highest when courses finish). Volunteers are highest in weeks 2–7 of the first two terms (exams in the third term). We estimate that we collected 350 bags of donations from the postgraduate room clearances, having distributed bags to 1,100 rooms. Note that we distributed 5,800 bags for the undergraduate room clearances, and estimate an effective return of 820–1,200 bags. I'll have worked at least 30 hours this week, and at least 45 hours last week (16-hour contract). I estimate that the undergraduate room clearances involved about 90 hours of voluntary overtime. Suffice to say, despite paperwork delays, when at the shop, I've been working almost non-stop for the past few months to cope with the room clearances.

This is due to the extreme pressure on the shop this week (the week before term starts). This week alone could easily beat August, coupled with the low availability of student volunteers who are starting new courses (currently we have two trained volunteers available, one of whom cannot use the till). The shop will then start having a donation drought. Due to the expected donations drought, we are storing some of the surplus in Cullen House, but we do not wish to do this for the books that we have an extreme demand for. Hence the stockroom is not accessible.

This week and the next two weeks are the shop's make or break weeks, and I need to concentrate on making money.

At least the author put his main points in the first paragraph (see chapter 16), but there's no wonder he's pressed for time.

Putting it all together

The chapter began by promising to cut more than a third from a letter to a mortgage payer. First, useless words can go:

Arrears ~~at present~~ subsist on your mortgage account ~~in the sum~~ of £1,032, with a further payment ~~becoming~~ due on ~~the~~ 11~~th~~ April. ~~In view of the account being a mortgage account~~, we are not in a position to stop interest being debited ~~each month~~ and ~~in order~~ to prevent the account ~~situation from~~ deteriorating, it is necessary that payments are received each month which represent the interest debit. At present this amount is £242 ~~and~~ therefore it is regretted that your offer to ~~make~~ pay~~ments in the sum of~~ £80 a month is not sufficient.

Then vigorous or useful words (underlined) can be grafted on:

The arrears ~~subsist~~ on your mortgage account ~~of~~ <u>are</u> £1 032, and ~~with~~ a further payment <u>is</u> due on 11 April. Regrettably we ~~are not in a position to~~ <u>cannot</u> stop interest being ~~debited~~ <u>charged</u>. Therefore, to prevent the ~~account from deteriorating,~~ arrears <u>growing</u>, ~~it is necessary that~~ <u>you will need to pay the interest charge</u> ~~are received~~ each month ~~which represent the interest debit~~. At present this ~~amount~~ is £242, ~~therefore~~ <u>so</u> ~~it is regretted~~ <u>we regret</u> that your offer to pay £80 a month is not sufficient.

So the final version is:

The arrears on your mortgage account are £1 032, and a further payment is due on 11 April. Regrettably we cannot stop interest being charged. Therefore, to prevent the arrears growing, you will need to pay the interest charge each month. At present this is £242, so we regret that your offer to pay £80 a month is not sufficient.

This is only 59 words, a cut of 38 per cent. It delivers the same facts and is just as courteous—perhaps more so. The ideal letter would also go on to offer the opportunity to discuss the matter and sources of help and advice.

Results from the focus group showed a strong preference for the final version over the original. The final version scored an average clarity mark of 17 points out of a possible 20, as against only 10 for the original. Twenty-nine people out of 34 preferred the final version.

4 Favouring the active voice

Guideline: *Prefer the active voice unless there's a good reason for using the passive.*

This sentence has an active-voice verb:

Fred is demolishing the building.

while this has a passive-voice verb:

The building is being demolished by Fred.

Instinctive use of the passive is widespread in business and government, fostered by bad teaching in schools and universities that equates good writing with excessive formality, obscurity, and Olympian detachment. Because the passive produces a style that helps students pass exams, many of them carry it into their working life where writing to inform—instead of writing to impress—should be their main goal. The boring, passive-infested style remains rife among academics, accountants, engineers, lawyers, and bureaucrats at all levels. So it's no surprise that an accountant's newsletter to clients includes this sentence in which five impersonal passives queue up to muddy the meaning:

Although the inflation factor can be used against bonds it can usually be assumed to be priced into the current yield of investment grade bonds the capital of which can be safely assumed to be repaid at maturity.

This chapter explains:

- the difference between active and passive
- how to convert one to the other
- why the active should be your first choice
- how 'I' and 'we' can make formal reports more readable, and
- when the passive can be useful.

Many writers have damned the passive voice unreservedly. In 1946, George Orwell wrote: 'Never use the passive where you can use the active'. But this is going much too far. Certainly the active tends to make the writing tighter, more personal, and introduces action earlier in sentences, while the passive tends to do the reverse. Yet the passive is still a valuable tool, as we'll see.

The words 'passive' and 'active' are well understood in their everyday meanings: 'Some men take an active role in infant care, but many are passive.' These everyday meanings differ from their grammatical ones. So, as you read this chapter, please suppress the everyday meanings as they don't apply here.

Recognizing active-voice verbs ('active verbs', for short)

Putting the 'doer' or agent—the person or thing doing the action in the sentence—in front of its verb will usually ensure that the verb is active. The following sentences all have active verbs (underlined) because the doers precede the verbs they govern:

> The President <u>wants</u> an improved health service.
> I <u>walked</u> up the stairs.
> She <u>hates</u> going to work.
> Ice cream <u>tastes</u> revolting.

Most of us favour active verbs when we speak. People would think you odd if you continually said things like 'The house is being bought by me' (passive) instead of 'I am buying the house' (active), though the meaning is the same if they are spoken with the same emphasis.

Occasionally a verb can be followed by a doer yet remain active:

> She used to hate going to work, said her sister.

Here 'her sister' follows 'said' but the verb is still in the active because 'said her sister' is grammatically identical to 'her sister said'.

In an example like 'Armies are on the march', the verb 'are' (part of 'to be') is called a linking or copular verb because there's no real action in it. It expresses a state and it's a bit like an equals sign. Linking verbs are always in the active voice. Other examples of them include 'seem', 'become', and 'get'.

Recognizing passive-voice verbs ('passive verbs', for short)

In most sentences with a passive verb, the doer follows the verb or isn't stated, as here (verbs underlined):

(a) Three mistakes <u>were admitted</u> by the director.
(b) Coastal towns <u>are being damaged</u> by storms.
(c) Verdicts <u>will</u> soon <u>be delivered</u> in the Smith case.

In (a) and (b), the doers ('director' and 'storms') follow the verbs through which they act. In (c), the doer is not stated; no one can tell who or what will give the verdicts.

To put (a) and (b) into the active, you simply bring the doer to the start of the sentence:

The director admitted three mistakes.
Storms are damaging coastal towns.

To convert (c) into the active, you would need to know the doer:

[The judge] will soon deliver verdicts in the Smith case.

An almost infallible test for passives is to check whether the verb consists of:

- part of the verb 'to be' (though this is sometimes implied rather than stated, as in many newspaper headlines where space is tight – 'Explorer [is] attacked in jungle'), and
- a past participle.

This is an easy test to apply if you can already recognize parts of 'to be' and past participles. If not, here's how:

Parts of the verb 'to be'

Present tense (explained in chapter 13): am, is, are, am being, is being, are being.
Past tenses: was, were, has been, have been, had been.
Future tense: will be, shall be.
Infinitive (explained in chapter 13 and below): to be.

Be careful, however, not to confuse parts of 'to be' with parts of 'to have', which are 'has', 'had', and 'have'. The difference is clear from the expressions 'You are a frog' and 'You have a frog'. The first is about being, the second about possession.

Past participle

All verbs have a past participle. To find it, begin with the infinitive form of the verb, for example:

to attract   to annoy   to decide   to go

Cross out 'to' and send the rest into the past tense:

~~to~~ attract + ed   ~~to~~ annoy + ed
~~to~~ decide + d   ~~to~~ go + ne or **went**

The first three are past participles. In the fourth, you need to apply a tie-break by putting 'we have' in front of each phrase, producing 'we have gone' and 'we have went'. Only the first of these makes sense in standard English, so 'gone' is the past participle while 'went' is just a past tense. The tie-break is useful because some common verbs have two candidates for past participle: 'see' (seen/saw); 'eat' (eaten/ate); 'take' (taken/took); and 'give' (given/gave). Applying the tie-break reveals that the first alternative is the past participle in each case.

Applying the full test for passives to the example sentences, it's clear they all fulfil its criteria:

(a) Three mistakes <u>were admitted</u> by the director.
(b) Coastal towns <u>are being damaged</u> by storms.
(c) Verdicts <u>will</u> soon <u>be delivered</u> in the Smith case.

In (c) the fact that 'soon' is splitting the verb makes no difference—the verb 'will be delivered' is still passive.

Computerized grammar checkers search for passives by applying the same test. Unfortunately this will occasionally throw up phantom passives. For example, 'is tired' would be flagged as a passive in the sentence:

A man who is tired of London is tired of life.

as it appears to fulfil the criteria of having part of 'to be' and the past participle of 'to tire'. But it cannot be a passive because no doer can be attached to 'is tired' and none is implied. 'Tired' in each case is a description of the man, not part of the verb. The word 'is' is a linking verb in the active voice. The same logic applies to sentences like this:

The pilots are concerned about the new runway.

—where 'are' is active and 'concerned' is not part of the verb 'to concern' but a description of the pilots' state of mind.

Converting passives to actives

Though using the active in the examples that follow will produce only small gains in clarity and economy, a general preference for active over passive will significantly improve the readability of most documents.

A financial adviser writes to his client:

> **We have been asked by your home insurers to obtain your written confirm-ation that all their requirements have been completed by yourself.**

By applying the test, 'have been asked' and 'have been completed' are revealed as passives. Use of the active, putting the doers in front of the verbs, would give:

> **Your home insurers have asked us to obtain your written confirmation that you have completed all their requirements.**

Would the focus group prefer either version, as the only difference is in the use of active and passive? Though the group regarded both as clear (13 points out of 20 for the passive sentence, 17 for the active), 28 people out of 35 preferred the active—a striking result.

A safety official writes (passives underlined):

> **A recommendation <u>was made</u> by inspectors that consideration <u>be given</u> by the company to the fitting of an interlock trip between the ventilation systems to prevent cell pressurisation.**

Converting passive to active, the sentence becomes (actives under-lined):

> **Inspectors <u>made</u> a recommendation that the company <u>give</u> consideration to the fitting of an interlock trip between the ventilation systems to prevent cell pressurisation.**

Then, using the strong verbs hidden beneath 'recommendation' and 'consideration', the sentence becomes even crisper—and ten words shorter than the original:

> **Inspectors <u>recommended</u> that the company <u>consider</u> fitting an interlock trip between the ventilation systems to prevent cell pressurisation.**

In the focus group, 18 people out of 35 preferred this final version over the passive sentence. Nine preferred the passive, while the others couldn't decide.

Verbs provide so much useful information that readers often prefer to get them early in sentences; this tends to happen when the verbs are active. Placing an important verb late forces readers to store large chunks of text in their short-term memory while they wait to discover the doer and what the action will be. The problem is worsened if there are other hurdles, like brackets containing exceptions and qualifications:

> **If you decide to cancel your application, a cheque for the amount of your investment (subject to a deduction of the amount (if any) by which the value of your investment has fallen at the date at which your cancellation form is received by us) will be sent to you.**

'You decide' and 'has fallen' are active, while 'is received' and 'will be sent' are passive. 'Will be sent' should be converted into the active because it is too far (36 words) from the noun it refers to, which is 'cheque'. This single change would produce:

> **If you decide to cancel your application, <u>we will send you</u> a cheque for the amount of your investment (subject to a deduction of the amount (if any) by which the value of your investment has fallen at the date at which your cancellation form is received by us) ~~will be sent to you~~.**

This would be the first stage in a comprehensive kill of brackets and other debris that would produce:

> **If you decide to cancel your application, we will send you a cheque for the amount of your investment less any fall in its value at the date we receive your cancellation form.**

This is a third shorter than the original. Using the active voice has enabled other good writing practices to come in.

The passive voice tends to make companies look uptight, defensive, evasive, and unapproachable, as in this sentence in an annual benefits statement to an investor:

> **Benefits from contributions invested in the With-Profits Fund are not guaranteed and are dependent on the bonuses declared by us.**

The passives are '[are] invested', 'are guaranteed', and '[are] declared', while 'are dependent' is a feeble form of 'depend'. With five active-voice verbs the sentence would sound more open:

> **We can't guarantee the benefits you'll get from contributions we've invested on your behalf in the With-Profits Fund. These benefits will depend on the bonuses we declare.**

Using 'I' or 'we' in formal reports

The myth that 'I' and 'we' should be avoided in formal reports has crippled many writers, causing them to adopt clumsy and confusing constructions like referring to themselves as 'the writer' or 'the author' and using impersonal passives like 'it is thought', 'it is felt', 'it is believed', 'it is understood', and

It is considered that fluoridation of drinking water is beneficial to health.

from which readers have to guess who is expressing the view: the writer, wider scientific opinion, public opinion, or all three. In reports, readers should not have to guess. Attempts to ban 'I' and 'we' are particularly strange in that any other person, creature, or thing may be mentioned in a report. Oddly, one group of diehards against the use of 'I', 'me', and 'my' are newspaper columnists, who often refer to themselves as 'this columnist', 'this column', 'your correspondent', and even 'this sketch'.

The strength of opposition to personal pronouns sometimes gives the impression they are a daring and revolutionary device. Yet personal pronouns in official documents are nothing new. In 1877 the British government was eager to investigate 'mechanical contrivances invented for economizing the labour of writing by hand' and appointed a committee to 'inquire into copying machines, departmental printing, &c'. Its often quaintly written report, which includes such headings as 'The Type Writer', 'The Type Writer discussed', and 'Its adoption likewise advocated', regularly uses 'we' and 'our':

We have visited all the chief public Departments in London...
How far these objects have been satisfactorily attained, and how far such contrivances may be usefully applied in public Departments, it has been our duty to consider and report. We shall first briefly describe the various processes which have been brought under our notice.

If you are writing on your own behalf, use 'I' and 'my' when they help you to state your case, but don't overdo it for fear of seeming self-centred. If you are writing on behalf of two or more people, let 'we' and 'our' do the same job. If there is some overriding reason why these tactics are impossible, you should still make sure that most of your sentences have doers—perhaps the name of your section, department, or organization.

Writers of scientific and technical material will especially benefit from using 'I' and 'we', which are becoming commonplace in many journals including the *British Medical Journal*. Unless a journal specifically prohibits these words—and most do not—you should feel free to use them. It's true that you can often omit personal pronouns by careful rewriting:

We discussed the benefits of recycling nuclear waste by home-composting methods in paragraph 3.

which becomes

Paragraph 3 discusses the benefits of recycling nuclear waste by home-composting methods.

– but the outcome is not always as neat and clear as that.

Almost everyone who writes about scientific and technical writing recommends personal pronouns. As Turk and Kirkman put it in *Effective Writing* (Spon, 1989): '. . . there is no good reason why personal pronouns should be scrupulously avoided. Readers are aware they are reading about the work of people, and their assessment of the experimental work reported will include an assessment of the personal competence of the scientist. It is artificial to avoid personal references in scientific writing.' So don't be seduced by the idea that impersonal writing makes you sound more scientific: no one ever became a scientist by wearing a white laboratory coat.

Warning: passives can be useful

Passive verbs have their uses and it would be silly—as well as futile—for the style police to outlaw them. There are five main reasons for using them:

- To defuse hostility—actives can sometimes be too direct and blunt.
- To avoid having to say who did the action, perhaps because the doer is irrelevant or obvious from the context.
- To focus attention on the receiver of the action by putting it first – 'An 18-year-old girl has been arrested by police in connection with the Blankshire murders.'
- To spread or evade responsibility by omitting the doer, for example: 'Regrettably, your file has been lost.'

- To help in positioning old or known information at the start of a sentence or clause, and new information at the end.

The last point relates to an important benefit of the passive. Read these two sentences about a nuclear reactor:

> Concern has been raised about arrangements for gaining immediate access to the chimney. Winch failure or the presence of debris between the platform edge and the chimney internal wall may necessitate access.

The second sentence, written in the active voice, doesn't seem to follow from the first, whose primary focus—placed late in the sentence—is about gaining access. Now try it with the second sentence in the passive voice:

> Concern has been raised about arrangements for gaining immediate access to the chimney. Access may be needed if the winch fails or there are debris between the platform edge and the chimney internal wall.

The topic of the second sentence, access, is now introduced early in that sentence and developed. There's a clear link between the focus of the first sentence and the topic of the second—a common device that helps the writing to flow by taking the reader from the known to the unknown. As in the example, this can often be done best by using the passive.

Checking your passive percentage

Manually or by using a computerized language checker like Style-Writer or Word, you can see how many passives you use. Your passive percentage is given by the formula:

100 × (Number of passives ÷ number of sentences)

If you score over 50 per cent (that's one passive every two sentences) check your verbs carefully. Do you really need so many passives?

5 Using vigorous verbs, and untying noun strings

Guideline: *Use clear, crisp, lively verbs to express the actions in your document, and avoid using noun strings.*

Good verbs give your writing its power and passion and delicacy. It's a simple truth that in most sentences you should express the action through verbs, just as you do when you speak. Yet in so many sentences the verbs are smothered, all their vitality trapped beneath heavy noun phrases based on the smothered verbs themselves. This chapter is about releasing the power in these verbs.

Business and official writing uses plenty of smothered verbs:

- People don't *apply* for a travel pass, they make an application.
- Speakers don't *inform* the public, they give information.
- Officials don't urgently *consider* a request, they give it urgent consideration.
- Staff don't *evaluate* a project, they perform an evaluation.
- Scientists don't *analyse* or *review* data, they conduct an analysis or carry out a review.
- Citizens don't *renew* their library books, they carry out a process of library-book renewal.

In each case the simple verb (in italics) is being converted into a noun that needs support from another verb. The technical term for a noun that masks a verb in this way is *nominalization*. There's nothing wrong with nominalization as such—it's a useful part of the language. But overusing it tends to freeze-frame the action.

The examples in this chapter show how vigorous verbs can improve sentences containing nominalizations, making them more powerful and concise. I discuss three types of construction:

- Nominalization linked to parts of 'to be' or 'to have'.
- Nominalization linked to active verbs or infinitives.
- Nominalization linked to passive verbs.

Nominalization linked to parts of 'to be' or 'to have'

Parts of 'to be' include 'are', 'is', 'was', 'were', 'has been', and 'have been'. Parts of 'to have' include 'has', 'had', and 'have'.

Many sentences whose only verbs are parts of 'to be' or 'to have' are perfectly clear and crisp, for example:

All animals are equal, but some animals are more equal than others.
To be or not to be: that is the question.
Detailed management information is available.

In other sentences, the linking of such a verb with a nominalization is a good reason for suspecting that improvement is possible, as in this example from an official letter:

I have now had sight of your letter to Mr Jones.

The main verb is 'had' while the nominalization is 'sight', which smothers 'see'. So it would be simpler to say:

I have now <u>seen</u> your letter...

This example is from a business letter:

Funding and waste management have a direct effect on progress towards the decommissioning of plant and equipment.

The main verb is 'have' while the nominalization is 'effect', which smothers 'affect'. It is crisper to write:

Funding and waste management <u>directly affect</u> progress...

A combination of part of 'to be' and a nominalization is easy to see in this example:

The original intention of the researchers was to discover the state of the equipment.

The nominalization is 'intention', smothering 'intend', while 'was' acts as a prop. A revision would say:

Originally the researchers <u>intended</u> to discover...

This example is from a report:

There is therefore an expectation on our part that the land will be used for building.

which becomes:

> So we <u>expect</u> that the land will be used for building.

Nominalization linked to active verbs or infinitives

This construction is easy to rewrite as the presence of active verbs usually enables the word order to be preserved.

A group of conservationists is writing to a local government department:

> The group considers that the director of community services should proceed with the introduction of as many mini-recycling centres as the budget allows.

The nominalization is 'introduction', supported by 'proceed with'. The rewrite would use the active voice to revive the smothered verb 'introduce':

> The group considers that the director of community services should <u>introduce</u> as many mini-recycling centres as the budget allows.

A company report explains what some of the staff do:

> The team's role is to perform problem definition and resolution.

Two nominalizations, 'definition' and 'resolution', are supported by 'to perform'. Using the smothered verbs 'define' and 'resolve', this becomes:

> The team's role is to <u>define</u> problems and <u>resolve</u> them.

or

> The team's role is to <u>define</u> and <u>resolve</u> problems.

or, risking a slight change of meaning:

> The team <u>defines</u> and <u>resolves</u> problems.

A government department writes:

> The policy branch has carried out a review of our forms and procedures in order to effect improvements in the reporting of accidents.

Here there are two nominalizations, 'review' and 'improvements', supported by 'carried out' and 'effect' respectively. Using vigorous verbs would produce:

The policy branch has reviewed our forms and procedures in order to improve the reporting of accidents.

or, putting the purpose first:

To improve the reporting of accidents, the policy branch has reviewed our forms and procedures.

It's also possible to convert noun-heavy writing into bullet-point lists. Instead of:

Meeting the new lead-in-water standards requires a combination of plumbo-solvency reduction and lead pipework replacement operations.

it would be simpler to write

To meet the new lead-in-water standards we are:

• reducing the level of dissolved lead in the water, and
• replacing lead pipework.

Nominalizations linked to passive verbs

This construction is harder to revise because changing from passive to active disrupts the original word order. To compensate, though, the satisfaction is usually greater.

A housing association writes:

Notification has been received from the insurers that they wish to re-issue the Tenants Scheme Policy.

The nominalization is 'notification' and the passive is 'has been received'. Using the smothered verb 'notify' produces:

The insurers have notified us that they wish to re-issue the Tenants Scheme Policy.

A safety officer writes:

An examination of the maintenance records for the plant was carried out by Mr Patel.

This becomes, by the same technique:

Mr Patel examined the maintenance records for the plant.

A company writes:

A reduction in payroll costs can be achieved if payslip printing is no longer required.

The nominalizations are 'reduction' and 'printing', supported by 'be achieved' and 'is required'. Making the writing more verby will produce:

Payroll costs will fall if payslips are no longer printed.

or

If we stop printing payslips, our payroll costs will fall.

When the going gets tougher

Sometimes the difficulties are harder to spot. But remember the common signals—nominalizations (often ending in -*ion*), passive voice, the verbs 'make' and 'carry out', and verbs derived from 'to be' or 'to have'.

A local government department writes:

The committee made a resolution that a study be carried out by officials into the feasibility of the provision of bottle banks in the area.

The rewriting task can be split into three operations:

1 The nominalization 'resolution' becomes a strong verb: 'The committee *resolved* that'.
2 The nominalization 'study' becomes the active verb 'study': 'officials should *study*'.
3 The nominalization 'provision' becomes a present participle (see chapter 13): 'the feasibility of *providing* bottle banks in the area'.

So the complete rewrite is:

The committee resolved that officials should study the feasibility of providing bottle banks in the area.

or

The committee resolved that officials should investigate whether it is feasible to provide bottle banks in the area.

An accountant writes:

> The incidence of serious monetary losses in several transactions entered into by the firm during the year is causing us great concern.

'Incidence', meaning 'rate of occurrence', isn't derived directly from a verb. Here it is probably used as a posh way of saying 'occurrence'. The verb of choice would be 'occur', so a rewrite could say:

> The serious monetary losses that have occurred in several transactions entered into by the firm during the year are causing us great concern.

Then, reorganizing this so that the main doer comes first, the result would be:

> We are very concerned about serious monetary losses in several of the firm's transactions during the year.

or

> The firm has lost large amounts in several transactions this year, which concerns us greatly.

These word-savings would be too small a gain to justify the effort, if brevity was the only criterion. More important is that the sentences can now be read without stumbling and backtracking to get the meaning.

Untying noun strings

In most well-written sentences, nouns tend not to lie next to each other. Normally starved of familiar company, when they are eventually bundled together by an unthinking author, they often couple promiscuously and spawn that loathsome love child of business writing, the noun string. Here are a few such:

- National Performance Framework Service Delivery Plan
- Employee Job Consultation (Appraisal) Scheme
- community capacity enhancement initiative
- Voluntary Accidental Death and Dismemberment Plan
- affordable housing special/specific needs provision targets
- advanced practice succession planning development pathway

and, in a surprising job advertisement from Manchester City Council in 2008:

- Teenage Pregnancy Implementation Manager.

What to do about them? Try to break them up. Instead of 'service user suggestion scheme', try 'suggestion scheme for users of our service'. Instead of 'advanced practice development needs analysis tool', try 'needs analysis tool for advanced practice development'. In other words, try to figure out what the noun string means (if anything), then add new words to help readers get the idea.

6 Using vertical lists

Guideline: *Use vertical lists to break up complicated text.*
Vertical lists have become a common feature of many documents
since the 1970s, helping to present complex information in manageable chunks. For example, instead of saying this:

> The Moorside Plan is a new way of planning for the future of our area. It will set
> the framework within which we plan for the future and includes important
> choices about development within Moorside. It will provide us with a clear
> vision to guide development to 2016 and will promote measures to improve
> our economy, provide the homes we need, and protect our environment.

we could say this:

> The Moorside Plan is a new way of planning for the future of our area, which
> will:
>
> - set the framework within which we plan for the future
> - include important choices about development in Moorside
> - give us a clear vision to guide development to 2016, and
> - promote measures to improve our economy, provide the homes we need,
>   and protect our environment.

Though this takes a bit more space, it's very easy to grasp.

Vertical lists can cause problems in three areas:

- keeping the listed items in parallel
- punctuating the listed items, and
- numbering the listed items.

Let's examine each in turn.

Keeping the listed items in parallel

A dietitian is explaining how a patient should cut her salt consumption:

> To restrict your salt intake, you should:
>
> - not add salt at the table
> - use only a little salt in cooking

- do not use bicarbonate of soda or baking powder in cooking
- avoid salty food like tinned fish, roasted peanuts, olives.

All the listed items are understandable individually and they are all commands, so to that extent they are in parallel. But the third point doesn't fit with the lead-in or 'platform' statement. Together they are saying:

you <u>should do not use</u> bicarbonate of soda or baking powder in cooking

which is nonsense. Obviously, 'do' should be struck out to create a true parallel structure:

To restrict your salt intake, you should:

- not add salt at the table
- use only a little salt in cooking
- not use bicarbonate of soda or baking powder in cooking
- avoid salty food like tinned fish, roasted peanuts, olives.

But the job isn't complete, as there's now an odd mixture of positive and negative. The best solution may be to shift the remaining positive statement into the platform:

To restrict your salt intake, you should use only a little salt in cooking and you should not:

- add salt at the table
- use bicarbonate of soda or baking powder in cooking, or
- eat salty food like tinned fish, roasted peanuts, and olives.

Sometimes a platform needs to be created to maintain the parallel structure. Here, a clerk is being told how to do a task:

- You should check that the details on the self-certificate or medical certificate match those on the person's information card.
- You should check that the certificate has been completed correctly and conforms to the rules on validity.
- That the certificate covers the period of absence.

By the third item the writer must have become tired of writing 'you should check that'. Rather than omit it, he or she should have converted it into a platform, producing:

You should check that:

- the details on the self-certificate or medical certificate match those on the person's information card

- the certificate has been completed correctly and conforms to the rules on validity, and
- the certificate covers the period of absence.

Often a vertical list is easier to read if each listed item has a similar grammatical structure. For example, they could all be statements that begin with infinitives or active verbs or passive verbs or present participles (see chapter 13 for explanations). In the following list, all the listed items are passive-verb statements, underlined for ease of reference:

The inspector should check that:

- the vehicle is properly marked with hazard plates
- the engine and cab heater are switched off during the loading and unloading of explosives
- any tobacco or cigarettes are kept in a suitable container and matches or cigarette lighters are not being kept in the cab[, and]
- the explosives are securely stowed[.]

There would be no harm in adding some active-voice statements as long as they made sense when linked to the platform:

- there are no unsecured metal objects in the vehicle's load-carrying compartments, and
- the vehicle is carrying one or more efficient fire extinguishers.

When statements with different grammatical structure are mixed haphazardly, the reader has to stop and backtrack. In this example, the listed items have infinitives, actives, passives, or no verbs at all:

When the committee began work, it established the following aims:

- make the regulations simple to understand and up to date in structure and layout
- to update forms and leaflets where necessary with details of current fees
- the effects of competition will be considered
- the creation of a document summarizing details of the regulations, which will enable people to focus on key issues and requirements
- recent changes in legislation should be taken into account.

As these points are supposed to be aims, they could all be written as infinitives:

When the committee began work, it established the following aims:

- to make the regulations simple to understand and up to date in structure and layout

- to update forms and leaflets where necessary with details of current fees
- to consider the effects of competition ~~will be considered~~
- to create ~~the creation of~~ a document summarizing details of the regulations, which will enable people to focus on key issues and requirements
- to take account of recent changes in legislation ~~should be taken into account~~.

Readers get used to the pattern here; they can then concentrate better on the meaning.

Punctuating the listed items

Vertical lists need punctuating as consistently as possible so that readers get used to a pattern and are not distracted by deviations. Here is a typical example of inconsistency:

The new job-holder will:
- develop a set of guidelines for clean wastepaper recycling
- Introduce green bins for clean wastepaper at appropriate places;
- monitor compliance with departmental targets.

Two of the listed items begin with a lower-case letter and one with a capital. One of them ends with a semicolon, another with a full stop, and the first with nothing at all.

For greater consistency, I suggest a two-part standard for all except legal documents.

The first part of the standard is that when a listed item is a sentence or sentence fragment that relies on the platform statement to give it meaning, it should begin with a lower-case letter and end without punctuation—except for the final item, which should normally end with a full stop. This produces the following result:

The new job-holder will:
- develop a set of guidelines for clean wastepaper recycling
- introduce green bins for clean wastepaper at appropriate places
- monitor compliance with departmental targets.

You could add a comma and 'and' after each of the first two items or, more conventionally, after the second item only. If you wanted to show that only one of the jobs had to be done, you would put 'or' after each comma or, more conventionally, after the final comma only:

The new job-holder will:

- **develop a set of guidelines for clean wastepaper recycling**
- **introduce green bins for clean wastepaper at appropriate places, or**
- **monitor compliance with departmental targets.**

Alternatively you could use this kind of set-up, which stresses the 'or':

The new job-holder will:

> - **develop a set of guidelines for clean wastepaper recycling,**
>
> or • **introduce green bins for clean wastepaper at appropriate places,**
>
> or • **monitor compliance with departmental targets.**

Rarely will you want to continue a sentence beyond a list as this could overburden the reader's short-term memory. If you do, your last listed item can end with a comma and the sentence should continue with a lower-case letter:

The new job-holder will:

- **develop a set of guidelines for clean wastepaper recycling**
- **introduce green bins for clean wastepaper at appropriate places, and**
- **monitor compliance with departmental targets,**

but the work must always take place within existing budgetary limits.

The second part of the standard applies to listed items that are complete sentences and don't depend on the platform statement to give them meaning. These should begin with a capital and end with a full stop. For example:

The speaker made three points:

- **Aboriginal people across the world have been persecuted in the name of civilization and religion.**
- **Even so-called enlightened governments have broken treaties made in good faith by aboriginals.**
- **Despair among aboriginals will lead either to their cultural disintegration or uprisings against authority.**

This treatment is particularly useful when a listed item is long and detailed, perhaps with several separate sentences, as it would seem odd if the listed item began with a lower-case letter and went on with a new sentence.

The two-part standard above differs from that given in earlier editions of the book, which used more semicolons at the end of listed items. This is because people seem to prefer the cleaner, more informal look that comes from using less punctuation in vertical lists. In legal documents, though, it is probably safer to use semicolons after all items in the first part of the standard. So a typical list would be:

The tenant must:

- **keep the garden and communal areas tidy and free of rubbish;**
- **pay the rent on time; and**
- **allow our staff to enter the property immediately without notice in an emergency.**

Numbering the listed items

There's no need to number the listed items if you or the reader won't need to refer to them again or if you wish to avoid suggesting that the items are in order of priority. Instead, just use a dash followed by a space, or a bullet •.

Other options are arabic numbers (1, 2, 3) or bracketed letters (a), (b), (c) or, as a last resort, bracketed roman numerals (i), (ii), (iii). Roman numerals can be used if you need to put a list within a list—more common in legal documents than in everyday writing:

The court may in an order made by it in relation to a regulated agreement include provisions:

(a) **making the operation of any term of the order conditional on the doing of specified acts by any party;**

(b) **suspending the operation of any term of the order:**
    (i) **until the court subsequently directs; or**
    (ii) **until the occurrence of a specified act or omission.**

Seeing the possibility for vertical lists

Sometimes the only method of enlivening and clarifying a piece of dreary text is a vertical list, so you need to be alert to the possibility. The following example is the first part of a local authority's

information leaflet to students explaining whether they are entitled
to some money:

Maintenance grants when studying abroad
Students of modern languages
A student of modern languages is defined by the regulations as a student
whose course 'includes the study of one or more modern languages other
than English for not less than half of the time spent studying the course and
which includes periods of residence in a country whose language is a main
language of the course'.

This seems at first to be beyond improvement—it is almost a
straight quote from a regulation so a paraphrase may have unwanted
results. Yet if you examine it from the reader's viewpoint, hope
begins to emerge. You can see that the focus should really be
on the effect of the regulations on the student, not on what the
regulations say, while 'includes' is used twice, suggesting the possibility of a vertical list. Using these levers, you can personalize
the information, switch it into question-and-answer style, and introduce a list. Through a bit of trial and error, you can produce something like this before getting your in-house lawyers to check it
for accuracy:

Maintenance grants when studying abroad
Who can get a maintenance grant?
You can get a grant if you are a student of modern languages. According to
the regulations, this means that your course must include both:

- the study of one or more modern languages (except English) for at least
  half the course time, and
- periods of residence in a country whose language is a main language of the
  course.

7 Converting negative to positive

Guideline: *Put your points positively when you can.*

'You've got to accentuate the positive, eliminate the negative', according to the Johnny Mercer song popularized by Bing Crosby in the 1940s. In writing, negatives include 'un-' words like 'unnecessary' and 'unless'; verbs with negative associations like 'avoid' and 'undo'; and the obvious ones like 'not', 'no', 'except', 'less than', 'not less than', and 'not more than'. When readers are faced with a negative, they must first imagine the positive alternative, then mentally cancel it out. So when a newspaper declares:

> It is surely less painful to be unemployed if one is not sober, drug-free and filled with a desire to work.

or when a gardening leaflet advises novice growers:

> Do not assume that if the weather is not warm the soil is not dry.

readers have to work very hard to get the meaning, and they are likely to make the wrong guess. Does the gardening sentence mean 'your soil could be dry even in cold weather', or does it mean 'your soil could be wet even in cold weather'? The context gives little help.

A single negative is unlikely to cause problems, though many a British voter has paused, pen poised, when confronted with the polling-booth challenge:

> Vote for not more than one candidate.

instead of the plainer and positive:

> Vote for one candidate only.

When two, three, or more negatives coexist in the same sentence, meaning may become obscure, as in this note from a lawyer to his client, an underwriter:

> Underwriters are, we consider, free to form the view that James Brothers have <u>not yet proved</u> to their satisfaction that the short-landed bags were <u>not discharged</u> from the ship, and were <u>not lost</u> in transit between Antwerp and Dieppe, when they were <u>not covered</u> by this insurance policy.

—a rodeo ride that perhaps only the lawyer who created it could negotiate without falling off. The going is almost as difficult in this pension contract:

> 'Dependent relative' includes a member's child or adopted child who has <u>not attained</u> the age of 18 or has <u>not ceased</u> to receive full-time education or training.

Put positively this would say:

> 'Dependent relative' includes a member's child or adopted child who is <u>aged 17 or under</u> or is in full-time education or training.

Just as 'at least' is a good alternative to 'not less than', the word 'only'—which is positive but restrictive—is a useful converter of negative to positive:

> The government will not consent to an application if those with a legal interest in the common land object to the application, except in exceptional circumstances.

'Not' and 'except' both vanish under the influence of 'only':

> Only in exceptional circumstances will the government consent to an application if those with a legal interest in the common land object to the application.

or

> If those with a legal interest in the common land object to an application, the government will consent to it only in exceptional circumstances.

This note was sent to a parent of a child with special needs (learning difficulties) by a local education authority:

> It is unusual for us not to be able to find a place for a child with special needs in one of our schools.

People can easily misinterpret the double negative as a single negative and think it means 'We cannot usually...', especially if they are used to getting negative replies from authority figures. The intended meaning, of course, is positive:

> We can usually find a place for a child with special needs in one of our schools.

Some bodies, particularly ombudsmen and tribunals, seem addicted to elaborate negativity:

- I see no reason why the firm should not require properly prepared supporting bills.
  (Meaning: 'It is reasonable for the firm to ask you for proper receipts.')

- The authority's actions do not appear to be unreasonable in the circumstances.

  (Meaning: 'The authority seems to have acted reasonably.')

- It is difficult to say what, if any, difference this information would have made to the councillors' assessment of your request. However, I do not believe I can safely say that it would definitely have made no difference.

  (Meaning: 'I do not know whether this information would have affected the councillors' assessment, but it might have done.')

- Having reviewed the application, the Board is not of the view that there is no reasonable likelihood that the applicants can establish a violation of the Act based on the allegations they have made in the application. Accordingly, the request by the responding party to dismiss this application at this stage is hereby dismissed.

  (Which seems to mean: 'The Board has reviewed the application. It has decided that the applicants are reasonably likely to be able to establish a violation of the Act based on their allegations in the application. The Board therefore dismisses the request by the responding party to dismiss the application. So the application stands.')

Clearly there can be a difference in meaning between an action being 'not unreasonable' and just plain 'reasonable'. But always ask yourself whether such distinctions are worth making in the particular case.

Negative words sometimes obscure a positive message. Here, a housing association is writing to local residents:

> Although we have developed alternatives where traditional residents associations are not well supported, four well-run and representative associations are active and continue to receive our support at Halfwood, Sockam, Haig Green and West Evesham.

Which could be put more positively as:

> We continue to support four active, well-run, and representative associations at Halfwood, Sockam, Haig Green, and West Evesham. Where traditional residents associations are not so well supported, we have developed alternatives.

And words like 'unless' and 'unlikely' cast such a pall of gloom that readers are as likely to slit their wrists as take the matter further:

> Unless you are qualified it is unlikely that you will be able to offer professional support.

—which may mean, more cheerfully:

> **To offer this kind of paid support, you will usually need to be professionally qualified.**

Rules from the European Commission are a fertile source of multiple negatives, as in this 67-word sentence from, ironically, a regulation on public access to documents (EC1049/2001):

> **Even though it is neither the object nor the effect of this Regulation to amend national legislation on access to documents, it is nevertheless clear that, by virtue of the principle of loyal cooperation which governs relations between the institutions and the Member States, Member States should take care not to hamper the proper application of this Regulation and should respect the security rules of the institutions.**

—which, with fewer negatives and a vertical list, could become:

> **This Regulation does not amend or seek to amend national legislation on access to documents. Yet the principle of loyal cooperation that governs relations between the institutions and the Member States means that Member States should:**
>
> **(a) take care not to hamper the proper application of this Regulation; and**
> **(b) respect the security rules of the institutions.**

Negatives are, of course, useful. Many commands are more powerful in the negative, which is why they have a place in procedures and instruction manuals. Even a double negative like:

> **Do not switch on the power unless you have made all the necessary checks.**

is probably more forceful than

> **Only switch on the power when you have made the necessary checks.**

Negatives also contribute to the vein of sardonic wit in the British character. Oscar Wilde, for example, described fox-hunters as 'the unspeakable in full pursuit of the uneatable', while Winston Churchill described Montgomery, one of his most successful generals, as 'in defeat unbeatable; in victory unbearable'. Double negatives are a staple of songwriters' exotic grammar, as in the Leiber and Stoller hit 'Hound Dog' (1952):

> **You ain't nothin' but a hound dog/Cryin' all the time/You ain't nothin' but a hound dog/Cryin' all the time/Well, you ain't never caught a rabbit/And you ain't no friend of mine.**

But avoid overusing negatives if clarity is the aim, and make sure that those you use are necessary.

8 Cross-references, cross readers

Guideline: *Reduce cross-references to a minimum.*
The British government has sent me a 26-page form that includes 183 questions, 70 separate paragraphs of notes, and about 125 cross-references from questions to notes. A tax schedule to the Finance No 2 Act of 1992 includes about 40 internal cross-references, forwards and backwards. In both cases, I am hurled from point to point like a pinball from the flippers.

In any complex document some cross-references are inevitable but they should be kept to the minimum. Unless they are carefully controlled, this kind of horror from a pension policy is the likely result:

> In the event of the policyholder being alive on the vesting date and having given (or being deemed to have given) appropriate notice in accordance with provision 11.4 the provisions set out in this provision 5 shall apply provided that where by reason of the policy-holder's exercise of the option under provision 6.2 or 6.3 the vesting date is a day which is not the specified date, provision 5 shall apply subject to any consequential alterations arising under the relevant part of provision 6.

Plain English can't improve this very much. The only hope is to scrap it and start again. If the point can't be made in a way that people can understand, it may not be worth making at all: the scheme underlying the policy might need to be simplified.

Skeins of cross-references are not always so hopelessly tangled. Here's an example from an investment policy:

> If you choose to receive income payments from your investment within the policy, subject as provided in clause 12, income (including tax credits) will be paid to you (subject to such sums being available first to pay any sums due to Unicorn Unit Trusts Limited under clause 9) monthly or quarterly and at any level you choose between a minimum of 5 per cent and a maximum of 10 per cent (in increments of 0.5 per cent) based on either a percentage of your original investment or the value of your policy at the time you choose to start making withdrawals.

To isolate and jot down the main points in this 101-word sentence is not easy but it will go a long way towards clearing up the mess:

1 If you have chosen to draw income from the investment, we'll pay it to you, monthly or quarterly.
2 How much we pay you could be affected by clause 12 and by Unicorn's charges set out in clause 9.
3 We'll pay you whatever percentage you choose—within certain limits—of your original investment or of the value of your investment at the time you start to make withdrawals.

By putting these points in 1–3–2 order, the cross-references can be grouped into a separate sentence at the end. The result might say this, using short sentences and paragraphs:

If you choose to draw income payments from your investment in the policy, we will pay them to you monthly or quarterly. The payments will include tax credits.

The payments you choose must be a percentage of your original investment or of the value of your investment at the time you start receiving the income. Your choice of percentage must be at least 5 per cent but not more than 10 per cent (using 0.5 per cent steps).

Payments are subject to clause 12 and are available first to pay any money owed to Unicorn Unit Trusts Limited under clause 9.

This is still not simple because the ideas themselves are complicated and, though the word count is the same, more space is needed. But now readers have a much better chance of understanding the points, and can ask sensible questions if they need more information.

9 Using good punctuation

Guideline: *Put accurate punctuation at the heart of your writing.*
Punctuation shouldn't cause as much fear as it does. Only about a dozen marks need to be mastered and the guidelines are fairly simple. You can buy a cheap punctuation lesson every day in the newspapers, where 99 per cent of it will accord with the advice given here. You'll also see the full range of marks, as journalists—especially the star columnists—use far more colons, semicolons, and dashes than business and official writers.

The rumour has got about that any old punctuation, or none at all, will do. This is as bad a fallacy as saying that any old words in any old order will do as long as readers can pick up the general idea. A good command of punctuation helps you to say more, say it more interestingly and exactly, and be understood at first reading. Punctuation is an essential part of the tool kit—as important as choosing the right words.

Consider these statements:

Father to be attacked on waste land.
Once she had the dress off she would go in search of matching shoes, gloves, and a handbag.

Without good punctuation they can be interpreted in different ways, distracting the readers and causing them to stop and backtrack. Punctuation helps to fix the meaning and smooth the path:

Father-to-be attacked on waste land.
Once she had the dress, off she would go in search of matching shoes, gloves, and a handbag.

The story is told of a school inspector who criticized a teacher for spending too much time on punctuation with his class. The teacher claimed punctuation was crucial to understanding, which the inspector denied. The teacher wrote on the whiteboard: 'The inspector said the teacher is an idiot.' He then inserted two commas, to give: 'The inspector, said the teacher, is an idiot.' Case proved.

Punctuation shows how words and strings of words are related, separated, and emphasized, so its main purpose is to help the reader understand the construction of the sentence. A lesser purpose is to act as a substitute for the devices we all use in speech, such as pausing and altering pitch; but an idea such as 'use a comma when you would have a one-beat pause in speech, a semicolon for a two-beat pause, and a full stop for a three-beat pause' is unhelpful because it can be interpreted in too many ways. Even so, you might want to read a sentence aloud to help you decide how to punctuate it.

Though this chapter describes the standards that most careful writers accept as sound, no two writers will ever agree on the position of every comma and full stop. So if you are editing someone's writing, be prepared for a bit of give and take.

Today, even careful writers have to face the fact that fine distinctions between such marks as colons and semicolons will be lost on many of their readers. Yet so long as readers regard a semicolon as a funny-looking comma and a colon as a bit like a full stop, that will usually give them enough to hang on to. So, even if you decide to use the less common punctuation marks sparingly when writing for a mass audience, there's no need to remove them altogether.

After a period when the teaching of punctuation seemed unfashionable in some British schools, children in the early 21st century are again learning the main rules. From the age of six or seven, they are also reading books showing the full range of marks, as in *The Green Cushion* by Margaret Joy:

> 'Let me think,' said Old Joey. 'Charlie from the chippy took one. Mrs Tomkins took one – she lives over at number nineteen; and Miss Wilson took the third one – she lives opposite at Rose Villa.'

Full stop (.)

The main use of a full stop (or, in the US, period) is to show where a sentence ends. For this reason, full stops should be the most common mark on the page.

There's no need to use full stops in people's names or in abbreviations or acronyms—*Mr J C Bennett, BBC, US, eg, ie, 8am, 9pm*—unless there's a genuine chance of ambiguity or you are having to follow a house-style manual that says otherwise. Headings in a report, letter, email, or memo don't need a final full stop. If a sentence ends with a website address, it's common to omit the full stop in case people think the stop is part of the address. But there's no more reason to do this than with a postal address.

Comma (,)

Single commas act as separators between parts of a sentence:

> Using accident and ill-health data and drawing upon my experience of inspecting slaughterhouses and meat-processing plants, I have prepared a list of hazards found in the meat industry.

or

> Although suitable protective equipment was available, most of the operatives were not wearing it.

or

> If you send the documents by Thursday, we will complete the sale by the following Monday.

Be sparing with commas. Using them every few words may prevent the reader getting the construction of the sentence. This, for example, is a mess:

> I have tried on a number of occasions to contact you at your office, without success and now resort, to writing to you, as these items should be dealt with urgently. You will appreciate the possible problems involved, if these units become occupied, before we have had a chance to check for their compliance with standards, and I would be obliged, if you could respond, by complying with my inspector's original request for compliance, as any further delay, could result in the start of disciplinary action against your company.

Almost every comma could go and the long final sentence could be split using the techniques in chapter 1.

A pair of commas cordons off information that is an aside, explanation, or addition. Readers can, if they wish, leapfrog the cordoned-off area and still make sense of what is said:

> Holmes, having searched for further clues, left by the back door.

Often the position of commas will change the meaning, so be careful with them:

The girls, who will join the team next week, are fine players for their age.

Here, the information between the commas comments on 'the girls', but is not essential to the main point of the sentence, which is that the girls are fine players. This kind of insert is said to be a commenting clause. Compare this, without commas:

The girls who will join the team next week are fine players for their age.

Obviously the meaning has changed: the words 'who will join the team next week' now help to define the girls. They are essential to our understanding of what kind of people they are. The clause is said to be defining and does not need a cordon of commas.

Commas are helpful in separating listed items:

Staple foods include rice, wheat, sorghum and millet.

No comma is needed after *sorghum* (though such a 'serial comma' is usual in US English and also forms part of the Oxford University Press house style), but when the penultimate or final listed item includes *and*, a comma in the right place can help the reader to see the meaning immediately:

To get an award, you must obtain a pass on theory, practical knowledge and application, and health and safety.

A comma can also help to create special effects like suspense. Compare this:

They crept into the room and found the body.

with

They crept into the room, and found the body.

Finally, ignore the advice often heard on writing courses: 'Use a maximum of one comma per sentence.' It's just plain silly.

Colon (:)

A colon is used to introduce direct speech, as an alternative to a comma; and to separate a main heading from a subtitle, as in 'Elephants: the full facts'. Colons have three other main purposes:

1   To introduce a vertical list (as in the line above) or a running-text list where there is a substantial break after the introductory phrase, such as:

She has several positive characteristics: charm, dignity, and stickability.

For notes on the punctuation of vertical lists, see chapter 6.

2   To act as a drum roll (mark of announcement) or a 'why-because' marker that leads the reader from one idea to its consequence or logical continuation, for example:

There's one big problem with tennis on radio: you can't see it.

3   Much more rarely, to separate two sharply contrasting and parallel statements as in the example always quoted in punctuation guides, 'Man proposes: God disposes.' Here is a more secular colon:

During Wimbledon, television is like someone with a reserved ticket: radio is the enthusiast who has queued all night to get in.

A weaker contrast might be signified by a semicolon; there is some overlap in meaning between the two marks.

In all these uses, the colon will usually follow a statement that could be a complete sentence. After the colon the sentence will usually continue with a lower-case letter.

A colon does not need support from a dash (:–). This nameless thing is not acceptable to most publishers, wastes a key stroke, and looks repulsive in most word-processed documents.

Semicolon (;)

Consider these sentences from a notice next to an ancient cathedral clock:

The large oak frame houses the striking train of gears, these parts have been painted black and are the early parts of the clock. In this same frame on the left between two posts is a going train (a time piece), this has been painted green.

Both commas are wrong and should be semicolons or full stops. To use semicolons safely—ignoring for the moment their use in lists—you need to satisfy two criteria:

1 The statements separated by the semicolons could stand alone as separate sentences.
2 The topics mentioned in the two statements are closely related.

So the paragraph would say:

> **The large oak frame houses the striking train of gears; these parts have been painted black and are the early parts of the clock. In this same frame on the left between two posts is a going train (a time piece); this has been painted green.**

The confusion between semicolons and commas is widespread and even afflicts the secretariat of 10 Downing Street (the UK prime minister's office). When Labour took power in 1997, there was concern about the fate of Humphrey, the resident feline, as the prime minister's wife was known to dislike cats. An artist tried to find the truth by offering to paint the beast, and received this reply in which all three commas are wrong because they stand between full sentences:

> **Thank you for your recent letter addressed to the Prime Minister, I have been asked to reply.**
> **Your portfolio of pen portraits was very impressive, however we already have a portrait of Humphrey hanging on the walls of the Cabinet Office. An artist sent it in two years ago, she copied his likeness from press photographs.**

These 'run-on' sentences need separation by full stops or semicolons. One way would be:

> **Thank you for your recent letter addressed to the Prime Minister. I have been asked to reply.**
> **Your portfolio of pen portraits was very impressive; however, we already have a portrait of Humphrey hanging on the walls of the Cabinet Office. An artist sent it in two years ago; she copied his likeness from press photographs.**

Another way would be to adjust the sentence boundaries by adding a few words:

> **Thank you for your recent letter addressed to the Prime Minister, to which I have been asked to reply.**

Your portfolio of pen portraits was very impressive but we already have a portrait of Humphrey hanging on the walls of the Cabinet Office. An artist sent it in two years ago, having copied his likeness from press photographs.

A semicolon can often seem less curt than a full stop. Instead of starting a letter:

Thank you for your letter of 10 December. We apologize for the delay in replying.

it would sound more relaxed to write:

Thank you for your letter of 10 December; we apologize for the delay in replying.

A comma would be wrong in that position because it cannot sustain such a long pause. Rarely is a comma enough to separate complete sentences.

Semicolons can also be used instead of commas to separate items in a list, especially where the items have their own commas:

Lunch at Henry's comprised all the ingredients for a happy and contented life: wine from the grapes of Tuscany; tropical avocados, seductively soft and yielding; French king prawns, clothed in a luscious sauce; a multitude of meaty snacks for carnivores and nutty nibbles for vegetarians; and the company of all the beautiful people of the town.

In a long, catalogue-type list, semicolons are ideal dividers:

Target audiences for the new manual will include other companies in our group, both European and US-based; business leaders, top politicians and other leading opinion-formers; consultants of proven expertise; and local schools and colleges.

To use merely commas as dividers would produce chaos because commas already exist within some of the listed items. An introductory colon after *include* would be unnecessary—there is no substantial pause at that point.

Dash (–)

Dashes are sometimes used singly to indicate the start of an aside, explanation, or addition:

> Justifying their case, smokers introduce a herring so red that it glows like coal: that if their illnesses are self-inflicted, well, so are most people's – look at traffic accidents, look at potholers.

They can add emphasis, too:

> He shot big game for status, pleasure – and greed.

When used in pairs, dashes draw special attention to the phrase they surround (compare 'Brackets', below):

> Visitors may stay overnight – or for as long as they wish – in the hostelry run by the friars.

A pair of commas or a pair of brackets would have done just as well, but the dashes emphasize the point.

It's all right to use more than one pair of dashes in a sentence but take care that the meaning doesn't disintegrate. Here's an awkward, if playful, use of two pairs of dashes by a columnist on *The Times*:

> Volkswagen is in trouble – terrible trouble – very terrible trouble, and we can sit on the sidelines – entry free – and bask in somebody else's trouble for hours on end.

Perhaps he should have read his paper's own guide on the subject of dashes which, happily, the journalists ignore:

> Dashes are sloppy punctuation, ugly in narrow columns of newspaper type. They often indicate that a sentence is badly constructed and needs rewriting.

In word processing (typing on computer), it is customary to use a hyphen with a space either side (in the US, a double hyphen is common for this purpose). In typesetting or desktop publishing, most publishers use a spaced 'en rule', as in the Volkswagen example above. The en rule (or en dash) is not obvious on most keyboards but may be an option under the hyphen key. On a PC keyboard, press Ctrl and the minus key on the number pad.

Some publishers, including Oxford University Press, use an 'em rule' (or em dash), which is slightly longer than the en rule, for all the purposes described above. An unspaced en rule is often used to show a range of dates or other figures, e.g. '1958–2004' or 'rats aged 6–9 months were used in the experiment'.

Square brackets [ ]

Square brackets (or, in the US, brackets) show that the text within does not belong to the document or quotation but is being inserted for clarity:

He [Mr Smith] told me to go home.
They saw it [the pheasant] as fair game.

Brackets ( )

Brackets (also called round brackets or, in the US, parentheses) surround an aside, explanation, or addition that is relatively unimportant to the main text (compare 'Dash', above):

The biker fell off at 160 mph, suffering an open fracture of his tibia (lower leg) and losing two inches of bone in the process. Only ten years ago, four out of ten open tibial fractures (in which the bone comes partially out of the leg) resulted in amputation.

Well-placed brackets can prevent the meaning of a sentence disintegrating, even if the result looks cluttered:

The problem is tidal flooding along the river. Many plans have been studied but the agreed solution is a system of river mattressing (to avoid breaches) and embankment raising (to avoid exceptionally high-tide flooding).

If a sentence begins within a bracket, it should start with a capital and end with a full stop inside the bracket. A comma should rarely precede a bracket but there is no harm in putting one after the closing bracket if this aids understanding.

If you are going to use an acronym several times and the reader is unlikely to know what it means, spell it out on the first occasion and put the acronym in brackets:

Agency Services Limited (ASL) has tendered for the work.

Other types of bracket are brace or curly brackets {which are used in maths} and angle brackets <used in linguistics and other specialisms>.

Capitals

Capital letters (upper case) defy any would-be rule-maker, as some decisions on whether to dignify a word with an initial capital have to be left to the individual writer. Use them sparingly though, and err on the side of lower case. Writing afflicted with random capitalitis just looks silly:

Please Complete One Line For Each Person Normally Living At This Address, including those who are temporarily living away. Include Everybody – Yourself, All Adults, whether entered or not on the Electoral Registration form, All Younger Persons, Children and Babies.

Headings in business and scientific reports tend to suffer from the same disease, with writers making invidious distinctions between words they capitalize and words they don't. Compare the distracting:

Factors that May Affect the Success of the Strategy

with

Factors that may affect the success of the strategy

In the US, headings in books often use 'title case', where the initial letters of nouns and adjectives (and sometimes even verbs) are capitalized. Title case spills over into reports and letters and, under the influence of Microsoft Word, is often seen in British home-cooked documents. It lends a rather self-important air, especially when applied to all the subheadings as well as chapter or section headings. It also gives an inconsistent look because words in lower case in the main text suddenly assume a higher status in headings. The world may yet be saved from the horrors of title case; authors and publishers just need to revolt.

People: Use an initial capital for ranks and titles when attached to a person's name, thus *Prince William* but *the prince*, *President Obama* but *the president*, *Judge Wright* but *the judge*. Offices of state in the UK such as *home secretary* and *chancellor of the exchequer* are lower case in *The Economist* and the *Sunday Times*, but confusingly become *Home Secretary* and *Chancellor of the Exchequer* in *The Times*. I prefer lower case. Titles that look odd in lower case need capitalizing, hence *Master of the Rolls*, *Lord Chief Justice*. In some organizations, job titles like *managing director* and *housing manager* are given initial capitals but this is poor practice—at what rank do you stop? It helps if the organization issues a style guide stating its house rules on this. Beneath the signature in a letter, job titles in lower case look odd so it's reasonable to use title case for them there (but only there).

Organizations and government departments generally take initial capitals only when their full name or something similar is used. Thus *Metropolitan Police* but *the police*; *County Court* and *Court of Appeal* but *the court*; *St John's Church* but *the church*. Because it helps to distinguish between an Act of Parliament (a statute) and an act of parliament (something done by parliament), upper case is better for the statute. A newspaper would usually print *Blankshire District Council* but *the council*. The council itself, however, might prefer to use a capital *c* whenever it referred to itself. Confusion sets in when it then refers to another council, to which it will invariably give a lower-case letter. The result is an apparent inconsistency, and the main merit of a general preference for lower case is that it tends to produce a much more consistent-looking text.

Trade names take upper case: *Hoover* but *vacuum cleaner*, *Xerox* but *photocopier*, *Penbritin* but *ampicillin*.

The names of wars and historical periods normally take an initial capital: *Iron Age fort*, *Vietnam War*.

Acronyms usually take all capitals: BBC, EU, USA, TUC, FBI. The publisher OUP's preferred style for acronyms that can be spoken as words is also all capitals: NATO, UNICEF, and UNESCO. Most newspapers use Nato, Unicef, and Unesco.

Hyphen (-)

Hyphens make links. For example, they link words that form a composite adjective before a noun: *computer-based work*, *short-term goals*, *half-inch nail*, *three-year-old child*, *out-of-hours work*, *low-power-consuming light-emitting diodes*, *no-go area*, and *couldn't-care-less attitude*. This kind of hyphenation helps to reduce ambiguities and stumbles.

The presence or absence of a hyphen can easily change the meaning. Compare:

The pop group reformed to The pop group re-formed.
The atrium has no smoking areas to The atrium has no-smoking areas.
A cross party spokesman to A cross-party spokesman.

The partnership was disrupted by extra marital sex to The partnership was disrupted by extra-marital sex.
There are no good lawyers in that firm to There are no-good lawyers in that firm.

Though their logic is clear enough, hyphens that hang in a permanent state of separation from their companion are sometimes hard to justify, as in this sentence from *The Times*:

A typical day's intake for me would include oat bran porridge for breakfast, flavoured with maple syrup, five wheat-, yeast- and sugar-free oatcakes mid-morning, baked potato, olive oil and salad for lunch, and hot vegetable stock at intervals until evening.

Consider this extract from a business proposal:

Normally on oil and gas related enquiries, a briefing meeting is convened at the client's request.

Gas related comes before *enquiries* and is effectively one word, so it needs a hyphen. But there are oil-related enquiries too in the sentence, because *related* is implied after *oil*. So the sentence should say, with a hyphen hanging after *oil*:

Normally on oil- and gas-related enquiries, a briefing meeting is convened at the client's request.

or

Normally on oil-related and gas-related enquiries, a briefing meeting is convened at the client's request.

It is difficult to use hyphens consistently, and there is usually someone to disagree with your best efforts. The treasurer of the World Pheasant Association might be peering over your shoulder:

[Your] article...refers to the endangered 'white-eared pheasant'... The hyphen is incorrect. The pheasant in question is a white pheasant with ears. There are also blue eared pheasants and brown eared pheasants. The taxonomic similarity is that all the three pheasants have ears and all the ears are white.

When a woman was assaulted by a London taxi driver a newspaper described the attacker as a *black cab driver*. But which was black, the driver or the cab? The paper had meant to say *black-cab driver*, leaving his skin colour out of the question. Had it really wanted to mention his colour, it could have written *black black-cab driver* or *white black-cab driver*, but perhaps then it would have decided to recast the sentence.

It's normally unnecessary to hyphenate when one of the words is an adverb (see chapter 13):

rapidly growing economy; carefully crafted answer

though some newspapers routinely do this.

When nouns or adjectives, words with 'self' should be hyphenated: *self-esteem, self-employed, self-contained, self-centred, self-explanatory.* As *non-* is a hyphenated prefix, its hyphen is always present: *non-partisan, non-violent, non-qualifying, non-capital offering, non-aggression pact, non-aligned countries.* When attached to another adjective, *mid* always takes a hyphen: *mid-Victorian pottery, mid-ocean ridge, mid-engined vehicle.* A good dictionary will show which words are inherently hyphenated.

Some nouns formed by two or more words need hyphens: *set-up, set-to, run-up, build-up, free-for-all, call-out, punch-up.* Without a hyphen, there is ambiguity in sentences like:

Last week there was a bust up in the street.

where the possible meanings include fight, drug bust, or a piece of sculpture.

Verbs rarely need hyphenation, so all three hyphens in this advertising leaflet are unnecessary, while a hyphen should have been included to create *high-street bargains*:

With inflation decreasing, the press and politicians are spelling-out the message that the recession is over . . . Now is the time to think about making cash available for the numerous high street bargains and to begin paying-off some of the commitments that have built-up in this tough period.

In those cases, *spelling out, paying off,* and *built up* were simply phrasal verbs (a verb followed by a particle). Verbs that do need hyphenating are usually compounds and are shown hyphenated in the dictionary, like to *fine-tune* a car, to *force-feed* a prisoner, to *freeze-frame* the action, to *fine-draw* two pieces of cloth, to *double-check* an answer, or to *copy-edit* some text.

Apostrophe (')

The apostrophe is now so widely misused—an errant tadpole, one columnist calls it—that its eventual death seems inevitable. Alongside their no-smoking stickers, companies could soon be declaring themselves apostrophe-free zones. This would be a pity, as the correct use of apostrophes conveys meaning and prevents ambiguity, while misplaced apostrophes make the reader stumble and backtrack.

The main rules on apostrophes are very simple and cover more than 99 per cent of cases. The few exceptions are more difficult and have to be memorized. The main rules deal with two matters, *possession* and *contraction*.

Possession

Follow a two-stage approach:

- First, find the possessor(s).
- Second, put an apostrophe immediately after the possessor(s).

For example, in:

The judges wig was eaten by the generals horse.

it's clear that the judge possesses the wig and the general the horse, so the sentence becomes

The judge's wig was eaten by the general's horse.

In:

The peoples leader ignored the childrens opinions.

it's clear that the people possess the leader and the children the opinions, so the sentence—note carefully the position of the apostrophes—becomes

The people's leader ignored the children's opinions.

The same rule applies to such sentences as:

The three inspectors' cars were attacked.
Several players' houses were daubed with paint.

where the apostrophe goes immediately after the possessors.

It's a little more complicated when the singular form of a word ends in *s*, but you either add *'s* or just an apostrophe. Both these forms are correct:

I sent you Mr Jones's copy of the lease yesterday.
I sent you Mr Jones' copy of the lease yesterday.

Words that end in *ss* or *x*, like *boss*, *business*, or *fox*, also take *'s* in possession:

The boss's failure to act led to orders being lost.

This surreal, apostrophe-free message is to be seen roaming Britain on a fleet of lorries:

COLLECTING TOMORROWS
DELIVERIES TODAY

As the deliveries belong to tomorrow, there should be an apostrophe between the *W* and *S*.

Contractions

Use an apostrophe to show that at least one letter is missing:

Today's the day for a fresh start (Today is . . .)
It's no concern of mine (It is . . .)
Doesn't anybody have the results? (Does not . . .)

Remember that pronouns—words in place of nouns—like *his*, *hers*, *ours*, *yours*, *theirs*, and *its* don't need apostrophes. They are words in their own right—no letters are missing and the possession is built into the word. (The only exception is *one's*, as in *one's head is aching*.) So it would be correct to write:

The cat wandered in, its wet paws patterning the carpet.

Though the wet paws belong to the cat, there is no apostrophe in *its* because the possession is built into the word. Only insert an apostrophe in *its* when the word is short for *it is* or *it has*.

In some expressions of measurement and time, apostrophes are conventional:

They took a week's holiday without permission and the firm then gave them two weeks' notice.

It's difficult at first to see the logic in this usage, but in the first example *holiday* in a sense belongs to the *week*. Without the apostrophe it would say:

a weeks holiday

which would mix a singular *a* with a plural-looking *weeks*. So, if it's logical to write a *week's holiday*, you should move the apostrophe along one letter when the possessor ends in *s*, as in *two weeks' notice*. This, however, is becoming extinct, whatever the logic, with even the more careful newspapers dropping the apostrophe from time to time.

Generally, don't use an apostrophe in a plural:

In the 1990s, people made more, spent more, and saved less.

unless there is possession:

Six MPs' offices were ransacked.

Refuse to be led astray by any shop notice proclaiming:

Shrimp's, prawns', pears', orange's and sandwich'es.

These are all straightforward plurals—no apostrophe is needed. Sometimes an exception to the rule is demanded by the need to avoid ambiguity. Hence:

Mind your p's and q's
A list of do's and don'ts
The first animal in the dictionary has three a's in its name.

are preferable to:

Mind your ps and qs
A list of dos and don'ts
The first animal in the dictionary has three as in its name.

Occasionally you meet a rarity where at first the apostrophe looks superfluous:

Maria's lasagne was better than the chef's.

Clearly the lasagne belongs to Maria, so the first apostrophe is fine. But what belongs to the chef to deserve an apostrophe? Lasagne, again, because that word is implied. Had there been more than one chef, the apostrophe would have followed the *s*. The same thing happens with some shop names. *Lewis's*, in Liverpool, England means the shop belonging to Lewis.

In some cases, an apostrophe might seem appropriate but is unnecessary. If you call your office guidance on word processing a *Typists Handbook*, you could argue that it's a handbook *for* typists not *belonging* to them, so an apostrophe is not needed. The same could be true of *cashiers office*, and may explain why the National Association of Citizens Advice Bureaux has no apostrophe in its name—the bureaux do not *belong* to citizens, they are *for* citizens to use. In *six weeks pregnant*, an apostrophe isn't needed because pregnancy is a state and there's no possession. The same applies to *six weeks late*.

A final point: many keyboards hide true apostrophes and curly quotation marks but seductively offer instant access to the marks for feet (′) and inches (″). Seek out the proper marks—they'll usually be hidden under another key.

Ellipsis (. . .)

The ellipsis has two purposes:

1 To show that material is missing, perhaps from a quotation. It is customary to put square brackets around this ellipsis, to avoid confusion with the second use of the ellipsis.
2 To indicate suspense:

    He said: 'And the winner is . . . Sydney, Australia!'

There should be three dots in the ellipsis, not two, five, or seven. However, a book reviewer tells me that when a phrase trails off unfinished, the US practice is to use four dots.

In typesetting or desktop publishing, there is often a word space before and after each one, so . . . not. . .Some typesetters insist on adding a fourth dot when a sentence ends with an ellipsis, the fourth dot being set tight on the third to show its different character. Others are quite sure that the dots in the ellipsis should *not* have word spaces between them, but a word space before the first dot and after the last. The fire of controversy rages among the three or four people who care, and consistency is hard to achieve in this as in so many things linguistic.

Quotation marks (' ')

These, also called quotes, quote marks, speech marks, or inverted commas, indicate the opening and closing of direct speech:

'There is no alternative,' said the prime minister, 'so we will go on as before.'

Or, if a sentence ends after the first statement:

'There is no alternative to our policy,' said the prime minister. 'Tomorrow we will continue as we did today.'

Note that in both cases the first comma comes within the closing quote in British English, as does the full stop after *before*. The logic of this is easy enough to remember, as the comma is placed where an exclamation mark or question mark would go.

Most books and newspapers use single quotes, reserving double quotes for a quotation within a quotation. The reverse is acceptable, though, and widespread in children's books and the US.

Quotes are also used to clothe a word in irony or, usually unnecessarily, to apologize for some clumsy or supposedly colloquial usage:

I have been 'toying' with the idea of buying a plasma TV and wondered if you were going to sell them.
In this first phase I also 'touched base' with other interested people.

Quotes are common when drawing attention to the first use of a technical term:

This kind of score is known as the 'median'.

In British English, when quoting a full sentence from another source, put your closing full stop inside the closing quotes:

We agree with the president when he says, 'New Coke is best.'

When quoting a sentence fragment, the closing full stop goes outside the closing quote:

He told us to 'get a life' and 'pay less attention to punctuation and more to growing the business'.

Just to confuse things, in US English that final quote mark would go outside the full stop (period), and the quote marks would usually be double. Moreover, in quoted sentence fragments that need to be followed by a comma, the comma will come inside the quote marks in a formation that looks as bizarre to British eyes as the opposite must look to Americans:

> Naturally the telemarketeer must be prepared for all possible answers like 'in the morning,' 'on weekends,' 'after midnight,' or 'between 3 a.m. and 4 a.m.'

(Gary Blake, *Quick Tips for Better Business Writing*, McGraw-Hill, New York, 1995)

Exclamation mark (!)

Use this to follow exclamations of surprise, shock, or dismay, but sparingly and singly!!! Using the mark to signal a witticism or acute observation not only deprives readers of the pleasure of noticing it for themselves, but suggests they are too slow to see it without your expert help.

Question mark (?)

Use this after direct questions. There is no need for one if the question is really a polite demand:

> Will you please let me have your reply by 6pm today.

In informal writing, a bracketed question mark is useful for drawing attention, perhaps facetiously, to a doubtful claim:

> His department is addicted to cutting-edge (?) technology.

10 Pitching your writing at the right level

Guideline: *Remember the average reading age of the population: about 13 years.*

A piece of writing is likely to go unread or be misunderstood if the intended readers find it too long, complicated, and boring. It's easy to overestimate their level of reading skill and perseverance. So if you're writing for a mass audience, it's a good idea to pitch it at or below the level of reading skill of the average person.

But how do you know what the average person can read or will persevere with? You can analyse your own experience of what you find difficult, which will help. But often you'll move in a highly literate world where people know an apostrophe from a semicolon and may be interested in the difference between 'discreet' and 'discrete'. You may read only the 'quality' newspapers. So it's possible to get out of touch with the mass of readers. And all of us find it easier to blame people who can't understand our writing for being stupid, ill-educated, or unwilling to try hard enough, than to pitch our writing at a lower level.

It helps if we jettison the 'gaining marks' mindset, which is a hangover from school and university. No more are we writing to impress lecturers by our command of technical detail. No more are we parading our profound knowledge in front of someone who knows the subject backwards. Suddenly we're trying to inform people who may know next to nothing about a topic. The skills are very different.

This chapter looks at:

- the average reading age of UK adults (about 13 years)
- examples of text written at the UK average level
- readability tests that can help you check the level of difficulty.

Average reading age

By definition, a 13-year-old child with average reading abilities has a reading age of 13. Skilful teachers can pick a particular book and be reasonably sure it will be readable by an average 13-year-old. (Whether the topic will interest them is another matter.)

For adults, it's also convenient to use reading age as a proxy for reading ability. A reading age of 16 will be adequate for most daily purposes. Few people will have a reading age much beyond 21. A person's reading age changes little after they stop full-time education unless a job or pastime requires them to read harder texts. Someone's reading age may decline if they read little. Most people prefer to read text that is below their reading age.

The UK's National Literacy Trust website shows what research has found on adult reading ages. If we ignore people who can read nothing or very little in English, the figures suggest a national average of 15–16 (GCSE grades A* to C). If we err towards pessimism and accept that most people prefer to read texts that are easier than their reading-age level, then the average UK adult has a reading age of 12–14, say 13 to keep things simple (US school grade 8). This equates to three years below the current legal school-leaving age. However, this is an estimate only, and adults may bring prior knowledge to a reading task that a typical 13-year-old will lack.

Thirteen is certainly not a high figure, being only two or three reading-age years above the generally accepted definition of 'functional literacy'—the level people need to cope with everyday life. But it far exceeds some of the wilder estimates. One company in the plain-language field has put the average reading age at 9.5 (US grade 4–5). This would mean the average Briton, after at least 12 years of formal schooling, was nearly two years below functional-literacy level. Were the figure true, it would mean that much of the education budget for the last 50 years had been wasted. But there's nothing to support it in adult literacy research. The National Audit Office regards the average adult as being at 'level 1' for literacy, based on Department for Education and Skills figures from 2003. Level 1 equates roughly to a reading age of 13–15.

Examples of text written at the average level

To give an idea of what level to aim at for a mass audience, the two following passages from schoolbooks are at about reading age 13 (US grade 8), though the second is rather more difficult than the first:

1/ While all this is happening, the embryo is getting longer. Now the tail bud begins to develop, and the embryo develops suckers beneath the place where the mouth will be. Although it is only about twenty-eight hours old and barely recognizable as a tadpole, the embryo now hatches. Toad embryos emerge very early, while frog and salamander embryos are further along when they come out of their jelly prisons. The small embryos hang by the suckers to the jelly. It will be five more hours before they can move their muscles at all.

When they are a little more than a day and a half old, their hearts begin to beat. Soon the blood begins to circulate through the gills, the developing eyes can be seen, the mouth opens, and the suckers begin to disappear. At two and a half days of age, when the blood starts circulating in the tail, they really look like tadpoles.

(Patent, Dorothy Hirshaw. "Frogs, Toads, Salamanders, and How They Reproduce." New York, NY: Holiday House, 1975.)

2/ As we have seen, a neutron star would be small and dense. It should also be rotating rapidly. All stars rotate, but most of them do so leisurely. For example, our Sun takes nearly one month to rotate around its axis. A collapsing star speeds up as its size shrinks, just as an ice-skater during a pirouette speeds up when she pulls in her arms. This phenomenon is a direct consequence of a law of physics known as the conservation of angular momentum, which holds that the total amount of angular momentum in a system holds constant. An ordinary star rotating once a month would be spinning faster than once a second if compressed to the size of a neutron star. In addition to having rapid rotation, we expect a neutron star to have an intense magnetic field. It is probably safe to say that every star has a magnetic field of some strength.

(*Discovering the Universe*, Kaufmann WJ 1990, p.290, pub WH Freeman.)

The first example has an average sentence length of 17.5 and there's only one passive-voice verb ('be seen'). The second has a similar average sentence length and no passives.

So these examples are typical of what the average adult can read. Remember, though, that plenty of people are reading below this level. So if you can clarify things further without losing the flow or resorting to nursery-school language, so much the better.

In the UK, mass-market material like *The Sun*, *Mirror*, and *Reader's Digest* are all written at a little above this level (UK reading age 14, US grade 9) according to Bill DuBay, who used readability tests to check a 4 000-word sample of each for his book *Smart Language* (2007). I used similar tests to analyse a *Times* editorial headed 'The risks of currency weakness' (21 November 2008, available on the paper's website). It needs a reading age of about 17. Its average sentence length is 20 words, which helps to compensate for fairly high-level language. Even for a well-educated audience, it's unwise to be writing much above this level.

Readability tests that can help you check the level of difficulty

Several formulas aim to measure the readability of writing. Most use only two variables to produce a score: sentence length and vocabulary load (such as word length or rarity). The score corresponds to that of texts needing known levels of reading skill to achieve (typically) 80 per cent comprehension.

Microsoft Word includes two readability calculators, Flesch Reading Ease and Flesch–Kincaid Grade Level. The program can also calculate the average sentence length and the percentage of passives. However, the Word score ignores any text (like headings or bullet points) that lacks sentence-end punctuation like full stops and question marks. Word's readability scoring can be helpful if you use the table below to interpret it.

Programs sold by Editor Software Ltd (StyleWriter) and Micro Power & Light Co (Readability Calculations) offer other ways of scoring readability.

Flesch Reading Ease score	UK reading age	Equivalent US grade (Flesch–Kincaid Grade Level)
90–100	10	5
80–90	11	6
70–80	12	7
60–70	13–14	8–9
50–60	15–17	10–12
30–50	18–21*	13–16*
0–30	Graduate*	Graduate*

*A fault in older versions of Word prevents Flesch–Kincaid scores above US school grade 12.

If you lack access to testing software, you can use a reasonably simple manual test like this one based on the Fog (frequency of gobbledygook) Index devised by Robert Gunning:

1 Count a passage of text roughly 300 words long, ending with a full stop. Number of words = **A**.
2 Divide A by the number of sentences, giving average sentence length, **B**.
3 Count the number of words of three or more syllables, excluding those that:
   • start with capitals
   • have three or more syllables only because they have had *-ing*, '*-ed*', or '*-es*' added, or
   • combine two short words such as 'pro-choice' or 'photofit'.

   This gives you the number of 'hard' words. Multiply it by 100/**A**, to give **C**.
4 Then add **B** to **C** and multiply by 0.4.
5 This gives the lowest US school grade level that could easily read the text, so add 5 to give the British reading age.

Drawbacks and uses of readability tests

The formulas are blunt tools. They ignore the way text is organized, how it looks on the page, and the reader's motivation and level of prior knowledge. They only hint at how to write a text better, and they encourage the idea that a clear document is one that scores well on the formula. Most tests don't discriminate between easy long words like 'immediately' and hard ones like 'esoteric'. Because 'consider' has three syllables, authors seeking a good score on the formula are tempted to use 'think about', 'look at', or 'mull over'. But 'consider' is an easy word according to the research (see, for example, *The Living Word Vocabulary* by Dale E and O'Rourke J, 1979). A test like Smog (a simplified version of the Fog Index) relies mainly on syllable counting for its scores, so authors addicted to the tests tend to think they must omit most long words. This can lead to boring, wordy, and over-idiomatic writing in which phrases like 'if you abandon your home' become 'if you move away from your home for good and do not tell us', just to avoid a three-syllable word. Authors who catch the single-syllable bug will even replace a simple word like 'explain' with 'tell you of', or replace 'contact you' with 'get in touch with you'. But these are wordier and achieve nothing.

Test scores correspond to those for texts requiring known reading levels. These 'normed' texts come from well-written published books that are grammatically sound, well punctuated, and logically sequenced, like those above about tadpoles and neutron stars. So unless what you write is like this, you can get a false impression of its clarity. The Flesch tests will give the same score to any two 10-sentence passages with, say, 12 long words and an average sentence length of 18. So if you reverse the order of the sentences in the tadpole piece, you'll get exactly the same score as in the well-ordered piece. In other words, if writing is muddled, ambiguous, or misleading, the test score won't tell you.

The formulas can act as a rough yardstick. Say a firm does consultancy work for its customers and writes reports for them. It can decide that the reports must score below a certain level on the formula or they won't be published without further editing. The yardstick acts as a constant reminder to authors. They can then be encouraged to attend courses and read about good writing.

Even a yardstick can be used to beat people, though. If an agency sets a target that 'all our documents must score reading age 13 (US school grade 8) on Flesch–Kincaid', authors need some leeway if there are good reasons why this is impossible. For example, a leaflet may have to use multi-syllabic words like 'benefit', 'eligible', 'adaptation', or 'disabled'. A report on Islamic finance may have to use terms like 'ijara' and 'diminishing musharaka'. Medical leaflets may need to equip patients with terms like 'endometriosis' and 'vasovagal syncope'. These will wreak havoc with your Flesch score but they'll be unavoidable.

Rudolf Flesch, a developer of readability formulas, said they should not be worshipped: 'Some readers, I am afraid, will expect a magic formula for good writing and will be disappointed with my simple yardstick. Others, with a passion for accuracy, will wallow in the little rules and computations but lose sight of the principles of plain English. What I hope for are readers who won't take the formula too seriously and won't expect from it more than a rough estimate.'

The Flesch–Kincaid Grade Level of this chapter (excluding the extracts and tables) is 9.7 (UK reading age 14.7) and the Flesch Reading Ease score is 59.

11 Six writing myths explored and exploded

Guideline: *Avoid being enslaved by writing myths.*

A business writer once told me she'd been instructed by her English teacher never to begin consecutive paragraphs with the same letter of the alphabet. After 30 years of following this non-rule, she confessed to wondering if it was justified. A writer's path is steep enough without the burden of schoolroom mythology. This chapter examines some of the most tenacious non-rules.

Myth 1: Never start a sentence with 'But'

This is neither a rule of grammar nor even a widely observed convention. Yet the myth is hardy: even as late as 2008 I was nearly defenestrated by a bunch of lawyers for suggesting they occasionally begin sentences with 'But' instead of 'However' or 'On the other hand'. It may stem from primary-school teachers who (quite reasonably) seek to persuade children to connect the sentence fragments they tend to write.

Most influential authors in the last few hundred years have ignored the myth. In *A Vindication of the Rights of Woman* (1792) Mary Wollstonecraft regularly uses 'But' and 'And' to begin sentences. Jane Austen starts hers with 'But' on many pages of her novels, and occasionally uses 'And' in the same position, in the sense of 'Furthermore'. This is one of her *Buts* from *Mansfield Park* (1814), where it stops the bland first sentence running on too long and heightens its contrast with the ironic second:

> She had two sisters to be benefited by her elevation [marriage to a social superior]; and such of their acquaintance as thought Miss Ward and Miss Frances quite as handsome as Miss Maria, did not scruple to predict their marrying with almost equal advantage. But there certainly are not so many men of large fortune in the world, as there are pretty women to deserve them.

'But', like most sentence connectors, signals a shift in pace and direction. It may help in stating an argument or point of view, as in this example from a modern British journalist who, for emphasis, happily begins the final sentence with 'And':

> The children of MPs, royalty, journalists and other moral prodnoses do not need to read underclass horror-stories to find out about the lifestyle problems which adult sexuality inflicts on children. They are familiar with it all: access arrangements, vendettas, embarrassment, lawsuits, confusion, hypocrisy. 'I believe strenuously,' says Mrs Nicholson [a British MP], 'that every child deserves a mother and father'; and so say all of us. But the plain fact is that not every child has them to hand. And in family life, the golden rule is to start from where you are.

Even old-time grammarians begin sentences with 'But', and if it were a real rule they wouldn't. J C Nesfield, in his *Manual of English Grammar and Composition* (1915)—a 423-page small-print textbook for Edwardian 14-year-olds—says:

> ... it is convenient for the sake of brevity to say that 'a conjunction joins words to words, and sentences to sentences'. But this is not enough for the purposes of definition.

People sometimes plead that starting with 'But' is unbusinesslike, yet there's nothing so special about business English that the norm for every other kind of writing should be ignored. If, however, you are hog-tied by managers who insist on obeying their long-dead schoolteachers, you can circumvent them by slyly using 'Yet' as an alternative. It will often do the job and, like an actuary's abacus, has the rare merit of simplicity and underuse.

Some people like to extend their 'But' ban to 'So', 'Because', 'And', and 'However'. This is equally absurd. 'So' makes a crisp alternative to 'Consequently', 'Therefore', and 'As a result', and it also helps slow typists:

> So it would seem that the courts may override the words which the parties have used, in the process of interpreting a written contract, despite the powerful authorities which I have mentioned.

(Sir Christopher Staughton, former Lord Justice of Appeal, England and Wales, writing in *Clarity* 50, pp 24–29)

Seamus Heaney's fine modern translation of the Anglo-Saxon poem *Beowulf* (1999) begins with the dramatic one-word sentence, 'So.' And there are six other sentences starting with 'So' in his first eight pages. Hilary Moriarty, in the *Daily Telegraph* (2004), writes:

I may be a headteacher now, but I am an English teacher to the bone, with an honours degree in English, a master's in 20th-century English and American literature and more than 30 years in the classroom. So how come I do not recognise a single poem in the selection of eight my son is studying for his rapidly approaching GCSE in English?

It's also harmless to begin sentences with 'Because' as an alternative to 'As' and 'Since'. To write 'Because we want the project to succeed, we're willing to work overtime' is as grammatically sound as 'We're willing to work overtime because we want the project to succeed.' Every teacher knows this, yet many in secondary schools and universities continue to peddle the myth they heard as nine-year-olds. Even an occasional 'Or' can be used as a crisp first-word alternative to 'Alternatively'.

While obedience to myth may produce stale writing, advertisers and journalists sometimes write incomplete sentences in their desire for brevity, for example:

> **In truth, the British sandwich is now worse than ever. Because both the key elements, the bread and the filling, are invariably poor, and their quality is made worse by the methods of production.** (*Daily Mail*, 2004)

The 'Because' at the start of the second sentence misleads readers who, thinking there'll be a second part, crash unaware into the full stop. Better to have omitted the first full stop and let the sentence run.

To begin a sentence with 'And'—in the sense of 'Furthermore'—is common among journalists and novelists who want its extra dramatic effect, yet it remains rare among business writers. Here, Philip Howard of *The Times*, writing in 2004 about the altered meanings of military metaphors like 'putting yourself in the firing line', uses 'And so' (meaning 'Thus') to begin a sentence:

> **The first citation of the phrase comes from our defeat by the Boers at Majuba in 1881: "General Stewart was obliged to put every reserve man into the firing line." As rifles became more accurate, it was no longer necessary or tactically sensible to concentrate your rifles into a firing line. And so our firing line has changed from attackers to targets.**

Moriarty, in her piece mentioned above, also includes a sentence starting with 'And':

> Now, key scenes are identified, and it's horribly likely that, in many classes, those are the only ones that get taught. Pass the exam, blow the literature. And who can wonder if our very best students find it ridiculously easy?

The device is not new, even in prose that purples at the edges. Reporting the Coronation in 1953, *The Times* wrote:

> And already waiting for her, on every stretch of her way to and from the Abbey, is the homage of which flag and symbol and flower are no more than an expression – the love and loyal service of her people.

In his acclaimed biography of Samuel Taylor Coleridge (1989), Richard Holmes regularly begins sentences and paragraphs with 'And', 'But', and 'Because'. If it were bad English, the critics would have slaughtered him. When so many able writers disregard these myths, the best advice is that you may start a sentence with any word you want, as long as it hangs together as a complete statement. *The Times* even wrote an editorial about it:

> But of course you can start an editorial with a "but". But us no buts. The Bible is full of the usage. But the taboo against it is a lingering superstition, dreamed up by prescriptive Victorian grammarians who tried to make English run on railway lines instead of an open road.

Myth 2: Never put a comma before 'and'

Many folk insist that putting a comma before 'and' is bad. Ignore them as Nesfield did in the paragraph quoted under Myth 1. Though a comma is usually unnecessary before 'and', it may help readers to see how the sentence is built, or pause them for a moment. This is because 'and' can be a separator as well as a joiner. Here are a few examples:

> It was a bright cold day in April, and the clocks were striking thirteen.
> (First line of Orwell's *Nineteen Eighty-Four*)
> Parents shop around. They send for a clutch of prospectuses, see what's available in both the public and private sectors, and are prepared to switch their children between the two at different stages in their education.
> (The Times, 1994)
> When I assumed command of the Eighth Army I said that the mandate was to destroy Rommel and his Army, and that it would be done as soon as we were ready. We are ready NOW.
> (Field Marshal Montgomery of Alamein, eve-of-battle message, 1942)
> When we met last night, you explained that you no longer wished me to remain as Secretary of State for Education, and I am writing to say how glad I have been to serve in Her Majesty's Government.

(Letter of resignation from John Patten to the British prime minister, 1994)

And here is Beatrix Potter, in *The Tale of Peter Rabbit*:

He found a door in a wall; but it was locked, and there was no room for a fat little rabbit to squeeze underneath.

See also page 82 about the use of a comma before the final 'and' in a list.

Myth 3: Never end a sentence with a preposition

A few fossils believe that a sentence is bad if it ends with words like 'on', 'in', 'out', 'down', 'at', 'to', and 'over' (prepositions—see chapter 13). The poet Dryden probably started the myth in a 17th-century essay. Its continuing force was ably stated by a letter-writer to the *Mail on Sunday* in 2005:

I vividly recall two items of English grammar that were drummed into me – that there are 26 letters (including a T) in our alphabet and that one should not end a sentence with a preposition...Yet...prominent newscasters and presenters frequently end their sentences with prepositions, although alternative phrasing is readily available.

And this is still being taught in schools. In *Could do Better! Help your Child Shine at School* (Doubleday, 2007), secondary school Teacher of the Year 2004 Phil Beadle unwittingly put his finger on the snobbery and one-upmanship of this variety of stickling: '... it is still perceived in some educational establishments as being the height of naughtiness, and is clearly the kind of grammar up with which any English teacher worth his salt will not put. To rid yourself of this unappealing habit...[etc.]' Beadle instructs children to learn how to alter the sentence 'Jimmy came first: Joseph came after' so that it reads 'Jimmy came first. After, Joseph came.' Doubtless this was a big relief for them both, but such nonsense risks alienating children from grammar for ever. Worse still, 'after' is not even a preposition in Beadle's original sentence—it's an adverb.

What torment it must be for pedants to open their *Hamlet* at Act 3 Scene 1 and find Shakespeare breaking the alleged rule in the most famous soliloquy in English:

> **To die, to sleep –/No more; and by a sleep to say we end/The heart-ache and the thousand natural shocks/That flesh is heir to.**

then to notice the *Daily Mail* columnist and playwright Keith Water-house doing the same:

> **I can only imagine that Saddam needed that clock to stare at.** (2003)

and then to see a *Daily Telegraph* sketch-writer, Andrew Gimson, catching the bug:

> **Initiation through hardship is the British way. The general idea is to be atrociously brutal to recruits, not so much because one enjoys flogging them (though that could be an incidental advantage), but in order to find out what sort of stuff they are made of.** (2004)

In fact, when using a conversational style that adopts some of the rhythms of speech, it's normal to end a few sentences with prepositions. For example, it seems harmless to write:

- **There are certain values that people should all be prepared to stand up for.**
- **The council decided this was the right system to invest in.**
- **It is very important to ensure you have listed everyone you owe money to.**

It's true that the first could be recast as:

> **There are certain values for which people should all be prepared to stand up.**

but this would still annoy anyone who thinks 'up' is a preposition here (actually it's a particle attached to the verb). There's no point changing a sentence that reads well, sounds right, and says what the writer wants to say, just because it contravenes the myth. Of course, some sentences ending in prepositions *do* need to be recast, but this is because they read awkwardly, not because they break a rule. These sentences, for example, come to a feeble end:

> **Get clean photocopies of the forms you want to make changes to. Make sure there is enough white space to mark your alterations on.**

Better to write:

> **Get clean photocopies of the forms you want to change. Make sure there is enough white space for marking your alterations.**

Also a bit feeble is this from the *Daily Mail* (2005) about handwriting:

The main problem is that many of the teachers and parents weren't taught to write properly themselves. It's a vicious circle in urgent need of being broken into.

Just omit the last word.

Myth 4: Never split your infinitives

Splitting the infinitive means putting a word or phrase between 'to' and the verb word, as in:

The department wants to <u>more than</u> double its budget.
The passengers were asked to <u>carefully</u> get down from the train.

If you think a sentence will be more emphatic, clear, or rhythmical, split your infinitive—there's no reason in logic or grammar for avoiding it. The examples above seem better split than not. Take care, though, lest the gap between 'to' and the verb word becomes too great, as the reader could lose track of the meaning. A *Times* editorial says:

The most diligent search can find no modern grammarian to pedantically, to dogmatically, to invariably condemn a split infinitive. Rules are created to aid the communication of meaning. In the cause of meaning they can sometimes be broken.

Though this is excellent, it encourages the idea that to split an infinitive is to break a rule. There is no such rule, merely a superstition that arose in the 19th century when grammarians sought to impose Latin rules on English. In Latin, a present-tense infinitive is always a single, unsplittable word: *amare, cantare, audire.*

If you can't bring yourself to split an infinitive, at least allow others the freedom to do so. For example, Byron, with his:

To slowly trace the forest's shady scene.

Phrases like 'I easily won the race' and 'he quickly drove away' are not split infinitives as there is no infinitive present.

There is good news. The most ardent defender of the split-infinitive myth, the *Daily Telegraph*, has hoisted the white flag. In an editorial on 31 July 1995 the paper had condemned the first edition of this book as the devil's work (I exaggerate only a little) for its view that split infinitives were OK. Yet on 12 December 2006 its leader-writer Christopher Howse posted a blog headed 'Why on earth do people think that splitting an infinitive is wrong?' and remarked:

> **When writing journalism I generally avoid a split infinitive because it annoys people, but there is no grammatical objection to it. The best reason objectors seem to find is that they were taught not to do it at school. It is no use arguing that an adverb between "to" and the infinitive form of the verb is illogical, or breaks up a semantic whole.**

You'd imagine there'd be nobody so boring as to have collected examples of the *Telegraph*'s split infinitives in a little jacket file since 1995. You'd be wrong, though, so here are a few of them: *to twice trip them up*; *to suddenly become inspired*; *his 42-year-old knees started to really creak*; *to seemingly last the course better*; *ready to strenuously deny the charge*; *to somehow swallow the disappointment*; *to instantly place him among the pantheon*; *resigned myself to never experiencing*; *to ever see themselves in such a light*; *to still be in the team*; *to radically reform the Independent*; *to still earn his devotion*; *failing to fully disclose*; *M&S would be unable to successfully fight*.

Myth 5: Never write a one-sentence paragraph

If you can say what you want to say in a single sentence that lacks a direct connection with any other sentence, just stop there and go on to a new paragraph. There's no rule against it. A paragraph can be a single sentence, whether long, short, or middling.

Myth 6: Write as you speak

This advice is widely heard, but take it with a large pinch of salt. True, many writers would benefit from making their writing more conversational, using more personal pronouns and active verbs. But this is not the same as writing as you speak. Most of us don't speak in complete sentences—a transcript of our talk usually reads like gibberish on the page. Even what is said in Parliament is tidied up by the Hansard writers so it makes some kind of sense. Good, clear writing is much more than speech transcribed; it is speech organized, worked, and refined for smooth reading.

12 Clearly non-sexist

Guideline: *Try to avoid sexist language.*
Trying to sell cat litter through posters on the London underground may not be easy, and since many cats are owned by women, the task becomes harder if the wording of the posters excludes them:

> Keep your fur on. Your owner is as concerned with hygiene as you are, which is why he buys Catsan Hygiene Cat Litter...In fact, Catsan works so well that it actually produces less odour after six days than ordinary cat litters do after only one day...Which means your owner will have to change it less often. Allowing them to get on with their life and you to get on with yours, all nine of them.

Though sexist usage is not strictly a matter of clarity, any writing habit that builds a barrier between you and half your readers must reduce the impact of your message. So even if you disagree with the view that sexist writing reinforces prejudice and unfair discrimination, it is still wiser to use inclusive language. Occasional silliness apart ('the art of one-upping' doesn't have quite the same ring as 'one-upmanship'), inclusive writing usually makes more sense and more accurately reflects reality.

Using sex-neutral terms

Using sex-neutral terms means avoiding words suggesting that maleness is the norm or superior or positive and that femaleness is non-standard, subordinate, or negative. Sex-specific terms like 'businessmen', 'firemen', 'poetess', 'headmaster', and 'sculptress' can be replaced by less restrictive words: 'business people' (or 'executives'), 'firefighters', 'poet', 'headteacher', and 'sculptor'. It's almost unthinkable today for Sylvia Plath to be called a poetess as she was in *The Times* in 1960. Some sex-specific terms may survive this trend, such as 'actress'—which perhaps lacks some of the negative echoes of low status and low pay—though some actresses specifically refer to themselves as 'actors'. 'Fishers' and 'fisherfolk' seem unlikely to gain popular acceptance as alternatives to 'fishermen' on the open sea, yet 'anglers' is a convenient sex-neutral term for those who fish for sport. The term 'purseress', which was used in a BBC broadcast of 1968 about the first voyage of a cross-Channel hovercraft, seems laughable today when 'purser' would be the obvious sex-neutral term. The *Daily Mail* used 'seductress' in 2008, presumably as a more seductive alternative to the sex-neutral 'seducer'. On the airlines, the sex-neutral 'flight attendant' seems to be vanquishing 'steward' and 'stewardess'. A BBC commentator on the 2008 Olympics caused wry amusement by describing a female North Korean soccer player as her team's 'taliswoman'. If 'talisman' can be sexed up like that, can 'womanic depression' and 'ewomancipation' be far behind, ask the cynics who forget that 'woman' and 'man' stem from different root words.

There seem not to be any palatable alternatives for such terms as 'manned space flight' and 'craftsmanship', and 'dominatrix' continues to cane any alternatives that rear their handsome heads. On the vexed question of chair, chairman, or chairwoman, the British socialist Barbara Castle used to say she didn't mind what people called her as long as she was in the chair.

Sex-specific words	Sex-neutral words
authoress	author
aviatrix	aviator
chairman, chairwoman	chair (or ask what they prefer)
clergymen	clergy, clerics
comedienne	comedian
craftsmen	craft workers, artisans
executrix	executor
forelady, foreman	supervisor, head juror (law)
heroine	hero
layman	lay person
man, mankind (humans)	the human species, human beings, people, humans, humanity

Sex-specific words	Sex-neutral words
man (noun)	person, individual, you
man (verb)	operate, staff, run, work
manageress	manager
man-hours	working hours, work hours
man-made	manufactured, artificial
parliamentary draftsman/ draughtsman	parliamentary counsel/drafter
policeman, policewoman	police officer
salesman, salesgirl	sales agent/representative/consultant
testatrix	testator, will-maker
workman	worker

Using titles or 'he or she'

It is better to avoid 'he', 'his', or 'him' when you intend to include both men and women. Instead of:

> Solvent abuse is not a crime but if a police officer finds a young person under 17 sniffing solvents, he should take him to a secure place such as a police station, home, or hospital.

you could repeat the short titles of both people:

> Solvent abuse is not a crime but if a police officer finds a young person under 17 sniffing solvents, the officer should take the person to a secure place such as home, a police station, or a hospital.

Using 'he or she' and 'him or her' is also feasible here—perhaps, to avoid confusion, for just one of the people:

> Solvent abuse is not a crime but if a police officer finds a person under 17 sniffing solvents, he or she should take the person to a secure place such as home, a police station, or a hospital.

Repeated use of 'he or she' and similar terms becomes clumsy and obtrusive. The alternatives, 's/he' or 'he/she', look ugly and cannot be spoken easily.

In guidance to police officers, it would be feasible to use 'you':

> Solvent abuse is not a crime but if <u>you</u> find a person under 17 sniffing solvents, <u>you</u> should take <u>him or her</u> to a secure place such as <u>his or her</u> home, a police station, or a hospital.

In a booklet issued to parents about schools, one British local education authority avoided the problem neatly for many years by referring to 'your child' as 'he' on odd-numbered pages and 'she' on even-numbered pages. This fix was explained in the introduction. The 2008 edition, however, uses 'your child' throughout.

Using the plural

A further alternative, and often the best, is to use the plural:

> Solvent abuse is not a crime but if <u>police officers</u> find a person under 17 sniffing solvents, <u>they</u> should take the person to a secure place such as the person's home, a police station, or a hospital.

Using the plural helps to disentangle difficulties such as this:

> If the court grants immediate possession, the tenant and anyone else living with him or her is required to leave his, her or their home immediately. If he, she or they do not do so, the court bailiffs will evict him, her or them but there is usually a delay before this happens.

This could become

> If the court grants immediate possession, the tenant and anyone living with them must leave their home immediately. If they do not do so, the court bailiff will evict them but there is usually a delay before this happens.

or, with further gymnastics:

> If the court grants immediate possession, the tenant must leave his or her home. If the tenant does not do so, the court bailiff will evict him or her. The same applies to anyone living with the tenant.

Using plurals as singulars

It's becoming more acceptable to flout the grammatical conventions set in the 18th century by male grammarians and to do what Shakespeare did when he wrote:

God send everyone their heart's desire.

– in other words, to revive the old use of 'they', 'them', and 'their' as singulars, as in these examples from forms and standard letters:

1 Give details of your partner's income. If <u>they</u> have been unemployed for more than 12 months ...
2 Your child has been chosen to take part in a class to further support and consolidate <u>their</u> creative writing skills.
3 You may find that an individual has levels of competence in several skills beyond those required in <u>their</u> current role. This will occur when the person has developed <u>their</u> skills and potential in readiness for other opportunities.

To me, these read smoothly enough, though the third may be better wholly in the plural:

You may find that <u>individuals</u> have levels of competence in several skills beyond those required in their current roles. This will occur when <u>they</u> have developed their skills and potential in readiness for other opportunities.

'Everybody' and 'everyone' are clearly singular in appearance but for centuries have often been followed by a plural pronoun in speech and writing, which avoids the need for 'his/her':

Every one Sacrifices a Cow or more, according to their different Degrees of Wealth or Devotion.
(Dr Johnson, 1735—note the now-strange capitalization and ancient split of 'Every one')
Everyone was absorbed in their own businesses.
(Andrew Motion, poet laureate 1999–2009, 1989)
Every body does and says what they please. (Byron, 1820)
Everybody seems to recover their spirits. (John Ruskin, 1866)
Everybody has a right to describe their own party machine as they choose.
(Winston Churchill, 1954)

It's worth remembering that using the plural as a singular still infuriates some diehards. If you can sensibly avoid it, do.

Postscript: the alternatives are worse

To reject all the ideas as bad compromises means accepting the kind of writing found in this advert from the 1920s, in which all typists are assumed to be women and all managers men:

By dictating [...] you enable your typist to be typing all day, not wasting half the morning taking notes [...] She writes more letters and does her work more easily and accurately. Also the Dictaphone saves the time of the chief. We hardly like to talk about the 'after-hours' work, but it is acknowledged that closing time is the time when men who bear the real burdens oftentimes get down to their serious work. Then is the time when a man can concentrate, when there are no interruptions, no clicking of typewriters, no buzz of conversation to disturb his train of thought. Minds become decisive, delicate situations are mastered, and tactful, forceful phrases find shape. Here it is that the Dictaphone comes into its own; it records the accumulated letters for the typist first thing in the morning, the chief's desk is clear—his mind relieved, and he arrives next day with only the 'current' matter to receive his attention.

In 1987, the *Sunday Times* wrote the kind of paragraph that would be regarded as ridiculous today:

Twenty years to the month after the Torrey Canyon disaster...mankind is still incapable of cleaning up one of the largest messes he is capable of making. All he can do, if wind and waves are on his side, is limit the damage.

Today it is much more likely to be written as:

Twenty years to the month after the Torrey Canyon disaster ... people are still incapable of cleaning up one of the largest messes they are capable of making. All they can do, if wind and waves are on their side, is limit the damage.

As late as 1998, this example of sexist writing appeared in a company report written by a female middle manager:

He asked me to speak to Jane and Alice. I asked the girls if they had been using the business transfer form supplied during my previous visit. They said they had. Michael asked the girls to think of the names of some of the policies that should be on the quarterly list. The girls agreed, then left the room.

Modern business practice is to give Jane and Alice surnames when they are first mentioned, then to use 'them', 'they, 'his assistants', or 'Jane and Alice'. If this seems pernickety, try inserting male forenames and 'boys' at the appropriate places. 'Boys' and 'girls' are widely regarded as demeaning terms in the workplace.

13 Conquering grammarphobia

Guideline: *Use good grammar even if you don't know hundreds of grammatical terms.*

Grammarphobia—an irrational terror of grammatical terminology—is common among those who underwent grammar lessons at school and those who did not. The first group might regard grammar as just one more abstract ritual to be endured while the sun shone outside; the second group might see it as a magical key to successful writing, unreasonably withheld from them by malevolent educationists—especially, in the UK, from 1960–90.

A little grammar goes a long way. It is not necessary to know much beyond well-taught primary-school grammar in order to write plain English, but it's helpful to know a few terms if only to get the most out of books in this field. This chapter provides a brief glossary of the grammatical terms in most common use. When reading it, remember that many words change their grammatical character depending on their role in a sentence. Just because 'progress' is a noun in this sentence:

We will make progress on the project next week.

doesn't stop it becoming a verb in this one:

I have progressed further than expected.

Adjective A word of description. In 'local residents have demanded safer streets', 'local' and 'safer' are adjectives describing their respective nouns.

Adverb Most adverbs end in *-ly* such as *certainly, quickly, sadly, probably*, but non *-ly* forms include *often, soon, away*. There are two types. First, verb-phrase adverbs that say how the action in the verb takes place, such as the words underlined here:

The politician <u>quietly</u> but <u>firmly</u> argued for more investment in the railways.

Second, sentence adverbs that show the speaker's attitude to what's being said:

<u>Understandably</u>, the miners demanded better pay and conditions. The coal-owners, not <u>surprisingly</u>, refused.

Clause A group of words, often not a complete sentence, containing such things as a doer and verb. There are two clauses in: 'If there were no bad people, there would be no good lawyers.'

Contraction A word with one or more letters missing and replaced by an apostrophe, for example: *don't* (do not), *won't* (will not), *haven't* (have not), *can't* (cannot), *I'd* (I would or I should, or I had). In informal and semi-formal business writing, contractions can add a little conversational warmth. The more unusual ones, like *you'll* (you will), *you've* (you have), *there'll* (there will), *there're* (there are), and *you'd* (you would or you had), will be difficult for people with very low literacy (see chapter 23) and look odd in formal letters and reports. If you use them, make sure the apostrophes go in the right places.

Coordinator A word that links two or more words, sentences, or clauses, for example: *but, when, and, yet, if, although.*

Doer The person doing the action in a sentence, also known as the agent. In 'The publisher sent the contract', 'publisher' is the doer.

Grammar The body of rules and conventions by which words are grouped in a way that is meaningful to other people. For example, the sentence 'Paris look a beautiful city' is ungrammatical—if standard English is the criterion—as it breaks the rule that a singular doer must govern a singular form of the verb. Non-standard English uses different grammar, which can be just as effective in the right circumstances. Bob Marley, the Jamaican reggae musician (died 1981), sang of his ancestors: 'Pirates, yes they rob I/Sold I to the merchant ships/Minutes after they took I/From the bottomless pit.' Usage changes over time: Queen Victoria (died 1901) was quite happy to write 'The news from France are very bad' because in her day 'news' was an accepted plural. Grammar also changes from place to place: in British sports commentary, national and local teams tend to be plural—'England are winning 2–0'—while in Australian commentary, teams are usually singular.

Imperative The form of the verb that gives commands, for example: *go, eat, push, don't jump, let them go, let me see, don't be deceived.*

Infinitive The basic form of the verb, made up of *to* plus the verb word. Present-tense infinitives include *to go, to eat, to dream.* Past-tense infinitives include *to have gone, to have eaten, to have dreamt.* Passive-voice infinitives include *to be eaten*, *to be attacked*. See chapter 11 for split infinitives.

Nominalization A noun phrase formed from a verb, for example *preparation* (from *to prepare*), *renewal* (from *to renew*). See chapter 5.

Noun A word that signifies a person, thing, place, activity, or quality, for example *axe*, *beacon*, *carrot*, *dam*, *eating*, *frill*, *gerbil*, *happiness*. Proper nouns are specific names of people, places, and the like: *Christmas*, *Canberra*, *Canada*, *Caroline*.

Object The thing to which some action is done: 'We destroyed the *ship*.'

Paragraph A sentence or group of sentences separated in some way from the rest of the text and dealing with a particular part of the topic being discussed.

Participle The present participle adds *-ing* to the verb, hence *going*, *finding*, *sleeping*. The past participle adds *-d* or *-ed* to most verbs, as in *worked*, *decided*, *starved*. See chapter 4 for the way other past participles are formed.

Particle Many words that act as prepositions can also be adverb particles. In 'The relationship was broken off' and 'My car has broken down', the words 'off' and 'down' are particles. You can tell this because they lack objects. See Preposition.

Plural More than one. 'Frogs' is the plural of 'frog', which is singular. Where optional plurals are available for words of Latin or Greek origin, it's usually better to favour the English. Hence *referendums* not *referenda*, *forums* not *fora*, *stadiums* not *stadia*, *formulas* not *formulae*, *bureaus* not *bureaux*. But *criteria* not *criterions*, *phenomena* not *phenomenons*.

Preposition A word that usually comes immediately before a noun or pronoun, such as *in*, *down*, *up*, *under*, *of*, *with*, *by*, *to*, *from*, *at*: 'My car rolled *down* the hill and *under* the bridge.' Prepositions have objects, 'hill' and 'bridge' being the objects in that sentence. See Particle.

Pronoun A word that stands in place of nouns, for example *he*, *she*, *it*, *him*, *you*, *I*, *me*, *they*, *anyone*.

Sentence A statement, question, exclamation, or command—usually starting with a capital letter and ending in a full stop—which is complete in itself as the expression of a thought. Grammarians differ on what constitutes a sentence, but it is easiest to think of it as a finished utterance that makes sense in its context. Thus it will usually have a finite (finished) verb. These, for example, are sentences:

Having succeeded in its first two years, my business will keep growing.
Referring to your letter of 21 January, I can see no cause for alarm.

My business will succeed, no matter what [where 'happens' is implied].

But these are not sentences:

Having succeeded in its first two years.
Referring to your letter of 21 January.
My business will succeed, no matter what anyone [where it's not clear how the sentence would be completed].

Examples like the following can be classed as sentences even though they lack verbs, provided they make sense in context. The verbs are implied and shown here in square brackets:

[This is] Not so.
[That would happen] Over my dead body.
[This has been] A great success for all concerned.

Singular See Plural.

Subject The noun or pronoun that agrees with the verb. In 'My elephant needs water' and 'The postilion has been struck by lightning', the words 'elephant' and 'postilion' are the subjects.

Tense This refers to when an action occurs:

- Present tenses: *he goes*; *he is going*; *she survives*; *she is surviving*.
- Conditional: *she would go*; *they would see*.
- Future tense: *he will go*; *she will survive*.
- Past tenses: *he went*; *he has gone*; *he was going*; *he had gone*; *she survived*; *she has survived*; *she was surviving*; *she had survived*.

Verb Verbs express an action (*eat*, *sleep*) or a mental state (*know*, *believe*), so they are often described as doing words. A more accurate description is time-action words because the action takes place in past, present, or future time. In active-voice verbs, the doer normally comes in front of the verb: *Goats destroy vegetation*; *Pigs might fly*. In passive-voice verbs, the doer normally comes after the verb: *Vegetation is destroyed by goats*, or is not present at all. See chapter 4 for more on this.

14 Sound starts and excellent endings

Guideline: *In letters and emails, avoid fusty first sentences and formula finishes.*

In letters and emails the best place to start being straightforward is at the beginning. Your first sentence should be clear, complete, concise, and written in modern English. This is easily done if you steer clear of three common traps.

Trap 1: Writing half a sentence instead of a full one

All these first sentences are incomplete:

> **Further to your letter of 3 February concerning the trustees of the P F Smith 1982 Settlement.**
> **With reference to our previous correspondence notifying you of the transfer of the administration of the above policy to Norwich Union Healthcare with effect from 9 January.**
> **In response to your letter to Mr Jones dated 19 February.**
> **Regarding your claim for attendance allowance.**
> **Referring to your letter dated 10 July about delayed frequency allocations.**

Each statement needs to be continued and completed, inserting a comma instead of a full stop. For example:

> **Further to your letter of 3 February concerning the trustees of the P F Smith 1982 Settlement, I am pleased to enclose the form you requested.**
> **Regarding your claim for attendance allowance, I need to ask you for some more information.**

Alternatively, you could insert a main verb at the start to complete the sentences:

> **Thank you for your letter of 3 February concerning the trustees of the P F Smith 1982 Settlement.**
> **I refer to your claim for attendance allowance.**

Other verbs that will do a similar job include 'I acknowledge'; 'I confirm'; 'I write to explain'. These alternatives are preferable for another reason: they use personal words like 'I', 'you', and 'we'.

Don't be afraid to write a one-sentence paragraph at the start of a letter:

Thank you for your letter dated 13 May.

If you are taking the initiative—rather than responding to someone's enquiry—these phrases may be helpful to get your first sentence off to a sound start:

You are warmly invited to . . .
You may be interested in . . .
This is an opportunity to . . .
Now is a good time to consider . . .

Or you could ask a question—preferably one to which the reader will answer yes:

Does your office have old and outdated law books gathering dust in corners?
Would you like to create some extra space for yourself, and see those books go to a good cause at the same time? If so . . .

Trap 2: Repeating the heading

Most business and official letters and emails benefit from a heading, as it introduces the topic and saves having to write a long first sentence to cover the same ground. The heading might even run to several lines:

Curtis Brothers Ltd
Lease Agreement No. 727-252-8978
Goods: Touchtone Telephone System
Installation address: Piller House, Crook Street, Downtown DW5 9JK

Whether the heading is short or long, don't keep referring to it with such phrases as 'with reference to the above-mentioned equipment', 'regarding the above-numbered agreement', 'the above matter', and 'in connection with the aforementioned'. Let's say you are selling property and someone has phoned for details of a house. Instead of writing:

Dear Ms Widdicombe
'The Tree House', 67 Larch Avenue, Poplar
I refer to your enquiry yesterday in relation to the above-mentioned property, and enclose details as requested.

it is crisper to write:

> **Dear Ms Widdicombe**
> **'The Tree House', 67 Larch Avenue, Poplar**
> **I refer to your enquiry yesterday and enclose details of the property as requested.**

or

> **Thank you for your enquiry yesterday about this property; details are enclosed.**

or

> **Thank you for your enquiry. I am pleased to enclose details of this spacious and well-situated house.**

This last suggestion has the advantage of mentioning some of the key selling points immediately.

Trap 3: Archaic usage

Avoid fusty usage like:

> **Our recent telephone discussion <u>refers</u>.**

Modern readers find 'refers' very odd in this position. Use 'I refer to...' or 'In our recent telephone conversation, we discussed...'. In an internal email you could merely say 'We spoke about this', when the heading will provide enough context for what you spoke about.

Just as fusty is:

> **<u>Re</u> your letter of the 10th, <u>the contents of which have been noted</u>.**

'Re' is Latin for 'in the matter of' and is best avoided. When responding to someone's letter it is stating the obvious to say that you have 'noted the contents'. And anyway, the phrase sounds bureaucratic and disapproving—avoid it. Similarly, avoid the old-fashioned 'instant', 'ultimo', and 'proxime', which some writers still use to mean 'this month', 'last month', and 'next month' respectively, as in 'Thank you for your letter of the 15th instant'. This immediately marks you as a dinosaur.

Finishing well

Keep the finish simple and sincere. In a sales letter you could reiterate an important action point:

> **I look forward to receiving your application soon, then you can begin to benefit from all our services.**

You could even add a PS beneath the signature. Useful non-selling sign-offs include 'I hope this is helpful' (which is much better than the negative and servile 'I am sorry I cannot be more helpful'); and 'If you need more information, please contact me' (which is better than waffle like 'Should you require any further assistance or clarification from ourselves with regard to this matter, please do not hesitate to contact the writer undersigned').

If you are trying to close a correspondence with a difficult customer, you could try:

> **I hope you will understand our position, and I regret that we cannot help any further.**

If a complainant won't take no for an answer and you have nothing more to say, ever, you can try:

> **Unless you provide some new information, I regret that we will not respond to your letters about this matter.**

Remember: these are only suggestions. Compose your own phrases to suit your own circumstances and personality. Make it sound individually crafted if you can—you are not a robot.

Conventions on opening and closing

If you start with 'Dear [first name]', 'Dear [Mr/Mrs/Miss/Ms]', or 'Dear [first name and surname]', the conventional endings are 'Yours sincerely', 'Sincerely yours', or 'Yours truly'. Alternatively, use a sensible sign-off of your own making: 'Kind regards' and 'Best wishes' are now common among people well known to each other. 'Regards' and 'Kind regards' are common in informal and semi-formal emails.

If you begin 'Dear Sir' or 'Dear Madam', the traditional formal ending is 'Yours faithfully' or, in the US, 'Yours truly'. An alternative opening is to use the organization's name: 'Dear Express Bus Company'.

In British English, the 'Dear...' salutation is followed by a comma or nothing. Whichever is used, the pattern is repeated after the 'Yours...' closure. In American English, the salutation is usually followed by a colon (formal) or comma (informal) and the closure by a comma.

Esquires were originally the shield-bearers of knights, or men in royal or noble service. Once a favoured courtesy title after a man's name, 'Esq.' is now rarely seen in the address block of a letter. It is perhaps thought over-formal or servile. The title is not applied to a woman's name except, oddly, among US lawyers, where both sexes use it when writing to each other. Nor does it traditionally follow 'Mr', so 'Mr J Smith Esq.' is unusual.

Punctuation can be omitted from the address block in British English (though it's still common in the US), so this is now normal style:

Mr J H Author
34 Ivory Towers
Watership Down WD2 0NN

In the UK, with its complicated honours system and welter of titles for royalty, the peerage, and religious office-holders, the usually simple jobs of addressing an envelope, greeting a correspondent, and closing a letter can be hazardous. If your work requires you to write to peers, presidents, mayors, and magistrates, you'll find a helpful path charted for you (and as much feudal wisdom as you can stomach) in the 240 pages of *Titles and Forms of Address* (A&C Black, 2007) and the 384 pages of *Debrett's Correct Form* (Headline, 2002).

15 Planning effectively

Guideline: *Plan before you write*.

'I don't know how to get started' is a common complaint. In the 'weaknesses' section of her pre-attendance form, one of my writing-course students declared: 'Before I start I often have to think for some time about what I am going to write.'

Thinking before writing is usually a strength, and many people find that the best way to start writing (or dictating) is not to write but to plan. The first stage of planning is to think out:

- who's going to read the document
- what they'll be expecting to get from it
- in what circumstances they'll be reading (in their leisure time; at work in a quarry or on a building site; on a website; underwater)
- what you're trying to achieve.

It is better to plan on paper or on a computer screen than in your head. This is because most people's brains are better at marshalling ideas when they are set down on the page. It's difficult to hold twenty points in your head while simultaneously assessing them for strength and relevance and grouping them into bundles of related points. For one thing, you're having to assess which of the two million billion possible ways of ranking the points is the best.

For a short document, keep the plan simple. Make a list or bubble diagram containing all the points you expect to make, *in no particular order*. (On the next page is a bubble diagram of my first thoughts for writing chapter 24.) Cross out the irrelevant points. Link the rest into groups of related points. Rank them using one of the structures in chapter 16. Then you will have a good framework from which to write or dictate. Don't skimp this stage, but don't overdo it to the point of boredom.

Longer documents benefit from fuller planning. If your managers ask you to write a report, discuss exactly what's wanted so that you're clear on the purpose and the amount of detail expected—otherwise you'll waste time on soul-destroying rewrites. If your managers don't

Simple plan: a bubble diagram

really know what they want, you should investigate the topic thoroughly and return with a core statement (explained next) which sets out the purpose of the document as you see it.

Creating a core statement and horizontal document plan

A core statement says what you'll cover in the main section of the document—normally the discussion section. It helps you to focus on the task and the audience. Sharpening your focus in this way will save you researching topics that don't need to be covered. The core statement also builds your confidence as it provides your first glimpse of the finishing line.

The core statement is a rigidly constructed sentence in seven segments, as shown next. The oblique strokes separate alternative words and phrases that you might use:

Core segments	Typical phrases
1 Type of document	This report/paper
2 Your readers	to the head of the legal department
3 Verb	describes/assesses/explains/analyses/evaluates /considers/investigates
4 Topic	possible improvements to the clarity of our insurance policies
5 Linking phrase	in terms of/with reference to/under
6 Number of sections	six main lines of enquiry
7 Main headings	– benefits and dangers
	– what documents we would need to rewrite
	– implications for staff training
	– other companies' experience
	– how to comply with the EC directive on plain language
	– costs (internal and external)

Don't expect to write the core statement in ten seconds. You may need several attempts at choosing the best verb in segment 3. Discuss the core statement with your manager, agree any changes, and get him or her to sign it off. This reduces the chance of creating a report nobody wants.

The core statement underlies the next stage of planning—the horizontal document plan. Regard this as a series of related boxes into which you slot all the points you expect to make under the headings set by the core statement. The main practical points are as follows:

- Use a big sheet of paper (prefer A3 to A4).
- Rotate the page so that the longer edge is nearer to you (landscape).
- Set down your headings along the top.
- Jot down all the points you can think of under that heading. Usually you'll want to create a system of subheadings within each section: boxes nested within boxes.

Let's assume the core statement said:

This report to the head of the legal department describes possible improvements to the clarity of our insurance policies under six main lines of enquiry: benefits and dangers; what documents we would need to rewrite; implications for staff training; other companies' experience; how to comply with the EC directive on plain language; costs (internal and external).

A much-simplified (and tidied up) horizontal document plan for two sections of the report might look like this:

You can then assess the points for strength and relevance and, if necessary, group them under further subheadings. Gaps in your knowledge may be revealed; you may need to fill them before proceeding. Next, put the headings and points in order, perhaps using one of the structures in chapter 16. Show a tidy version of the plan to your manager. Discuss it with him or her. Get it signed off.

The writing itself can now begin. As you write the first draft you'll probably change your mind about the order of points, and add to the plan. This is fine—the plan is meant to be a working document. When you do start to write, there's no need to begin at the beginning.

Provided they are self-contained, the bits you are confident about and know best can be written first. Then you'll be less anxious about tackling the rest.

I've assumed that you're the sole writer on this project. If you're part of a team, the core statement and horizontal document plan can be prepared collaboratively, using a whiteboard or similar. Then all the team members can take part in creating a common purpose and plan for the report, and will write individual sections with a better awareness of how their part fits into the whole.

Alternative approaches to planning

Writers I've worked with seem to perform better when they plan. They also *believe* they write better and more quickly. But not everyone is happy to plan to the same extent: there are differing approaches, all with their followers. For convenience, four main labels can be used to represent these approaches: 'architects', 'watercolourists', 'oil painters', and 'bricklayers'. You may like to consider which category you fit into and whether the alternatives might suit you better. Bear in mind, though, that most writers fit into two or more of the categories from time to time.

- **Architects** tend to take a three-stage approach to writing: planning, writing, and revising. They don't try to perfect the writing as they create the first draft. They prefer to leave a draft and come back to it later, revising thoroughly on paper or on screen.
- **Watercolourists** try to produce a complete version rapidly at the first attempt, with little revision. There may have been little planning on paper but long mental incubation of the document. Some literary writers are said to favour this, believing that it keeps their writing spontaneous and true to feeling. Jack Kerouac wrote his novel of the beat generation, *On the Road*, at 6 500 words a day using a typewriter with a single roll of paper and making few corrections.
- **Oil painters** tend to jot down ideas and then organize and repeatedly rework them. On paper there is little planning. Rewriting seems to help oil painters to find out what they think, rather than helping them to focus on the readers' needs.

- **Bricklayers** tend to polish every sentence before going on to the next, in a careful process of building block by block. This means they revise very little once a first draft has been prepared. Bricklayers tend to plan and have a clear idea of what they want to say from the outset. They tend not to regard writing as an aid to thinking.

Given the importance of careful thought about the readers' needs when preparing plain-English documents, the architectural approach, with its bias towards planning, seems to be the most suitable. Again, though, you should be ready to experiment, use different strategies for different tasks, and do whatever will get the writing job completed to a satisfactory standard with the minimum of effort.

If you can't see yourself in any of the above categories, here is another way of looking at it, based on the ideas of Dr Betty Sue Flowers, once a University of Texas English professor. Her paradigm (or writing model) separates writing into four stages, each requiring the writer to take a different approach and assume four different personalities. They are described thus by the Australian plain-language practitioner, Christopher Balmford:

- **The madman** who brainstorms, takes notes, and is enthusiastic, experimental, and above all creative.
- **The architect** who reviews the information that the madman has created and gathered, and uses it to develop an outline of the document.
- **The carpenter** who fleshes out the structure by writing the text and producing the first (however many) drafts.
- **The judge** who edits and reviews [the] drafts.

All the personalities are vital to the writing process, but the architect has the key job of dividing, classifying, and sequencing the information.

Strategic planning: learning from readers

A strategic plan may be necessary, especially when preparing a major document for internal or public use. The plan below relates to the preparation of a booklet for staff joining a company pension scheme, but many of its points are universal. The plan builds in plenty of reader involvement—essential unless secrecy, deadlines, or costs prevent it.

Pre-production stage

- Decide the purpose. Why is the booklet needed? Would something else do a better job?
- Determine the content. At this stage, just outline main points.
- Define the audience. Consult staff to see what they expect from the booklet. Discuss the outline. If possible, get an idea of how they would like the information organized and even what they'd like it to say.
- Consider how the booklet fits into the system. How will it be distributed, used, stored? Will it be downloadable from your company website? How will it be amended in future and by whom? What organizational politics will need to be dealt with and how?

Production stage

- Fill in the outline of the content. Decide what structure is most suitable.
- Write the draft. Include headings and subheadings but don't worry about adding too many layout features at this stage.
- Evaluate the draft with staff—include some who haven't yet been consulted. Use a questionnaire to test comprehension. Iron out problems by redrafting and restructuring.
- Consider using an external editor to clarify the text and make its grammar and punctuation more consistent.
- Prepare an appropriate layout. Use professional help if necessary. Evaluate the layout with staff.
- Consider using an external proofreader and, for long documents, an external indexer.
- Give the booklet a reference number and date.

Post-production stage

- Final evaluation: after distribution, use a survey and face-to-face discussions to gauge reactions. Did the booklet do its job?
- Keep it up to date by regular reviews.

16 Using reader-centred structure

Guideline: *Organize your material so that readers can grasp the important information early and navigate through the document easily.*

You might be lucky. Your readers might regard your letter or report as the highlight of their day. They might give it the time you know it deserves. They might sit back in a comfortable armchair and browse through it contentedly for hours.

Or you might be like most other writers. Your document will be an interruption to your readers' busy day. They'll read it in haste, scribbling remarks on it and picking out important bits with a highlighter pen. And they'll be asking two questions with every sentence they read:

- So what?
- How does this affect me?

Answering these questions in plain words and short sentences won't always be enough. You'll also need to organize the material so that readers can extract what they want in the shortest possible time. This will increase the likelihood of getting your ideas read—the first step in getting them accepted. And a crucial way of organizing material well is to put the big news early. Then readers can see, right from the start, exactly what you're getting at. This is particularly important on Web pages, where limited screen space means that the top half of a page is more likely to be read (see chapter 21).

This chapter shows ten ways ('models') of organizing your information. Don't feel that you have to force your writing to fit the models or, where headings are suggested, that you have to use the exact words. Quarry them for ideas that will suit your own way of doing things.

Model 1: Top-heavy triangle

Put your most important point first, follow it with the next most important, and so on, until your last paragraph includes relatively minor points. You may need to do a bit of scene-setting to start with—use the first sentence or the heading for this:

John

Request for leave from 25 March – 12 April

Scene-setting	Thanks for your email yesterday.
Big news	The managing director has agreed to your request to take special unpaid leave immediately after your visit to Athens. It is vital, though, that we have a brief written report of your key findings as soon as the business part of the trip is completed. Will you please email or fax this to us on 24 March.
Less important	As your flight was booked some time ago, please liaise with Michael South about rearranging the return leg.
Minor points	Hope this helps. We'll speak again after Tuesday's meeting.

Even unwelcome news should usually be delivered early. You may need to soften it, though:

John

Request for leave from 25 March – 12 April

Scene-setting	Thanks for your email yesterday.
Big news	The managing director considered your request carefully but I'm sorry to tell you that he has had to say no. He feels that the launch of the new product at the end of March really demands your presence here.
Minor points	I realize you'll be disappointed but perhaps we can have a chat about things after next Tuesday's meeting.

I know of only one good reason for saving big news till the end—deliberate obfuscation, when delay will increase surprise, raise tension, or leave the reader with a sense of threat.

The top-heavy triangle is useful when you're asking for something your readers may be reluctant to give. The letter below is trying to get local traders to fill in a questionnaire. But where does this vital information come?

Dear Mr Jones

Our Sea Fishery Group is conducting studies in order to aid the development of a local Fishery Forum. The idea of a Fishery Forum is to promote the fishing industry of the north west and to stress the importance of a regional approach as this could attract support from the European Union.

The study is designed to help evaluate the monetary impact that fish landings from the north west fishing fleet have on the region as a whole. Also the study will assess the feasibility of placing a logo on local fish products so that their origins can be instantly recognized.

To gather information for the study, a questionnaire has been designed. It is hoped that a high proportion of these forms will be completed and returned so that the final analysis will be as detailed as possible.

All answers to the questionnaires will be confidential and only the combined figures for the whole region would be published.

I would greatly appreciate it if you could complete the enclosed questionnaire by 15 June and return it to me. If you have any queries about the study or the questionnaire, please contact me on the above number. Thank you for your help.

The readers only learn the main action point in the final paragraph, and they might never get there. It would have been better to begin with an explanatory heading and the plea for help.

Dear Mr Jones

Improving the prosperity of the north west: your help is needed

I'm writing to ask for your help with a venture that will improve the prosperity of our region and of every trader who does business here.

Our Sea Fishery Group is conducting research into setting up a Fishery Forum that would promote our local fishing industry.

As part of the research, I need your help. Would you please be kind enough to complete the enclosed questionnaire and return it to me by 15 June? [etc.]

In long letters or long emails that deal with several different issues, it's a good idea to use a heading for each issue. The heading can be placed between paragraphs or form the first few words of the paragraph, in bold or italic type. The top-heavy triangle can then be used when arranging the points in each headed section. When responding to long and rambling letters of complaint, ombudsmen and regulators often begin, 'From your letter, I understand that your main complaints are ...', followed by a bullet list. This is good practice: it sets out what issues will be dealt with and enables the complainant to object if the issues have been wrongly summarized.

Model 2: Problem–cause–solution

This is a simple model for short letters, emails and reports. First you state the problem ...

> **You asked me to find out how a batch of chocolate came to be contaminated during the night shift on 25 April.**

Then you state the cause ...

> **What seems to have happened is that some inadequately treated reclaimed chocolate was added to the mix. This occurred because the reclaimed chocolate was mislabelled and stored in the wrong part of the factory.**

Then you say what should happen in the future ...

> **The contaminated batch will have to be destroyed. The cost of the loss is about £2 800, taking everything into account. I have told supervisors to tighten their procedures for labelling and storage. They'll be reporting back to me next week.**

Model 3: Chronological order

This simply follows the time sequence of a series of actions or events, which can be paragraphed, numbered, or dated depending on the purpose. For more on using chronological-order instructions, see chapter 20.

Model 4: Questions and answers

Questions and answers help to break the information into small chunks. Here's an excellent example, which also benefits from short paragraphs and everyday English:

> **How do I make a complaint about the council's services?**
>
> If you have a complaint, please raise it first with the department that deals with the subject of your complaint. Contact them and try to get the problem settled there and then. Phone numbers of departments are shown at the end of the leaflet.
>
> **What if I'm still not satisfied?**
>
> If you're not satisfied or your complaint is complicated, please set out all the facts clearly by making a formal complaint in writing. You can do this on the pull-out form opposite. If you need help to complete the form, please ask at any council office. We'll acknowledge your complaint and keep you informed at every stage.
>
> **Where else can I get help?**
>
> If you're not satisfied with the way your complaint is dealt with, you could contact one of your ward councillors. A list is available at all our reception desks and from Member Services (telephone: Cadeby 4000).

Questions tend to provoke interest in readers by bringing them into the action. It's customary to reiterate at least part of the question when answering it. So the answer to 'What if I'm not satisfied?' begins 'If you're not satisfied ...'. This may be tedious but seems to help the readers. There's no harm in occasionally giving a short answer where it would be boring to repeat the question. So if the question were 'Can I claim housing benefit if I live alone?', the answer would be 'Yes.'

Questions are particularly useful if they use personal words. Compare:

Where can more information be obtained?

with

Where can I get more information?

Questions also convert dull, plodding label-headings into verb-rich information. Compare this heading:

Frequency of use by paramedics of aspirin in the treatment of heart-attack victims

with its equivalent question:

How often do paramedics use aspirin to treat heart-attack victims?

or, in the passive to put the stress on 'aspirin':

How often is aspirin used by paramedics to treat heart-attack victims?

Model 5: S–C–R–A–P (Situation, Complication, Resolution, Action, Politeness)

A corny mnemonic, but useful. A letter or email using this structure might say:

Dear Mr Soaring

Order for 5 Sky-Fly hang gliders, £2 500 each

Situation	Thank you for your order dated 17 December; my apologies for the delay in responding.
Complication	The manufacturers have recently withdrawn the Sky-Fly and now offer a much-improved model, the Sky Jet. I enclose a leaflet that gives details of all its features.
Resolution	Although the price of the Sky Jet is £255 more than the old model, I can offer it to you at a special introductory price of £2 600 until 10 January next. We could let you have immediate delivery.
Action	If you would like to order the new model at the discount price, do please contact us. We accept payment by cheque and all major credit cards. You can also buy online from our e-shop.
Politeness	I look forward to hearing from you.

Model 6: S–O–A–P (Situation, Objective, Appraisal, Proposal)

Here's a much-simplified short report that uses SOAP:

FALL IN SALES OF RABBIT CHOCOLATE BARS
Situation

- In the last three months, Rabbit has lost about 10 per cent of its share in the aphrodisiac chocolate bar market.

Objective

- To regain and improve market share in the next six months.

Appraisal

- The impact of our initial advertising and promotional burst has petered out. Research shows the recent price increase didn't affect sales very much but Rabbit has started losing ground to similar-priced competitors like the Hunky bar and the Rhino bar: people are seeing them as more sophisticated products.

Proposal

- Target the higher social groups with a more sophisticated campaign based on Beatrix Potter stereotypes, including special-offer shooting weekends in Brer Rabbit country.

Model 7: PARbox emails and memos

Some firms, infuriated at the time-wasting woolliness of inter-office emails and memos, insist that all begin with three standard boxes for Purpose, Action, and Response:

Purpose

To explain developments in the Savill fraud case

Action requested

Your help in unearthing missing documents

Response required

By 10 January

Readers can then immediately see the key facts and fit the request into their schedule. After the PARboxes will come a main heading and text as normal.

Model 8: The 5 P's (Position, Problem, Possibilities, Proposal, Packaging)

Using these headings, a short and very simplified report for a sports club might say:

UPDATE ON OUR LEAGUE PLACING

1   Position
1.1   With only 10 games to go this season, the team is close to the relegation zone.
1.2   The coach's contract has two years to run at £70K a year. He is widely respected in the town and throughout the sport.
2   Problem
2.1   Recent results have been very bad—9 defeats and 2 draws in the last 11 games. Attendances are down 10 per cent on last season's and our overdraft stands at £3m. The fans are restless and some have started barracking the coach.
3   Possibilities
3.1   We could buy new players before the transfer deadline—the coach's proposals are attached.
3.2   We could terminate the coach's contract immediately but this would be costly and very unpopular with most of the fans. It could also damage team morale.
3.3   We could leave things as they are.
4   Proposal
4.1   We should try to buy Player A to improve the defence. Apart from that, we should leave things as they are because:
   (a) there's little cash for new players or buying out the coach's contract
   (b) two key players will soon return from injury
   (c) the team has played better recently and the last two defeats were very narrow.
5   Packaging
5.1   It may be a cliché, but we need to express full confidence in the players and the coach and say that they would benefit from the continued support of the fans. We need to explain the club's financial position better. We need to reassure supporters that their views will continue to be considered.

In the report I've added a commonly used system of paragraph numbering. The aim is to help readers to navigate through the report and, if necessary, comment on it more easily. An alternative to a decimal system is simply to number paragraphs in 1–2–3 order. In either system, if you use a second tier of heading, you don't need to number it but you should distinguish it by layout, perhaps with bold type or underlining.

Avoid creating a third or fourth level of decimals (3.1.2 etc.) unless the amount of detail really demands it. Many readers will boggle at such complications.

Model 9: Correspondent's order

It's possible to respond to some letters or emails using the same order of points as your correspondent. Normally it's wise to say that this is what you're doing:

I'd like to respond to your points in the same order that you used.

Model 10: Full-dress report

A good arrangement for a detailed administrative or technical report or consultation paper is given below. Notice that the summary is placed early, though it will be written late in the process. A scientific report would also have sections for 'method' and 'results', which would follow the introduction. It might also have an abstract—a kind of condensed summary that can be included in a database of abstracts along with a list of key words and phrases that researchers will look for as they trawl the database.

Title

The title says what the topic is, briefly but not too cryptically. If necessary, add a longer subtitle. Also add the author's name, the date, and the distribution list.

Contents list

If included at all, a contents list deserves a page of its own. Its headings should replicate those in the body of the report as this makes them easy to find.

Summary

The summary delivers the report's most interesting must-read points in bitesize chunks. It should briefly set out the report's purpose, main findings, main conclusions, and main recommendations. It is designed to give an accurate and rapid understanding of the main issues, enabling busy readers to ignore everything else if they wish. Therefore any main conclusion or recommendation that is qualified elsewhere in the report should also be qualified in the summary. A summary may contain subheadings, which should differ from any other main headings in the report.

The summary should mainly be composed of informative not descriptive statements: 'Five staff should be transferred to Section X', not 'A recommendation is made about transferring staff'.

Remember that everyone who sees the report will read the summary, whereas perhaps only 30 per cent will read the full report—so allow proper time to prepare it well. In a short report (say, two or three pages), the summary can come after the conclusions and recommendations or be omitted altogether.

If you have written the report well, the summary should be easy to do because it is mainly a cut-and-paste exercise, with some fine-tuning and polishing.

The summary's position, substance, and brevity make it the most important part of the report. In a long document, you could summarize the big news of each section at the start of the section. Then the readers will know whether to bother reading further. You can then stitch together your section summaries to form the overall document summary.

If most readers are unlikely to want the full report, circulate only the summary with the title and distribution list attached. People can then call for the full report if they wish.

Introduction

The introduction describes the purpose, background, how the work was done, and what it cost. It may include brief, simple acknowledgements. Resist the temptation to include conclusions and recommendations here.

Discussion

The heading 'Discussion' need not appear if more specific alternatives are available. The discussion section sets out your main results, findings, arguments, options, and ideas, preferably under headings and subheadings so that readers can easily find their way around and skim from point to point. It is likely to be the longest section. See chapter 15 for how to plan it.

Conclusions

Conclusions are the inferences you draw from the discussion. They're not the same as 'concluding remarks' so there's no need to put them at the end. It may be convenient to include them in the discussion itself, while saying clearly that each is a conclusion. Putting them into a separate section may help the reader, though, especially in a long report.

Recommendations

Your recommendations are the steps you think should be taken, based on the conclusions. Again, it may sometimes be convenient to include them in the discussion, and again you'll need to make clear that they are your recommendations. To make clear their status, recommendations normally include 'should' or 'should be'. They can be numbered or bulleted to add punch.

Appendices

Any appendices provide a home for fine detail that readers won't need in order to follow the discussion.

Finally

Your writing will rarely be the most important thing in your busy readers' lives. Your main aim is to help readers to achieve their objectives in reading your work. Stated bluntly, these are to Get In, Get On, and Get Out—in other words, to access the information readily, progress through it quickly, and stop as soon as possible. Lucid language and structure will help them do so, and that can only be good for your reputation as a clear thinker.

17 Using alternatives to words, words, words

Guideline: *Consider different ways of setting out your information.*

The written word alone is not always the best way of communicating a message. Graphic devices such as tables, illustrations, pie charts, diagrams, maps, strip cartoons, mathematical formulas, and photographs can all help. The difficulty is knowing when to use them and which ones will suit the information. There's no rulebook. You have to be flexible and experiment a bit to see what works. And, ideally, you should test your decisions with typical readers.

Using tables

An insurance company wants to tell a customer how much her policies are worth, so it uses continuous text:

1/ You now hold three equity plans. The 2002 plan is mature and is valued at £462.08. The 2003 plan will not become mature until 1 January 2015 and is currently valued at £645.43. The 2004 plan will mature on 1 January 2016 and is currently valued at £438.45.

These sentences are short and simple enough for any investor who knows that 'mature' means that the policy is ripe for cashing in. (You noticed, though, that the last two sentences switched from negative to positive despite making similar points.) Using elaborate alternatives to text would be unjustifiable for such simple ideas. But a table would be feasible because the information in each sentence consists of a year, a value, and a maturity date. Creating a table is fairly easy in most word-processing packages, and might look like this:

2/ You now hold three equity plans, as follows:		
Year of plan	*Current value*	*Maturity date*
2002	£462.08	Already mature
2003	£645.43	1 January 2015
2004	£438.45	1 January 2016

Or you could try it this way:

3/ You now hold three equity plans, as follows:			
	2002 plan	*2003 plan*	*2004 plan*
Current value	£462.08	£645.43	£438.45
Maturity date	Already mature	1 Jan 2015	1 Jan 2016

Of the three possibilities, I prefer version 2, as it seems easier to compare the values and maturity dates in vertical columns than in continuous text or rows. The preferred table could be extended easily if, say, details of ten plans were being given. In continuous text this would be tedious, while you'd need a very wide piece of paper or a wide screen to accommodate ten tables in the style of version 3.

Exploring other possibilities

The more complex the information, the more the possible choices of presentation multiply, and there is rarely one perfect solution. To show this, here are five ways of presenting the same handful of facts about what a local government department will charge for hiring a hall.

Version 1: Continuous text—original version

This version is the real one being used by the department. Though far from total gobbledygook, it doesn't seem clear at first reading:

> Hiring fees of £100.00 or less must be paid in full at the time of booking. In the case of all hiring fees in excess of £100.00 the hirer agrees to pay £100.00 deposit at once on all bookings valued up to £200.00 or 50 per cent of the total hire fee as a deposit on bookings on or over £200.00 in value. The balance of the cost of each hiring must be paid at least 21 days before the date of the event.

I asked several writers to come up with alternatives. Shown below are the four main lines that emerged. In one or two, the tone of voice has changed with the use of 'please' instead of 'must'. (In a contract, 'must' would be necessary.) Otherwise, the content is the same, though sharp-eyed readers will notice that amounts from £100.01–100.99 aren't covered. At the end of all the examples, I'll give the verdict of our focus group. Which do you think is best?

Version 2: Continuous text—paragraphed version

This version paragraphs the information:

> If a hiring fee is £100 or less, please pay it in full when you book.If the hiring fee is from £101 to £199, please pay £100 deposit when you book, then pay the rest at least 21 days before the event. If the hiring fee is £200 or over, please pay half the hiring fee as a deposit when you book, then pay the rest at least 21 days before the event.

Because the sentence patterns are similar (all beginning with 'if' statements), readers can more easily pick out the details that are relevant to them.

Version 3: List

Version 2 could become a list:

> If the hiring fee is:
> - £100 or less, please pay it in full when you book.
> - £101 to £199, please pay £100 deposit when you book, then pay the rest at least 21 days before the event.
> - £200 or over, please pay half the hiring fee as a deposit when you book, then pay the rest at least 21 days before the event.

Version 4: Questions and answers

A question-and-answer set-up would also be feasible:

Is the hiring fee £100 or less?
Please pay it in full when you book.
Is the hiring fee £101 to £199?
Please pay £100 deposit when you book, then pay the rest at least 21 days before the event.
Is the hiring fee £200 or over?
Please pay half the hiring fee as a deposit when you book, then pay the rest at least 21 days before the event.

Version 5: Table

The final option is a table:

Hiring fee	Deposit	Balance to be paid
£100 or less	None – pay fee in full on booking	
£101 to £199	£100 deposit, pay on booking	At least 21 days before event
£200 or over	Half hiring fee, pay on booking	At least 21 days before event

The focus group's verdict

The focus group narrowly preferred version 4, giving it an average of 18 points out of 20 for clarity. The differences were small, though: version 5 scored 17; version 3 scored 16; and version 2 scored 15. In terms of first preferences, version 5 was the clear leader: 11 people out of 35 preferred it, while 8 preferred version 4. Version 1 was a distant fifth, scoring 6 points out of 20 for clarity and receiving no first preferences.

These results suggest that the focus group preferred plain English in whatever layout it appeared, but that they regarded layout as an important factor in their ultimate preference between the four plain-English versions. In practice, the best presentation would depend on the document's purpose and the readers' purpose. A question-and-answer layout might be seen as friendlier than a table, but friendliness would be more relevant in a sales leaflet than a legal contract. Readers wanting to get the answers to specific questions might perform better with a table, while those wanting to remember what they had read might perform better with questions and answers.

There are no easy solutions: writers need to know what presentation methods are available, be flexible in using them, and try to find out their readers' reactions to them.

Algorithms

An algorithm may be a good solution if the information aims to help people make a decision from a complicated range of possibilities, or to explain a complicated rule or procedure. Algorithms tend to occupy more space than text and may take a long time to write and lay out, but they can save the readers a great deal of effort. The main danger is that readers may be so put off by the unusual format that they will reject it immediately.

Case history: A charity wanted to gather donations in the most tax-efficient way. It explained several methods, 'Gift Aid', 'Deed of Covenant', 'Payroll Giving', and 'Deposited Covenant'. For simplicity, I haven't included the highly detailed explanations here. The fund-raising leaflet said this:

    If you pay UK income tax and:
- you want to make a one-off donation of £250 or more, please use Gift Aid;

or • you want to make a one-off donation of less than £250, please use a Deposited Covenant;

or • you want to give regularly and your employer has a payroll giving scheme, please use the scheme;

or • you want to give regularly and your employer does not have a payroll giving scheme, please use a Deed of Covenant.
    If you do not pay UK income tax, we will not be able to reclaim tax on your donation but please make a donation anyway.

This seemed easy enough to follow and the charity was satisfied with the level of donations. The next year, however, it decided to put the information into the algorithm shown below. Though other factors may have influenced the result, the charity found that its donations increased by a fifth.

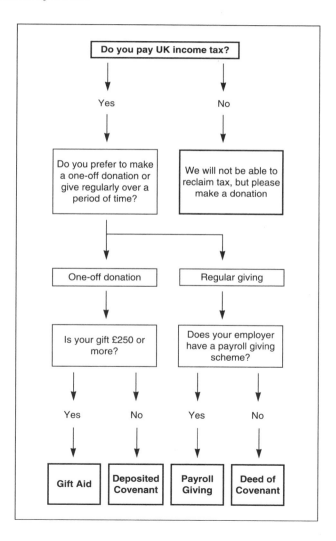

18 Management of colleagues' writing

Guideline: *Manage colleagues' writing carefully and considerately to boost their morale and effectiveness.*

The managing director of a prominent chain of high-street jewellery shops gave a speech in which he said: 'We also do cut-glass sherry decanters complete with six glasses on a silver-plated tray that your butler can serve you drinks on, all for £4.95. People say, "How can you sell this for such a low price?" I say: "Because it's total crap." '

A plain message, admirably candid, but the wrong message for someone trying to sell jewellery. Within a short time the firm's profits had slumped, he was out of a job, and his name was being removed from the shop-fronts in the chain.

Writers don't usually make such spectacular mistakes in letters and emails to customers, and even if they do, the results are rarely so disastrous. But, over time, the drip, drip, drip of weak writing erodes customer confidence and sullies the image of quality that most managers like to convey. This makes the management of writing a very important task, one that takes care and effort.

One approach is 'hands-off'—not intervening at all in the writing of the staff in the belief that they should take full individual responsibility. Absolute freedom sounds fine in theory but leaves quality to chance, because things that go uninspected tend to deteriorate.

Other managers are so hands-on that their paw prints are evident in every sentence. Whatever their staff write is returned with a mass of red-pen or track-changed amendments, schoolteacher style. This approach may spring from a good motive—the desire to produce lucid, unstuffy writing—or from a need to show who's in charge. Whatever the reason, the results are the same: managers spend too much time playing editor, and staff become demoralized because they don't know what's wanted or how to improve.

The rest of this chapter tries to chart a middle way.

Working with the team

For the sake of example, let's assume you're managing a team that answers complaints from customers. Though team members deal with many complaints by phone, they also write letters and emails. Here are a dozen things you could do.

1 Ask the team how they recognize a good complaint response when they see it. Usually they'll agree with you (and me) that the letter should be relevant, accurate, well organized, clear, and concise. It should seek to rebuild customer relations and even strengthen them beyond the pre-complaint level.

2 Ask the team what you can do to help them achieve these things. You may be told a few home truths about how you should supervise their writing but you may also get requests for extra training, style guides, books on better English, dictionaries, and electronic style checkers.

3 Show one of your own first-draft letters and ask the team to compare it with the final draft you sent. Ask for ideas on how the final draft could have been improved further. Be prepared to take criticism yourself without becoming defensive. Stress that nearly all writing can be improved by the injection of another person's ideas.

4 Show some of the team's letters and ask them to pick out strengths and weaknesses. If there are problems of spelling, punctuation, sense, and tone of voice, team members will realize for themselves that they'll have to improve. This can be painful at first, but foster an atmosphere in which writing can be discussed in an unthreatening way. If necessary, bring in a qualified outsider, such as a writing-skills coach or applied linguist, to take part in the discussion. The ghosts at the meeting will be typical readers but try to make sure their feelings and circumstances are represented.

5 Discuss the process of writing, particularly the need for planning by writers who use dictation machines or who type or speak directly on to word processors. Stress that planning will usually save time and raise quality.

6 When you ask a writer to respond to a long or difficult complaint, ask him or her to come back with a detailed plan of the key points. Discuss and agree it before the writer produces a full draft. This will make purpose and content clear at every step and ensure that the writer follows a clear track from the outset. (Chapter 15 can help authors to plan long documents.)

7 Explain what standards you will use to supervise writing. You will be checking for:

- *Purpose*: Is the reason for the letter clear to the reader?
- *Content*: Does the letter contain the right messages and deal with any relevant points the complainant made? Is it accurate, complete, and relevant? Is it defensible in the light of your organization's policies or the laws or regulations that govern you? If it is based on a standard letter, has it been tailored appropriately to the individual's circumstances? Does it say what, if anything, the reader should do next?
- *Structure*: Is the material organized in a logical sequence? Does it place the big news early? In a long letter, are headings used to help the reader navigate? If there's an apology, is it positioned early enough? (Refer to the various models in chapter 16.)
- *Style*: Are the points explained clearly in sentences of reasonable length with short paragraphs, active-voice verbs, and good punctuation? Have officialese and business clichés been removed? Is it as warm and friendly as the topic allows?

8 Say that you will try to intervene as little as possible in the writing and that your interventions will seek to make genuine improvements without nitpicking. Your overriding question will be 'Is this letter fit to go?', not 'Is it perfect?' or 'Is it how I would have written it myself?'

9 Promise that if you make substantial alterations to the draft your staff member provides, you'll explain why. This kind of feedback is vital.

10 Make available the tools and information that will help staff do a good job:

- Buy a good dictionary in book or electronic form.
- Copy and circulate press articles about words.
- Consider asking known good writers in your department to act as coaches and advisers.
- Make your copy of this book available to all. In fact, buy several.
- Add an effective style-checking program to your word-processing software. All style- and grammar-checkers have limitations because they can't assess the sense, logic, or structure of a document, but there are a few good ones. (StyleWriter has been favourably reviewed in the computer press

and is used by British and US federal government departments—www.editorsoftware.com).

- Take some of the free newsletter subscriptions from
editorial companies and circulate relevant extracts. In the
UK, *Pikestaff* (Plain Language Commission's newsletter) is available from www.clearest.co.uk. In the US, Impact Information produces a regular, thought-provoking despatch: www.
impact-information.com. Both rise above self-promotion and
offer a free archive of back issues.
- For six months or so, circulate letters from each month's
output that you think are particularly good. Discuss them at
your team meetings.

11 Trust your writers. With proper guidance, they should be able
to produce good work without constant supervision. You'll still
keep an eye on things by checking copy letters whenever you
want. The letters of some staff will need more attention than
those of others.

12 Do a survey of recent complainants that includes questions
about whether they thought the response letters were clear
and in the right tone of voice. Commission an annual audit of
a sample of your team's letters by a writing-skills consultancy or
an applied linguist.

Making the right interventions

Let's consider two examples of writing that should have been substantially improved before they went out.

Case history 1. In the late 1980s, the UK was convulsed by a health scare
about fresh eggs. Several people died and there were some 30 000
confirmed cases of food poisoning. The main cause was hens being
fed chicken remains and faeces, according to the health minister of
the day. One well-known firm of egg distributors (I'll call them Cockerel Brothers) asked hundreds of shopkeepers to reassure their customers by displaying this notice:

Dear Retailer
As a valued customer, for Cockerel Brothers. We would like to assure you
of our continual monitering for anything which could affect the quality of our
fresh eggs.

> Cockerels have just undertook a survey of all our feed mills which involved testing finished feeds and samples (scrappings) from the mills, and having them tested by the Public Health Laboratory. This has resulted in a programme of mill monitering to prevent any bacterial build-up in our mills. We do not use any raw poultry offal meat, and dried poultry manure in our mills. We are taking these precautions to endevour our feed is as free from harmful bacteria, as is humanly possible, and manufactured from only wholesome raw materials.

Reassuring, it certainly isn't. There is too much murky detail, and all the errors speak of the kind of carelessness that the notice is warning against, for example:

- the first sentence isn't complete and suggests that the writer is the customer, which would be nonsense
- 'monitering' should be 'monitoring'
- 'undertook' should be 'undertaken', in standard English
- 'endevour' should be 'endeavour'
- the commas after 'meat' and 'bacteria' are wrong and should be deleted
- it's addressed to the shopkeeper but ought to be addressed to the shopper
- implicitly the firm is admitting that harmful bacteria have been allowed to build up in the feed.

No supervisor of writing should have let the notice go out untouched. There should have been a friendly, tactful conversation in which improvements were discussed with the writer so that he or she could rework the text, perhaps trying to emphasize the whole someness of the product. It might have said:

> **Dear Customer**
> - Our eggs are fresh and healthy.
> - We give our hens high-quality food and continually monitor and test it.
> - We do not feed our hens on chicken remains or manure.
> - Our priority is to produce eggs that are healthy, wholesome, and safe.
> - Please contact us on 000 0000 if you would like any further reassurance.

A rival firm in similar circumstances to Cockerel Brothers decided that saying less was a far better way of saying more. Its notice simply said:

EDENDALE EGGS
Healthy Eggs from Healthy Hens.

Case history 2. A housing association is writing to several hundred tenants to explain why modernization work has been delayed. It's an important letter:

> Bathroom modernization
> First of all apologies for the delay in the start of the bathroom refurbishment programme which was due to start at the end of last year but because the costs came in over budget, further negotiations had to be entered into with the contractors and the extent of the work reconsidered.
> Although all the work to the bathroom will be undertaken as previously agreed, we will not be undertaking any work to ground-floor WCs which you may or may not have.
> Find attached a draft programme for the anticipated commencement date on your property and we anticipate that the work will take three or four days to complete. Your next contact will be by the contractor, GH Construction, who will contact you individually about a week prior to the start at your house.
> If you anticipate any problems with access arrangements or require any further information, please do not hesitate to call Jane Teal on Tameside 99099.

The first question a manager of writing needs to ask is 'Is this fit to go?' My answer would be no. The writer has arranged the points logically and there are plenty of personal words like 'you' and 'we', but officialese, jargon, passives, and long sentences are overused.

Great improvement is possible by following good writing tactics. Again you'd need to discuss the letter, praise its good points, but perhaps show a reworking of the first paragraph as an example of what to do with the rest. It would be useless—and demoralizing to the writer—to redraft the whole letter, though you could provide guidance notes in the margin. Helpful coaching, pleasantly given and cooperatively received, should enable the writer to produce a letter that you would be able to pass as 'fit to go'.

Taking one paragraph at a time, I've underlined possible insertions and shown deletions for the whole letter:

> Bathroom modernization
> ~~First of all apologies~~ I apologize for the delay in ~~the start of~~ the bathroom ~~refurbishment~~ modernization programme which was due to start at the

end of last year. ~~but~~ The delay has occurred because the costs ~~came in over budget,~~ were higher than we had budgeted for. ~~further negotiations had to be entered into~~ We have had to negotiate again with the contractors and reconsider how much work we could afford ~~the extent of the work reconsidered~~.

This splits the long sentence into three and puts the verbs in the active voice.

~~Although all~~ All the work to ~~the~~ your bathroom will be ~~undertaken~~ done as previously agreed~~, we~~. But unfortunately the extra costs mean that if you have a ground-floor toilet, we will not be ~~undertaking~~ able to do any work to ~~ground floor WCs which you may or may not have~~ it.

I've left the first verb in the passive because it will put the stress on 'all the work to your bathroom'. The other changes split the sentence in two and remove the burbling expression 'may or may not have'. (It would, of course, be preferable to send one letter to tenants with ground-floor toilets, and a slightly different letter to the rest.)

~~Find attached~~ I attach a ~~draft~~ programme ~~for~~ which shows the ~~anticipated commencement~~ likely starting date ~~for work~~ on your property. ~~and we anticipate that the work~~ We expect the work will take three or four days to complete.

This splits another long sentence and uses plainer English.

~~Your next contact will be by~~ You will hear next from the contractor, GH Construction, who will contact you ~~individually~~ about a week ~~prior to the start~~ before the work at your house ~~begins~~.

This strengthens the first verb and adds another in place of the noun 'start'.

If you ~~anticipate~~ think the contractor will have any problems with access ~~arrangements~~ to your house, or if you need ~~require~~ any ~~further~~ more information, please ~~do not hesitate to~~ call Jane Teal on Tameside 99099.

This costs a few more words in the cause of certainty but also gets rid of waffle. In the final, complete version below, the last sentence has been turned round so that the shorter 'please' clause comes first:

Bathroom modernization
I apologize for the delay in the bathroom modernization programme which was due to start at the end of last year. The delay has occurred because the costs were higher than we had budgeted for. We have had to negotiate again with the contractors and reconsider how much work we could afford.
All the work to your bathroom will be done as previously agreed. But unfortunately the extra costs mean that if you have a ground-floor toilet, we will not be able to do any work to it.
I attach a programme which shows the likely starting date for work on your property. We expect the work will take three or four days to complete. You will hear next from the contractor, GH Construction, who will contact you about a week before work at your house begins.
Please call Jane Teal on Tameside 99099 if you think the contractor will have any problems with access to your house, or if you need any more information.

The focus group were asked whether they perceived any difference in clarity between this last version and the original. The average clarity rating was 14 points out of 20 for the original, 17 for the revision. Twenty-five out of 35 people expressed a preference for the revision. The fact that eight people preferred the original (with two scoring them equal), and that the scores were so close, is a salutary reminder that no one can please all the people all the time and that audience reaction is rarely uniform. It might even suggest that the letter was fit to send in its original state—a rather depressing outcome for plain-English devotees.

Finally

Criticizing someone's writing can be unnerving for them. So, before you intervene, always consider how you would feel if you were on the receiving end. Remember also that editing is far easier than creating the first draft, so remember to give due praise.

It's fair for you to want a high standard of clarity and grammar from all who write for you. But remember that no two writers will ever use exactly the same words or tone of voice, so trying to impose uniformity will not only be demoralizing but futile.

For those whose writing is criticized, the director-general of the UK's Health and Safety Executive offered this comforting advice in 1988: 'If your draft is rewritten at a higher level, do not despair. Seek to learn from the experience. And bear in mind that a piece of work can be good (and may be appreciated as such), or be very helpful but not usable in its original form.'

19 Good practice with email

Guideline: *Take as much care with email as you would with the rest of your writing.*

Most of the other guidelines are relevant to email but this chapter offers further points specific to the medium.

Like a paper-based message, an email may be many things: a note to a colleague, a business letter to an external customer or partner, a response to a complaint, or a call for information. It may also become part of an email chain formed by several emails from different authors.

The main benefits of email are speed, ease of use, and the ability to attach separate documents, photos, and illustrations in their precise format from your electronic filing system. The possible drawbacks include:

- responding too hastily or angrily because a reply is so easy to send
- copying your email to the wrong people, such as a business rival or an opponent in a legal action
- sending libellous or indiscreet material that others may forward, perhaps to everyone in their address book
- sending messages that break data protection or obscenity laws
- copying your message to many people who will have little or no interest in it
- misjudging the level of formality required and being too friendly or too distant, and
- attaching lengthy documents to your message, just because you can, when these will be irrelevant to most of your readers and may even exceed their inbox capacity.

Moreover, because (like me) most email authors have never learned to touch-type and, if they proofread at all, they do so on screen, emails tend to contain mistakes that would normally be spotted in a print-out. These drawbacks need not reduce you to jelly whenever you press 'send', as long as you take reasonable care and follow any 'netiquette' rules your organization imposes.

Planning and structure

The on-screen window has an inviting space for typing, so the tendency is to type first and think later. Yet it remains a good idea to plan an email briefly at the outset if you have more than, say, six points to make. Planning helps you collect your thoughts, decide what you really want to say, and, in the final stage, use one of the structures in chapter 16 to organize the points. Your most usual structure will be the top-heavy triangle because you'll want your main points to be in the immediately visible part of the reader's screen, answering their inevitable questions:

- 'What's this got to do with me?'
- 'What do you want me to do about it?'

For a lengthy email you can use headings or reduce the length by adding an attachment that has its own system of headings.

At the least, your plan can be a typed list of points on your computer's notepad—put them in no particular order at first; you can organize them later. Alternatively your plan can be a bubble diagram on paper, as shown in chapter 15.

By all means write a quick first draft based on your plan but let it sit in your draft box for a while, then rework it. This enables you to smooth out rough edges that may confuse or offend, and to remove errors and ambiguities.

Standards to follow

A clear heading in the 'subject' line is a good start. To be predictive is more important than to be brief—in other words, you should specify what the email is about. So not 'Proposed meeting' but 'Proposed meeting with Alan Bennett, Gem Design, 22 May, 5pm.' If you're replying to an email, it's courteous to keep to the original heading unless it's obviously wrong or unspecific or puts words into your mouth with which you disagree. If the email requires an urgent response or is just for information, signal this in the heading. If your email program automatically inserts 'Re' as the first word of the heading, strike a small blow for conciseness by deleting it.

Use a greeting and sign-off. For a formal email that is effectively an external letter, follow letter conventions (chapter 14). So write 'Dear Mr Adamson' and 'Yours sincerely' and end with your name, job title, phone number, etc. (use the automated signature option available in most email programs). Although your email might not appear on your business stationery, it could be printed out by the recipient and circulated as a business letter. An alternative is to prepare a letter on your company's electronic letterhead, then attach it to a short covering email.

For a semi-formal email, use the style 'Dear John' or 'John' and 'Kind regards'. For an informal email, you can please yourself but 'Hi John' and 'Regards' are fairly standard forms.

Vary all these possibilities to suit your taste and to comply with your in-house rules. Staff in one British government agency routinely begin their business replies in the form 'Hello Mr Smith'. No one seems to object, but my preference would be for a more formal start.

Take care to type the salutation correctly. Having complained to an airport about lost baggage, I received an email headed 'Without Prejudice' (a lawyer's way of saying the email couldn't be used in legal proceedings), which then began 'Dear Mr prejudice'.

Though you may have a wide range of fonts, colours, backgrounds, and symbols available, be sparing with them unless they will genuinely help to fulfil your purpose. Some readers' software may not be able to display all your carefully crafted special effects.

Formality in the text

Email has become a more informal medium than a paper letter. As we've seen, you need to judge the right degree of formality in the greeting and sign-off, and make similar adjustments in the body of the email. If in doubt, err on the side of formality. Sometimes you'll want to keep a degree of distance from a customer who is seeking to draw you into a more informal business relationship than you want. Be aware that others may be reading over the immediate recipient's shoulder. As email is not a particularly secure medium, consider how your message might look on the front page of your local paper. If you're a lawyer, consider how it will sound when read in open court.

Checking carefully

In a note to busy colleagues, occasional spelling mistakes and the like will not cause much dismay as they all make mistakes themselves. But be careful not to be too slipshod, as you'll give the impression that you don't care enough about them or the topic to bother getting your words right. And some details do matter—the timing of a meeting, the date of a training course, an amount of money, a missing 'not'. Proofread carefully and slowly—you're not skim-reading for information, but checking for errors (see chapter 25).

This email from a social worker calls for various actions, but the stream-of-consciousness approach would entitle the reader to gently ask for a redraft:

> were anxious to experdite this matter and would be grateful to information requested and costings as soon as possible otherwise we will have to source other placements in addition K is currently placed at Shaw house were it is agreed his needs are not being met however the delay in providing the info and costing has necessitated K remaining her we would expect you to review the current fee structure at this placement since the delay in moving K i.e reducing them

After receiving a reply to this, the social worker responded. This time it was closer to English, but showed that her original freestyle was no fluke:

> Many Thanks For your information I am now in demand of a move date as K needs to be moved as a matter of Urgency now due to his needs not being met at his current placement

So check even your briefest emails before sending them. And be as punctilious with long emails as you would with paper-based documents. If necessary, print out your email, polish it on paper, then transfer the amendments to the screen.

Abbreviations and emoticons

Abbreviations are common in informal emails. Obvious ones include asap (as soon as possible), wd (would), u (you), pls (please), thnx (thanks), faq (frequently asked question), btw (by the way), fya (for your amusement), fyi (for your information), fwiw (for what it's worth), oic (oh, I see), rec'd (received), and yr (your). In semi-formal or formal emails, it's better to avoid using such abbreviations because some may not be understood and others will seem too casual.

As substitutes for facial expression or body language, emoticons or smileys have enjoyed some popularity but now seem as dated as catchphrases from the hippy era. The tone of a surly email is scarcely redeemed by a smirking :-) next to the signature. Let the words do the talking, especially in semi-formal and formal emails. For informal emails, here are a few of the more common smileys:

:-[	sad sarcasm
:-(	sad, angry
;-(	feel like crying
:-&	tongue-tied
:!-(	crying
:-<	very upset
:-*	kiss
;-)	winking
:-#	my lips are sealed
8-O	shocked, amazed

As ever, a sign communicates only if the readers can decode it. If in doubt, write some words.

Inserting your own comments (interpolations)

Email enables you to respond by inserting your own comments at various points in the incoming email and returning the whole thing as your reply. If you choose to do this, make clear where your comments start and finish. Using a second colour for your text can work well if it will show up on the reader's machine. Other good options are indenting your added text, enclosing it in square brackets (US, brackets), using a markedly different font, or some combination of these.

20 Writing better instructions

Guideline: *Devote special effort to producing lucid and well-organized instructions.*

Everyone has a favourite example of ambiguous instructions:

- On a Marks & Spencer's plastic bag: 'To avoid suffocation keep away from children.'
- On a bottle top: 'Pierce with pin, then push off.'
- On the door of a health centre: 'Family Planning—please use rear entrance.'
- In an aircraft maintenance manual: 'Check undercarriage locking pin. If bent, replace.' (The operator examined the pin. It was indeed bent, so he carefully put it back. The aircraft crashed.)
- On a chocolate-pudding tin: 'Before opening, stand in boiling water for ten minutes.'

A lifetime's experience of abysmal product instructions leads many people to read them only when all else fails. Hence the industry slogan 'RTFM'—Read The Flaming Manual. When his car clock failed, an executive of an American car-maker tried to reset it using the approved company handbook. He couldn't. Next day he began a project to rewrite the whole manual in language that a highly paid corporate captain could understand. Such searing personal experience is often the spur to writing better instructions. Unless some handbook or manual has made you want to disembowel every employee in the company responsible, you might never feel the urge to write it better.

An experiment by University of Michigan psychologists Hyunjin Song and Norbert Schwarz found that people equate the ease with which they read and process instructions with how complex they think the task itself will be. In other words, if the instructions look difficult, they think the task will be too.

Bad instructions are bad for business. Customers think twice about buying from a company whose instructions have proved useless before. In some countries, consumer protection regulations require that instructions and safety information accompanying a product are taken into account when deciding whether it is faulty. Manufacturers can be held liable for injury or damage caused by poor safety information. The selling of unsafe consumer goods can lead to criminal prosecution.

So, what goes wrong in the writing of instructions, and how can problems be put right? Usually some of the following six principles are broken.

Principle 1: Remember the readers

Usually readers haven't used the product before; that's why they're reading the instructions. But what else can you find out about them? Will they be technically knowledgeable or complete novices? Will they be children or adults? Under what conditions will they be using the instructions? Learning about these things and making the right assumptions will affect the words and structure you use. An experienced carpenter might readily understand the instruction 'screw pendant bolts into door plates using cheese-head screws', but most do-it-yourselfers would need an illustration of pendant bolts, door plates, and cheese-head screws. Everyone, though, will benefit if you say a little at a time. So instead of:

Placing the paper on a pasting table, use a pasting brush to apply the paste evenly, brushing towards yourself and making sure the edges are well covered.

you could write

Place the paper on a pasting table. Use a pasting brush to apply the paste evenly, brushing towards yourself. Cover the edges well.

Principle 2: Favour a basic style of language

This often means using the command form of the verb, known as the imperative, which states the action early and keeps the message simple:

Set this tool correctly for best performance. Read the instructions carefully before use.

instead of long-winded passive-voice writing:

> This tool needs to be set correctly if optimum performance is to be gained. It is recommended that the instruction booklet, located inside the packing, is read thoroughly before use.

Let's say you are instructing office staff how to fill in this box on a computer screen:

New Cost Centre Code
New Cost Centre Name
Parent Cost Centre Code

Using the passive voice you could write:

> The code of the new cost centre should be entered into the New Cost Centre Code field. The name of the new cost centre (maximum 40 characters) should then be entered into the New Cost Centre Name field. The code of the parent cost centre should then be entered into the Parent Cost Centre Code field. When satisfied, the 'Do' key should be pressed to commit the new cost centre to the database.

Or you could write it much more crisply in the imperative, with bullets:

- Enter the code of the new cost centre into the New Cost Centre Code field.
- Enter the name of the new cost centre (maximum 40 characters) into the New Cost Centre Name field.
- Enter the code of the parent cost centre into the Parent Cost Centre Code field.
- When satisfied, press 'Do' to commit the new cost centre to the database.

This is simpler because the readers know from the start of each sentence what action they have to take. Even simpler would be to assign numbers to the three fields:

New Cost Centre Code	[1]
New Cost Centre Name	[2]
Parent Cost Centre Code	[3]

and then write

- **Enter the correct code in field 1.**
- **Enter the correct name (maximum 40 characters) in field 2.**

and so on.

Principle 3: Split the information into chunks

Readers waste time and make mistakes if the information they need is buried in long paragraphs. In this example a local council inspector is encouraging a café owner, whose dirty kitchens she has been visiting, to do his washing-up hygienically. Notice there are no numbered steps or short paragraphs. It all looks too boring and complicated. If you feel like skipping it, that's probably what the reader and his staff thought too.

> **After the preliminary sorting of the utensils and scraping off of food residues into the refuse containers, the utensils should be washed in the first sink, piece by piece, in clean hot water at a temperature of about 60°C with a detergent added. This temperature is too hot for the hands and the operative should wear rubber gloves and use a dish mop. The water should be changed as often as it becomes dirty or greasy. After this, the utensils should be suitably arranged in the wire baskets available for immersion in the sterilising sink. The utensils should be placed so that no two pieces touch each other and that all the surfaces of every piece are exposed to the rinse water. The rinse will be ineffective if plates or saucers are piled on top of one another or if cutlery is merely heaped in the basket. The sterilising rinse in the second sink should be of clean hot water without added detergent or chemical and at a temperature of not less than 77°C and the utensils should remain in the water for a full two minutes. At this temperature care should of course be taken not to immerse the hands. The purpose is to raise the temperature of the utensils to that of the water so that they will air-dry almost instantly on removal. The temperature of the water should be maintained at about 77°C throughout and accordingly this sink should be fitted with a device to record the temperature of the water. When the two minutes are up, the basket should be removed from the sink and stood temporarily on a draining board and as soon as the utensils are dry and cool enough to be handled, they should be put in a clean place awaiting re-use.**

The words are reasonably plain, the punctuation is sound, and none of the sentences is impossibly long. But the whole thing needs splitting into short paragraphs ('chunking') and transforming into the imperative. First we need an introductory sentence, perhaps this:

You should make sure that your staff follow these instructions.

then the points need redrafting in the imperative:

1 Sort the utensils and scrape off waste food into the bins.
2 Wash the utensils in the first sink, piece by piece, in clean hot water at a temperature of about 60°C with a detergent added. This temperature is too hot for your hands, so wear rubber gloves and use a dish mop.
3 Change the water as often as it becomes dirty or greasy.
4 Put the utensils in the wire baskets available for immersion in the sterilising sink. Arrange the utensils so that no two pieces touch each other and that all the surfaces of every piece are exposed to the rinse water. The rinse will not do its job if plates or saucers are piled on top of one another or if cutlery is merely heaped in the basket. The sterilising rinse should be of clean hot water without added detergent or chemical and at a temperature of at least 77°C.
5 Put the wire baskets containing the utensils in the water for a full two minutes. At this temperature, take care not to immerse your hands. The purpose is to raise the temperature of the utensils to that of the water, so that they will air-dry almost instantly on removal. Maintain the water temperature at about 77°C throughout. To check this, make sure the sink is fitted with a suitable thermometer.
6 When the two minutes are up, remove the basket from the sink and stand it temporarily on a draining board.
7 As soon as the utensils are dry and cool enough to be handled, put them in a clean place awaiting re-use.

These improvements have arisen not from a total rewrite but from two simple structural tactics (chunking and numbering) and one simple style tactic, the use of imperatives. All 35 members of the focus group preferred the revision. They gave it an average clarity rating of 18 points out of 20, compared to a (generous) 10 for the original. The rewrite needs more work, particularly in paragraph 4, and headings could be used throughout. But it's going in the right direction.

Principle 4: Use separate headed sections

Normally it's wise to split the instructions into separate sections whose headings identify the purpose of each action.

A common sequence of sections is:

- *Introductory explanation, overview, or summary*: This tells readers the purpose of the activity, what it will achieve, and how long it should take. Sometimes users with experience of similar tools or equipment will benefit from a quick-start procedure. In long instructions, a contents list will help.
- *Tools or materials required*: Giving this information saves readers from having to stop the job whenever a new tool is needed.
- *Definitions*: These explain any terms the readers may not understand. Definitions may also be needed of everyday words carrying special or limited meanings in the instructions.
- *Warnings*: If these come after the instructions, they are useless and could be dangerous. Warnings should be given twice: once in the introduction and again just before the instruction to which they relate. Make clear that the warnings must be obeyed and are not just recommended practice. Could the product be modified to eliminate the hazard? Where possible, resist the desire to warn of the obvious in an effort to avoid lawsuits. For example, a label on a children's scooter warns 'This product moves when used'; a digital thermometer warns 'Once used rectally, the thermometer should not be used orally'; and a bag of cat litter warns 'should not be used as a traction aid on ice and snow'.
- *Main text*, split into headed sections.

The extract below from a factory notice shows one way of splitting up text by using headings. Like those in the notice, the headings should be predictive and, if possible, stimulating. Label headings like 'Spillages' or 'Storage' are weaker than 'What to do about spillages' or 'How much should be stored?'. The other main benefit of headings is that they force the author to group like with like.

Code for use and maintenance of Dominion ink jet printers

Type of substances

Dominion inks use the solvent base methyl ethyl ketone, 'MEK'. MEK-based inks and solvents are all highly flammable and pose a serious fire and explosion risk if not handled properly.

Is it dangerous to breathe near the vapour?

In normal use there is no health hazard from inhaling the vapour. If spills are being cleaned up, wear respiratory protective equipment.

Avoiding skin contact

Dominion inks and solvents are not very poisonous but you should still avoid skin contact. If there is a risk of spills or when cleaning up spillages, wear solvent-resistant gloves and goggles.

How much should be stored?

Store as little of these substances as possible in the workroom. Never store more than 50 litres (including waste liquids). Storage should always be in metal cabinets purpose-made for highly flammable liquids.

Clearing up spills

Mop up small spills with industrial wipes or other dry material. After use, put the wipes in a purpose-made fire-resistant lidded bin. Absorb larger spills using a non-combustible material such as sand or Nil-flam absorbent. Departments should ensure they have enough materials and equipment to deal with spills.

Dried inks

Deposits of dried ink are highly flammable, so take great care to avoid spills. Clean up dried deposits regularly using non-sparking scrapers. Dispose of the deposits safely.

Use of printers in safe areas

Printers should only be used and maintained in an area free from risk of ignition of flammable vapours. Keep the area well ventilated, particularly at low level. Eliminate sources of ignition such as naked flames and hot elements. Prohibit smoking. Use reduced-sparking tools where possible.

Fire

Suitable extinguishing agents are carbon dioxide, dry powder, alcohol-resistant foam and Halon. Large fires should only be tackled by trained firefighters. If containers get heated, isolate any nearby electrical supply. Then cool the containers by spraying them with water from a safe distance.

Principle 5: Use clear illustrations with good labels and captions

If a message can be simply conveyed in words, there's no need for illustrations (and vice versa). Words are good for getting abstract ideas across, for dealing with fine differences in meaning like 'could be' and 'might be', and for referring to things the reader has already learned about. Illustrations are good at showing what things look like and their relative size; this can save words and illuminate the words that remain. Sometimes illustrations can be so comprehensive you won't need words at all, which will save translation costs.

Whether you are buying illustrations from graphics professionals or drawing them yourself, you may like to consider such things as:

- using exploded-view format (useful for self-assembly products as they show how the item is put together)
- showing enlargements of particular parts so that readers can focus on the relevant point easily
- placing the illustration near the text—ideally people should be able to refer to it as they read
- presenting an object at an angle of view that clearly shows the parts concerned or the action to be taken
- keeping objects to scale
- ensuring that any typesetting included in the illustration will be legible if scaled down to fit the document.

The instructions below for maintaining a pressure cooker lid integrate text and pictures in a straightforward way.

Principle 6: Test with typical users

This is the most important principle, because users' performance is the key. Instructions for dangerous tools like chainsaws and for child seats in cars are rarely pre-tested with users. Many children are killed and injured every year because child seats are fitted wrongly. In 2008, Derbyshire safety officials found that of 193 seats they checked, 66 per cent were wrongly installed. In the US, where car crashes are the

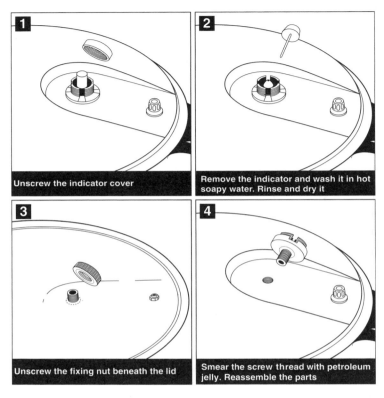

Instructions for maintaining a pressure cooker lid

leading cause of child deaths, a survey of 3 500 'child restraint systems' in 2006 found 73 per cent were badly fitted. Car-seat instructions are often baffling. This is from the top of the left-hand page of a two-page spread in a booklet from one of the best-known providers:

How to fit the Club Class Extra Rearward Facing
Have you checked that your baby weighs less than 13kg?
In this weight range you must only install the Club Class Extra rearward facing.

But at the top of the right-hand page, the booklet says:

How to fit the Club Class Extra Forward Facing
Have you checked that your baby weighs more than 9kg?
In this weight range you must only install the Club Class Extra forward facing.

Each part is clear but taken together they are nonsense because a child of, say, 11kg fits into both weight ranges. Readers get confused even before they've tried to fit the seat.

If your budget allows, hire a specialist usability company to test your instructions on real people. Failing this, give them to a focus group of typical readers—preferably unconnected with you or your work. Watch them trying to use the instructions with the product. Don't intervene unless asked (then give minimal help) or unless there's danger. Observe any false moves they make. Discuss how they got on, without leading them. Ask them about any misinterpretations they made. Redraft the instructions in the light of what you find. Test again if possible.

A company in New York found out how easily mistakes could occur if they didn't pre-test. As part of a school education programme, they distributed a batch of pencils carrying the slogan 'Too Cool to Do Drugs'. But schoolboy Kodi Mosier soon noticed that as he sharpened his pencil the message changed to become 'Cool to Do Drugs' and then 'Do Drugs'. The company recalled the pencils and reprinted the words with 'Drugs' at the sharp end.

21 Clarity for the Web

Guideline: *Don't waffle on the Web—put the big news early and make the style and structure punchy.*

You've visited plenty of websites, so you already know a lot about writing for the Web. What caught your attention, kept you reading, or turned you off? Maybe some of these:

Attention catchers

- Interesting and relevant content in highly legible type.
- Predictive headlines, saying what's to come without quirkiness or punning.
- Attractive graphics and pictures.
- Big news stated early on each page, perhaps with a summary of main points at the top.

Attention keepers

- Writing that's easy to read, flows logically, and is consistent in style—so 'sign in', 'sign on', or 'log in', not all three.
- Key words and phrases picked out in bold type.
- Short paragraphs (40–50 words), short sentences, active verbs, and personal words, particularly 'you'.
- Credibility and trustworthiness—increased by high-quality graphics, good writing, and the use of outbound descriptive hyperlinks, which suggest that authors have read widely and are happy for users to visit other sites.

Turn-offs

- The opposite of all the above.
- Spelling and punctuation errors.
- Links that fail.
- Puffery—pompous self-promotion and marketing hype.
- Pages that have too many eye-catching elements or are text-heavy.

Little new, then, here—most of the previous chapters are relevant to Web writing. But people do read differently on screen to how they read on paper, so some rethinking is needed. The main difference is that they tend to scan Web pages quickly and read far less than authors may like. Also, they'll take their own route through a website and it won't be as linear as if they were reading on paper.

This chapter:

- re-emphasizes some points that are important for Web writing
- examines research results on what makes Web writing effective
- considers some technical points that will make your writing more effective
- analyses some examples of Web writing.

The chapter gives brief points only. It's not a full technical guide to creating effective websites. For the amateur, there's probably no substitute for hiring good Web designers. Many of the points are meant for you to check with your chosen designer rather than to apply yourself.

A simple site map

Get help and plan

Hire a good Web designer, early. Check for competence by examining other sites they've built and asking how they'd tackle the issues in this chapter.

Write a mind map for your website—see chapter 15. This will give you a picture of everything you want to include. Transform the mind map into a plan that shows the hierarchy of the site. There's a simple site map for Plain Language Commission's website on page 177. More detailed site maps are often signposted on home pages; see, for example www.communitylegaladvice.org.uk and www.postoffice.co.uk.

Create scannable text

Most readers of paper documents won't pore over every word, following the argument in all its subtle detail and hoping that when they reach the end there'll be an appendix. Even more so with the Web. Busy and literate people rarely read Web pages word for word. Instead they scan, picking out individual words and sentences. In user-testing by Dr Jakob Nielsen of the Nielsen Norman Group (www.useit.com/papers/webwriting/) 79 per cent of people always scanned any new page they came across but only 16 per cent read word for word. This is partly because reading on-screen is uncomfortable for most of us, compared with reading on paper. With protruding belly and sore neck we perch on an office chair and stare wearily at low-resolution dots that pretend to be print. Most of us read on-screen to select and extract information, not for pleasure.

So Web pages should be easily scannable. This means using things like:

- keywords, highlighted by bold type, colour, hyperlinks
- meaningful subheads, not clever-clever ones
- bulleted lists
- one idea per paragraph—readers who aren't hooked by the first few words will skip the rest
- half or less of the wordage of paper texts—people read 20 per cent of the average Web page
- figures for numbers—eyetracking data shows that '23' catches more attention than 'twenty-three'.

Nielsen found that the inverted-triangle structure was best (see also chapter 16). This means starting with the big news (usually the conclusion) in the first two or three paragraphs. Early, you need to get across the five Ws and the H—who, what, where, when, why, and how.

Brevity and clarity are vital because if users don't find what they want almost immediately, they'll go elsewhere. They are window-shopping for information and spending their most precious asset—time—flitting between stores to see what takes their fancy. If you don't hook them, they'll go back to their search list and click through to another site.

Eyetracking studies show that Web users tend to scan pages in an F-pattern. They first read in a horizontal scan, usually across the top part of the content area—the top bar of the F. Next, they move down the page a bit and read across in a second horizontal scan that's typically shorter than the previous movement—the F's lower bar. Finally, they vertically scan the content's left side. This may be a quick scan or a slow and systematic scan that forms the stem of the F pattern.

There are clear implications for Web authors, says Jakob Nielsen: 'Start subheads, paragraphs, and bullet points with information-carrying words that users will notice when scanning down the left side of your content in the final stem of their F-behavior. They'll read the third word on a line much less often than the first two words.'

Studying performance, which he calls 'usability', Nielsen found a remarkable difference when users read varying styles of text on the Web. He averaged their scores on several measures including task time and errors on questions. One style of text was linear, promotional, wordy, detailed, and dull, like this:

Nebraska is filled with internationally recognized attractions that draw large crowds of people every year, without fail. In 1996, some of the most popular places were Fort Robinson State Park (355,000 visitors), Scotts Bluff National Monument (132,166), Arbor Lodge State Historical Park & Museum (100,000), Carhenge* (86,598), Stuhr Museum of the Prairie Pioneer (60,002), and Buffalo Bill Ranch State Historical Park (28,446).

A second style was more scannable and, though bland, used more concise and neutral language, like this:

In 1996, six of the most-visited places in Nebraska were:
- **Fort Robinson State Park**
- **Scotts Bluff National Monument**
- **Arbor Lodge State Historical Park & Museum**
- **Carhenge***
- **Stuhr Museum of the Prairie Pioneer**
- **Buffalo Bill Ranch State Historical Park.**

Nielsen found a 124 per cent increase in usability of the scannable text over the linear text. (The asterisk in each sample is to show that Carhenge was hyperlinked.)

Build attractive and accessible pages

Organizing material well

- Just as newspapers put their best stories 'above the fold', so you should put your best stuff in the top third of the typical user's screen, remembering that screens tend to be wider than they are deep (i.e. 'landscape') and that the browser's menu bar will occupy some of the screen. If users have to scroll down to find something, they may never see it. If possible, avoid the need to scroll unless the extra page-breaks that result would cause confusion.
- Articles, documents, and large bodies of information need summaries at the top to help readers decide whether to go further. The summary needs to be brief. Make some general points about the piece and some specific points to illustrate each general point.
- If you're a website editor, try to prevent being swamped by contributors who think their lengthy documents will inform the public. You'll need to shorten the text, split it into chunks, summarize, and add headlines.
- Research by the Poynter Institute in the US found that when people read newspapers online and in print, the 'story form' significantly affected their recall of facts. So, by including things like question-and-answer sections, timelines, lists, and fact boxes, newspapers could improve readers' recall as against the same story published in continuous text.
- A headline has to work harder because it may not appear only above the text it refers to. For example, it may join a contents menu, too. As usual, write the headline after you write the story. Make sure it can stand alone away from the story, if necessary, and still make sense. If headlines and subheads appear in a clickable list on another page, they may also need to make sense as a set.

Page design: key points

- Keep the page design simple. Put your important stuff in a single main column, so people don't have to scan several columns. This also helps users of low-vision aids.

- Make the navigation simple by placing the main choices in a linear menu. This helps users decide where to go next, so they don't have to scan the whole page for options. Put the menu on every page so users don't get marooned. This also helps users who don't enter the site via the home page.

- Keep the line length reasonably short, say 50–60 characters and spaces, and make the text left-aligned rather than centred—it will be easier to scan and read.

- Add space between paragraphs rather than indenting the first line; this enables people to locate the starting point more easily when scanning, and makes pages more spacious.

- Favour black type on a white background. White type out of a dark green background can also work well but makes the layout less flexible.

- Don't go berserk with colour. Use it functionally, say for a particular level of heading or in solid blocks.

- Use fonts that look highly legible on the Web. Verdana, Trebuchet MS, Tahoma, and Georgia are four such, and Verdana (which was designed for on-screen reading) works well at small sizes. These fonts are reasonably 'websafe', i.e. they are cross-platform for Microsoft and Macintosh (though less good on Linux). (Useful articles: www.yourhtmlsource.com/text/webtypography.html, www.ampsoft.net/webdesign-l/WindowsMacFonts.html, www.webspaceworks.com/resources/fonts-web-typography/41/.) You'll have these fonts on your computer or be able to see them on the Web (e.g. www.will-harris.com/verdana-georgia.htm).

- Use a limited palette of websafe fonts—perhaps one for headlines and one for body type. Where possible, use proportional font sizes. These enable users to increase the font size in their browsers while retaining most of the site format. Choose websafe fonts that, while highly legible, reflect the personality you want for the site.

- Use 'cascading style sheets' (www.howtocreate.co.uk/tutorials/css/fonts). These enable your site to meet different users' needs, where appropriate—for example, by being available in easy-to-print, mobile (handheld), or screenreader-friendly formats.

- Make the pages cross-browser compatible, e.g. on Firefox, Internet Explorer, Safari, Opera, and Google Chrome.
- Write an 'alt tag' (alternative text) for all images (e.g. 'image of . . .' or 'image linking to . . .'. This will help visually impaired users. Most screenreading software can't read text on images.
- Add informative captions to graphics. Even a picture worth a thousand words will often need some explanation.
- Optimize search. Ideally, a user's first search should answer the question. All search hits should yield a short, easy-to-read summary. Make your site tolerant of searchers' misspellings.
- Try to comply with one of the accessibility standards, so that users with impairments are not disadvantaged further. See, for example, www.w3.org/WAI/ and www.shaw-trust.org.uk/. Via W3C, you can get a free check of your site against its criteria.
- If you put audio files on your site, make transcripts available.
- Write informative links, not things like 'click here'.

Help people find your site: the essentials

People use search engines, directories, etc. to search for sites with relevant content. Unless your site is high in the search results, few users will click through to it. So there are some key things to do.

1 Try to get inbound links from high-status websites (e.g. newspapers). Major newspapers mirror some of their content online, so if they review an aspect of your business their review may include a link to your website.
2 Write first paragraphs for each page, and particularly the home page, that include the words people will use to search for the things you offer. Say you are running a small guest house in the Peak District of Derbyshire. Your first paragraph might say: 'Luxury bed-and-breakfast (B&B) accommodation in the Peak District of Derbyshire, with recently modernized en-suite rooms and free wireless internet. Business people, walkers, and tourists are welcome to our beautifully furnished Georgian farmhouse in the pretty village of Burbling-on-the-Water just off the A515. We're close to Buxton, Chatsworth, Bakewell, and the best scenery in the area.'
3 Write effective meta tags (data that helps some search engines to categorize your pages). The most important meta tags are:

- the page title (what the browser puts at the top of the screen), e.g. luxury bed and breakfast (B&B) accommodation, Burbling-on-the-Water, Derbyshire—homepage
- the site description, e.g. Miss Pelt's bed and breakfast, B&B accommodation at Burbling-on-the-Water in the Peak District National Park, Derbyshire, UK
- the site keywords, e.g. bed and breakfast, bed-and-breakfast, B&B, b+b, B & B, b + b, accommodation, Burbling on the Water, Burbling-on-the-Water, Peak, District, National, Park, Derbyshire, A515, Buxton, Chatsworth, Bakewell, Matlock, guest, family, room, luxury, tourist, tourism, information, business, commercial, special, events, retreat, weddings, weekend, break, holiday, market, secure, parking, acomodation, accomodation, acommodation. It's good to include common misspellings for the things you offer.

4 Add fresh content regularly; search engines find this attractive.

Check your site thoroughly for errors, nonsense, and officialese

Web English is far less clear and accurate than it should be. Even high-profile sites have gross errors of spelling and punctuation. These mistakes, which would live for years in a printed book, can be corrected quickly if they're noticed. Often, though, they disfigure a site for months. Here are some from the home page—basically the main shop window—of a housing trust, which, without irony, also carried the heading 'Need help with communication?':

- 'Choiced Based Lettings'
- 'Older Peoples Service'
- 'Feedback from our customrs'
- 'Complaints & Complements'.

Plain words are keenly needed, too. Here are a few examples of how verbose and muddled Web writing can be clarified. In each case, the same simple tactics help: think out the message; put the points in a logical order; use short sentences; favour the active voice; and read it aloud to see if it's conversational.

Original: Composting waste for subsequent use in the garden is also encouraged and composters will remain available for purchase at a heavily subsidised cost. Further information is available on composting garden waste and purchasing a compost bin. (Local authority)

Revised: It's easy and simple to compost waste for use in the garden. Ask us for a leaflet on how to do it. And buy a compost bin from us—we've cut the cost by [say how much].

Original: The brown bin option should be useful for those with bigger gardens or simply for those that want the convenience of a reusable container. (Local authority)

Revised: If you have a big garden or prefer a re-usable container, ask us for a brown bin.

Original: Subject to the valuer's judgement, a visual inspection is to be carried out of so much of the exterior and interior of the property as is accessible to the valuer without undue difficulty. (Law firm)

Revised: It's for valuers to decide what they inspect. But they will always look at all parts of the inside and outside of the property that they can see or get into safely and easily.

Original: Should you be a utility company, developer or member of the public seeking information regarding which Utility companies service any particular Essex district, then this site should help. (Local authority)

Revised: Use this site to find out which utility companies serve each district of Essex.

Cut waffle to make Web text more scannable

Here's a short example of how to examine a piece of Web text critically and, by cutting dross and putting the big news early, make it more scannable.

The clear and catchy headline in a financial newsletter is 'Corporate bonds could provide good value'. The first paragraph, though, is a letdown for the busy Web user:

> **Fixed interest investors can be excused for considering that the present financial crisis provides an excellent chance for showing their skills and the implementation of rational analysis.**

What's the big news here? That it's time for fixed-interest investors to show their skills (what skills?) in some unstated way? That it's time for them to rationally analyse something, again unstated? The next paragraph sheds little light:

> **While those favouring company shares, especially the devotees of 'growth', look askance at the sliding market indices, there is a very reassuring satisfaction at being able to look at the reliability of bond yields.**

The big news here could be that you might make more money if you invest in bonds not shares. But it's hard to know. The quote marks on 'growth' only add to the mystery.

The final paragraph is a tangle of words in search of a message:

> **They are, of course, heavily dependent on the course or, at least, the market's expectation of, interest rates and, over the last two years, these rates have oscillated several times between moving up and down.**

Over the three paragraphs the average sentence length is about 30 words—that's 50 per cent more than in the 'quality' newspapers. Any big news has been buried in verbiage and readers get a poor return for their effort. If they get beyond the second paragraph, they've done well.

Using the inverted triangle and being miserly with words, the author might have said:

> **Investing in corporate bonds is worth considering now.**
> **In a crisis, when share prices are on the slide, bonds can give you much more solid and reliable returns.**
> **But those returns will depend on what the market thinks will happen to interest rates—as well as what actually happens to them.**

In about half the words of the original, this gives the readers three simple messages: it may be a good time to invest in bonds; why this

212 Oxford Guide to Plain English

may be so; and one of the factors that may affect the prospects for bonds. The average sentence length is 17 words. By being clear and much more scannable, it's more likely to catch and keep the user's attention. The author can then give more detail on what corporate bonds are and how to buy them.

22 Lucid legal language

Guideline: *Apply plain-English techniques to legal documents such as insurance policies, car-hire agreements, laws, and wills.*

The way many lawyers write is disappointing to their friends and obnoxious to their clients. 'Excrementitious matter' and 'literary garbage' was how Jeremy Bentham described legal English in the 19th century. While every profession tends to cloak its mysteries in unusual language, lawyers have done so more thoroughly than most. Legalese is not sacred, though. Many lawyers despise it, realize it brings them into disrepute, and are working to remove it. Lawyers campaign for plain language through their umbrella group 'Clarity'. A former chairman, Mark Adler, asks:

> **Why do lawyers write so that no one can understand them? They say it is because they need to be precise, and that their language has been honed by centuries of litigation. But this is baloney. The real reason is that, although they are paid for their skill with words, most lawyers are dull and clumsy writers who have not broken the bad habits they learned as students.**

Fog in the law and legal writing is often blamed on the complex topics being tackled. Yet when legal texts are closely examined, their complexity seems to arise far less from this than from unusual language, tortuous sentence construction, and disorder in the arrangement of points. So the complexity is largely linguistic and structural smoke created by poor writing practices.

Legalese is one of the few social evils that can be eradicated by careful thought and disciplined use of a pen. It is doubly demeaning: first it demeans its writers, who seem to be either deliberately exploiting its power to dominate or are at best careless of its effects; and second it demeans its readers by making them feel powerless and stupid.

Training and long exposure to legalese have given many lawyers a deep emotional attachment to its antiquated forms. Weaning is vital, for the good of citizens and the profession alike. Lawyers need to be convinced that any fool can make a complex topic sound complex, but that it takes real skill to clarify.

A step forward came in 1999 when, among other reforms of the civil court system in England and Wales, the Lord Chancellor ordered antiquated Latin and English expressions to be replaced by more modern or exact English. Here are some of the changes:

Original	Modern
discovery	disclosure
ex parte	without notice
further and better particulars	requests for information
in camera/in chambers	in private
inter partes	on notice
interrogatories	requests for information
leave of the court	permission of the court
minor/infant	child
next friend/guardian ad litem	litigation friend
plaintiff	claimant
pleading	statement of case
subpoena	witness summons
summons/motion	application
taxation of costs	assessment of costs
taxing master	costs judge
writ	claim form

After four years' work by a committee of judges, lawyers, law professors, and a plain-language expert, the United States Supreme Court in 2007 approved a new clarified version of the 300-page Federal Rules of Civil Procedure. The rules govern the procedure in all US federal trial (district) courts. Judges and lawyers rely on them daily, the rules serve as models for state courts, and law students study them in a year-long course. Here's an example of the difference that plain language made:

Before 'When two or more statements are made in the alternative and one of them if made independently would be sufficient, the pleading is not made insufficient by the insufficiency of one or more of the alternative statements.' *After* 'If a party makes alternative statements, the pleading is sufficient if any one of them is sufficient.'

Since 2003, the Law Society of England and Wales has required solicitors (under the Solicitors' Charter) to communicate clearly. A similar duty has existed for solicitors in New South Wales, Australia since 1994. Some of the biggest London law practices describe themselves, with differing degrees of justification, as plain-language firms. One head of department told his staff: 'We are paid for the words on the paper and we should never forget that. We have spent a lot of money on our brand, and a key part of our brand is the clarity of our documents.' Denton Wilde Sapte employ a plain-language coordinator, who says: 'We have found that plain language editing always raises legal questions ... We end up with a better document, in substance as well as in style.' These firms realize that the more international they become, the more customers and colleagues want clarity of expression: legal matters that cross national boundaries are complex enough without obscure language adding to the muddle.

Similarly, organizations that want to win the confidence of customers should give them comprehensible legal agreements to sign. Now that there are many examples of clear, well-organized insurance policies, credit card conditions, and tenancy agreements, it is uncompetitive to be locked into legalese.

So the myth is slowly crumbling that obscurity is necessary or part of the price customers are willing to pay. Indeed, with some lawyers charging more for an hour's work than their customers earn in a week, it seems only right that the writing they provide as part of their service is easy to understand.

What can be done?

All the techniques described so far in the book can be used in legal documents, though they need to be harnessed to legal knowledge and a desire for precision and accuracy.

In the introductory chapter I said that readers needed to be coopera-tive and well motivated if they were to understand a text in the sense it was meant to be understood. With legal documents, the position is different: some readers will try to misinterpret a text in their favour. Certainty of meaning is therefore more important. But plain English, if well and cautiously used, can make an important contribution to certainty.

It's true that lawyers cannot blithely replace technical legal terms like 'negligence', 'indemnify', and 'estoppel' with one-word equivalents, though they can often provide separate explanations or glossaries. Yet in most legal documents only a few words are genuinely technical. The rest are plain words with ordinary meanings, or legal-flavouring words that smell of the law but can be replaced by plain words or simply struck out. This spells death, or at best very limited life, for the three ugly brothers 'hereof', 'whereof', and 'thereof', their kissing cousins 'herein', 'hereinafter', and 'hereinbefore', and their wicked uncles 'hereby', 'thereby', and 'whereby'. Such legal flavouring has virtually gone from modern UK laws, which proves how redundant it is elsewhere.

Even if you're not a lawyer, you can play a part in counteracting legalese by questioning its use wherever it appears. You may, for example, be asked to comment on documents written by your own organization's lawyers. Be prepared to comment on content as well as style and structure. The lawyers may not thank you for invading their territory, but you have something useful to offer—the ability to see the document as non-lawyers will see it.

The clarification of legal documents would make a book of its own, so I want to examine just four easy techniques:

- Replace or cut out legal flavouring.
- Chop up snakes.
- Put people into the writing.
- Add headings.

You may have seen worse examples of legal writing than those that follow, but I've chosen them because they're understandable to the gen-eral reader while still displaying many of the faults that need rectifying.

Replace or cut out legal flavouring

Case study 1. In this extract from a car-hire agreement, there's legal flavouring and pomposity (underlined):

> In the event of car breakdown the owners must at their own expense effect the collection of the car and perform repairs thereto.

The sentence is also ambiguous—lawyers will argue that only the collection would be at the owners' expense, not the repair. But let's assume that both collection and repair are free to the hirer. We can then replace the legalese with plain words. 'In the event of' becomes 'if'; 'thereto' becomes 'to it' or 'to the car'; and 'must effect the collection' becomes 'must collect'. Losing its ambiguity and making the point more briefly, the sentence becomes:

> If the car breaks down the owners must collect and repair it, both at their own expense.

Case study 2. A local government department is asking people who apply for a replacement car-parking pass to sign a form. The legal flavouring is underlined:

> I hereby declare that the information given above is correct to the best of my knowledge and that I have conducted a thorough search for the said pass and honestly believe that the same cannot be found by me. I agree that in the event of the said pass being found by me I will forthwith return the same to the City Engineer.

All the legal flavouring can safely be removed:

- 'Hereby' just means 'by this writing'.
- 'The said pass' is no more specific than 'the pass' since no other pass is in question. If there were several passes, you'd call them 'pass 1', 'pass 2', etc.
- 'The same' is legalese for 'it' or 'them'.
- 'Forthwith' has been given many different interpretations in the courts—so either use the simple 'immediately' or state a certain number of days.

The legal flavouring doesn't make the form incomprehensible and it may impress some readers. But is it any less impressive in plain English?

I declare that:

- the information given above is correct to the best of my knowledge
- I have conducted a thorough search for the pass and cannot find it.

I agree that if I find the pass, I will immediately return it to the City Engineer.

Case study 3. Pruning shears are the most appropriate tool for attacking this example, in which a city requires a householder to cut back his hedge. Again, the legal flavouring and pomposity are underlined:

> <u>Whereas</u> a hedge <u>situate</u> at Dean Road, Moreton belonging to you overhangs the highway known as Dean Road, Moreton <u>aforesaid</u> so as to endanger or obstruct the passage of pedestrians.
>
> <u>Now therefore</u> the Council <u>in pursuance of</u> section 134 of the Highways Act 1959 <u>hereby</u> require you as the owner of the <u>said hedge</u> within fourteen days from the date of service of this notice <u>so to lop or cut the said hedge</u> as to remove the cause of danger or obstruction.
>
> If you <u>fail to comply with</u> this notice the Council may carry out the work required by this notice and may recover from you the expenses reasonably <u>incurred</u> by them in so doing.
>
> If you are aggrieved by the requirement of this notice you may appeal to the magistrates' court <u>holden</u> at Moreton <u>aforesaid</u> within fourteen days from the date of service of this notice on you.

The legal flavouring falls prey to plain words:

- 'Whereas' is fairly common and well understood, but here its use is pointless and creates an incomplete sentence. It can be struck out.
- 'Situate' means 'situated' or 'at'.
- 'Dean Road, Moreton aforesaid' just means 'Dean Road, Moreton'. If there were two Moretons, the correct one would need to be specified by adding the county or postcode—'aforesaid' doesn't aid precision.
- 'Now therefore' is redundant.
- 'In pursuance of' can be replaced by 'under' or 'for the purpose of' or 'using'.
- 'Hereby' is redundant, as it means 'by this writing'.
- 'So to lop or cut the said hedge' just means 'to cut the hedge' or 'to trim the hedge'. The *Shorter Oxford English Dictionary* gives 'lop' as 'cut off the branches, twigs, etc., from (a tree)', so there is no need for both 'cut' and 'lop'. An alternative would be 'cut back'.
- 'Fail to comply with' is wordier than 'disobey'.

- 'Incurred' is an unusual though very useful word. For a mass audience, the sentence might need rewriting to remove it.
- 'Holden' is a medieval remnant, meaning 'held'.

With dross swept away and new words underlined, the notice could read:

~~Whereas~~ You are the owner of a hedge ~~situate~~ at Dean Road, Moreton ~~belonging to you~~ which overhangs the highway ~~known as Dean Road, Moreton aforesaid so as to~~ endangering or obstructing ~~the passage of~~ pedestrians.
~~Now therefore the~~ The Council ~~in pursuance of,~~ under section 134 of the Highways Act 1959, ~~hereby~~ requires you ~~as the owner of the said hedge~~ within fourteen days from the date of service of this notice ~~so~~ to ~~lop or~~ cut the ~~said~~ hedge, removing ~~as to remove~~ the cause of danger or obstruction.
If you ~~fail to comply with~~ disobey this notice the Council may ~~carry out the work required by this notice~~ choose to cut the hedge and ~~may~~ recover from you ~~the expenses reasonably incurred by them in so~~ its reasonable expenses in doing so.
If you are aggrieved by ~~the requirement of~~ this notice, you may appeal to the magistrates' court ~~holden~~ at Moreton ~~aforesaid~~ within fourteen days from the date of service of this notice on you.

That draft would be fit to show to a lawyer to check for legal accuracy. The focus group agreed that the revision was much clearer. The 34 who responded gave it an average clarity rating of 18 points out of 20. The original notice averaged only 8. Three police officers in the group, accustomed and perhaps a little loyal to the peculiarities of law language, each gave the original 15 points.

Chop up snakes

Long sentences are another blight in legal documents. Sentences in bank overdraft agreements have been known to stretch to 900 words, monstrosities that show contempt for the readers as well as befuddling them. This 77-word sentence from an office equipment lease between Bigg, the owner, and Tiny, the company renting the equipment, explains what happens if the equipment breaks down:

If the equipment shall go out of order, Tiny shall at its own expense have the equipment repaired by the person, firm or body corporate designated by Bigg and in the event of Tiny failing so to do then Bigg shall be entitled to take possession of the equipment and have it repaired at the cost of Tiny and during such possession and repair, the lease charges shall nevertheless accrue and be payable by Tiny to Bigg.

Clearly the sentence can be split into three where one part of the story finishes and another begins. This preserves the meaning of the original and all its word order:

> If the equipment shall go out of order, Tiny shall at its own expense have the equipment repaired by the person, firm or body corporate designated by Bigg. ~~and in~~ In the event of Tiny failing so to do then Bigg shall be entitled to take possession of the equipment and have it repaired at the cost of Tiny. ~~and during~~ During such possession and repair, the lease charges shall nevertheless accrue and be payable by Tiny to Bigg.

Then you can replace all the shalls with 'must' or a verb in the present tense, or both (see chapter 2). You can also rewrite legalese like 'in the event of' and 'nevertheless accrue'. The new text would say:

> If the equipment goes out of order, Tiny must at its own expense have it repaired by a person chosen by Bigg. If Tiny fails to do this, Bigg may take possession of the equipment and have it repaired at Tiny's expense. During such possession and repair, Tiny must still pay the lease charges.

A long sentence is sometimes unavoidable in making a complex point that has exceptions and qualifications attached. Then, it needs to be managed well, with simple construction, plain words, and perhaps a bullet list.

Put people into the writing

Most legal agreements are about what people on all sides of a bargain must and must not do. It makes sense to give these people convenient names at the start of the agreement and use them throughout. So 'John Fustian of 97 Sackcloth Court, Berwick' might be identified as 'Fustian', and this term, along with 'he', 'his', and 'him', could be freely used for the sake of brevity. In standard-form agreements it is now common to define the bargain-makers by personal pronouns and this can aid clarity. In an agreement to lease a vehicle, the two sides to the bargain could be defined thus:

> 'We' means the lessor, Misfit and Snaggs Motors plc, The Garage, Sumpcity. 'You' means the lessee, Paul Oilyhands, 7 Rag Street, Pumptown.

The words 'we', 'you', 'our', and 'your' could then be used, improving every sentence in which they appear. It would mean the end of this kind of thing:

The lessor will register details of this lease and the conduct of the lessee's account with any licensed credit reference agency. The lessor may also disclose this and any other information supplied by the lessee to any member or associated company of the Scottish Bank plc group of companies or to any person acting on the lessee's behalf for any purpose connected with the group's business. The lessor may also use the lessee's name and address to mail the lessee about services that may be of interest to the lessee.

Instead it would be possible to write:

We will register details of this lease and the conduct of your account with any licensed credit reference agency. We may disclose this and any other information you supply to any member or associated company of the Scottish Bank plc group of companies or to any person acting on your behalf for any purpose connected with the group's business. We may use your name and address to mail you about services that may interest you.

Add headings

In this deed, lawyers for the local authority involved are trying to rectify a mistake by using highly traditional and legalistic language:

THIS DEED IS MADE the tenth day of January 2001 BETWEEN THE MAYOR AND BURGESSES OF THE LONDON BOROUGH OF BOREHAM of Civic Centre Boreham BU8 2AW (hereinafter called 'the Council') of the one part and Brian Tony Taggart and Miriam Mary Taggart both of 22 Vernon Road Farfield (hereinafter called 'the Purchasers') of the other part.
WHEREAS:-
1) By a Transfer dated 27 May 1999 and made between the parties hereto the property known as 22 Vernon Road Farfield (hereinafter called 'the Property') was transferred to the Purchasers as therein contained
2) The said Transfer contains a plan purporting to delineate the property transferred
3) The said plan does not correctly delineate the property transferred and the plan annexed hereto and marked 'plan No. 2' signed by the parties hereto and dated the tenth day of January 2001 correctly delineates the property
NOW THIS DEED WITNESSETH:-
The said Transfer shall at all times be read and construed as if the plan therein referred to was the said plan No. 2 and not the plan originally annexed thereto but in all other respects the parties hereto confirm the said Transfer IN WITNESS whereof the Council has caused its Common Seal to be hereunto affixed and the Purchasers have set their hands and seals the day and year first above written

The points are not very complicated. There was a mistake in the plan attached to the original transfer documents. The parties want to rectify it by attaching a new plan. So Mr and Mrs Taggart would probably like a clearly written document they can take out of their files in a few years' time and understand immediately without going to a lawyer.

By grouping the information carefully under headings, this should be possible. Little legal flavouring is needed. As long as the document is signed as a deed and witnessed properly, it will work. A possible transformation into plain language would say:

Deed of Amendment
Date: 10 January 2001
Parties
1 **London Borough of Boreham, Civic Centre, Boreham BU8 2AW (the 'council').**
2 **Brian Tony Taggart and Miriam Mary Taggart, both of 22 Vernon Road, Farfield (the 'buyers').**
Background
1 A transfer dated 27 May 1999 between the parties transferred 22 Vernon Road, Farfield (the 'property') to the buyers.
2 The transfer contained a plan ('Plan 1') that showed the property incorrectly.
Outcome
The plan attached to this deed ('Plan 2') correctly shows the property. It was signed as correct by the parties on 10 January 2001.
The transfer is to be read as if Plan 2 and not Plan 1 had been attached to it. In all other respects, the parties confirm the transfer.
Signatures
Signed as a deed on 10 January 2001:
● **by the council's authorized officer—**
● **by the buyers—**
Witness to the buyers' signature—

Though this is only a short example, its use of headings and simple style can be applied when much more complex matters have to be expressed in legal terms.

23 Writing low-literacy plain English

Guideline: *For people with low literacy, cut out the fine detail, be brief, and test your documents with the real experts—the readers.*

Who needs this kind of writing?

Several groups of people cannot cope with materials written for average readers. One obvious group is those whose first language isn't English. They fall on a spectrum: at one end are people who use the Roman alphabet and can read a language with similarities to English; at the other are people lacking education and unable to read any language—they take much longer to learn and some may never become fluent readers.

Another group have reading difficulties arising from health problems such as stroke or brain injury. Heavy drug or alcohol misuse, and the lifestyle that sometimes goes with it, also affect reading. Old age, too, can impair reading as vision and memory fade. Some people's reading will be temporarily affected by stress that is short-term (such as a medical appointment or a police interview) or longer-term (such as living with an abusive partner or in severe poverty). People who quit school young may have weak skills; youngsters with problems such as dyslexia are often in this group.

And there are those with cognitive impairments. Some are only mildly affected, while others are so severely disabled they may never read. However, many can read to some extent and more could do so if the writing were simpler.

For each group there'll be some differences in the kind of writing they need. For instance, people learning English will benefit from text that is relatively formal, while people with cognitive impairments will do better with colloquial wording, as their verbal skills often far exceed their reading skills.

Testing is the key

The most important thing is testing, as people who read and write fluently can only guess what these groups can understand. They are the experts to consult.

For newcomers to English, hold focus groups. You can sometimes arrange these through agencies for immigrants. Sometimes a language class may try out the materials you're preparing, or maybe a special group can be convened. Many are happy to help writers, as they benefit themselves.

If it's impossible to run focus groups, a quick one-to-one test may be feasible, perhaps with someone you overhear speaking a language other than English. Or someone stuffing envelopes in an office (a job sometimes taken by people with cognitive disabilities) may help during a coffee break. Immigrant organizations or agencies for people with cognitive impairments may be able to find someone you can talk to, once they understand what you need. Just asking about one word is better than nothing. Ask the reader to describe the action they might take after reading the material; what the pictures are saying; and what they learned from the text.

For people with cognitive impairments, it's best to get them to work on documents with you, say in groups of about three. Try to find people whose reading ability is very limited. Support workers tend to suggest people who can read fluently, but these are not very useful because—like you—they are guessing what will be hard for others to read. Several meetings may be needed before people gain the confidence to speak up. They need to feel they won't lose respect if they admit they don't understand. You can overcome shyness by explaining that they'll be helping others. Ask them to use their own words to explain what they've read. One person, asked what *values* meant, said *jewellery* (i.e. valuables). Ask for suggestions for clearer words.

Sometimes complete non-readers can also take part in the sessions. They're often skilled in commenting on pictures. A group with mixed abilities is best. Ask those who can read to speak the text aloud, as this helps to expose problems.

Keep sessions shorter than two hours, as the work is intensive and tiring. Payment is vital. It helps to keep people interested in what can be tedious work, and raises their often low incomes.

Preparing low-literacy materials

Prepare the materials in the same way as for average readers, only more so. The same principles apply: short paragraphs, very short sentences, familiar words, active voice, and good layout. There's one major difference: with most plain language for average readers, you're aiming to replicate most of the meaning in what you are clarifying, while for low-literacy readers, near-equivalence is rarely possible or even useful. Explaining or clarifying every word and phrase in a legal document, for example, may triple the length of the original and still not be readable. For low literacy, you have to consider how much text the readers will tolerate and whether even a definition will be enough to explain harder terms. To help people cope, you have to cut. It's better to include the minimum and add a phone number so people can call for more information if they need it. A four-pager that's read is more use than a twenty-pager gathering dust. A two-fold leaflet is a good size for many people. If needed, you can create a family of leaflets or really short booklets with text on related topics. A person can read them at different times, rather than being hit by a blockbuster.

Using difficult terms

Sometimes you have to use a difficult term. This is better than baby language. Immediately include an explanation (in brackets or a separate sentence). After all, readers will probably hear the word in daily life. So you could describe a *counsellor* (a hard word) as someone who is trained to listen and help sort out problems. Terms familiar in a person's life may be fairly easily learned in print. So, for instance, people with Down's syndrome can often read *syndrome* and even *chromosome*, while immigrants often recognize *immigrant* and *sponsor*.

Even so, minimize the number of difficult terms. A glossary at the end will help people learning English. Others are less likely to use it and need the definition immediately. Dictionary definitions are seldom helpful to readers as they use equally hard words. Sometimes a children's dictionary can help you, as can some of the plain-language lists available. You may just have to manage on your own, with the help of your testing teams. When all else fails, sleep on the problem. A new dawn may bring a solution just as you are burning the toast.

Language that's dumbed down or cleared up?

Low-literacy plain language is indeed more stilted than would probably be used otherwise; sentences are shorter and don't always flow. Sometimes the words may look repetitive or over-simplified. This is why some people complain about language being dumbed down. You don't need to use baby words (*bunny* instead of *rabbit*) but yes, the style may seem awkward compared with normal speech. But those who need the simple language won't complain.

Often, you'll need not merely to remove one harder word and insert a simpler one, but to alter the entire phrase or sentence. So, for a committee's duties, instead of *Terms of reference*, you can say *What we do*.

You'll need to decide what to do with stuff that's interesting but not vital—perhaps park it in a side panel. Often there's a compromise between lots of good information and just enough.

Short words help, but aren't enough. For instance, many people with cognitive impairments struggle with both *decide* and *choose*. You can substitute *pick*, but even that occasionally causes confusion—not that it's hard to read, but because a literal thinker will be looking for an object to pick up. A good alternative may be *you can make up your own mind about* ...

Simple tenses help. Words ending in *-ing* often cause difficulty for people with cognitive impairments and for newcomers to English. So, instead of *Are you going to do this soon?* you can say *Do you plan to do this soon?* Not the same, but close enough.

If necessary, use more than one term to suit various types of reader. Native speakers will probably understand *split up with* to describe the end of a relationship, but newcomers to English will need the more formal *separation* or *divorce*.

Use repetition—don't try variations to be 'interesting'. A car is a car and doesn't have to be a vehicle. Some people will fail to read *vehicle*, and some will assume you mean different things.

Keep your language as concrete as possible for readers who don't grasp abstract ideas easily, which is usual among people with cognitive impairments. So *Use a condom when you have sex* is clearer than *Practise safe sex*.

Don't use contractions. They look friendly but are harder to read. This is important for both readers with English as a second language and readers with cognitive impairments. Write *do not*, not *don't*. Do write *OK*—it's almost always understood.

Avoid metaphors. To say something is *a piece of cake* will have newcomers to English expecting cake. Sports-related sayings may not be understood by non-sports enthusiasts, so *level playing fields*, *sticky wickets*, and *end runs* need translation. Other sayings are old-fashioned, such as *grist to the mill*, *pig in a poke*, and *it went like clockwork*.

Use hyphens freely to break a word into chunks. Instead of *coworker*, say *co-worker* (and not *colleague*); and *by-law*, not *bylaw*; *web-site*, not *website*; *day-care*, not *daycare*; *tree-tops*, not *treetops*; *mouth-piece*, not *mouthpiece*; *coordinate*, not *coordinate*; and *health-care*, not *healthcare*. But never split a word over two lines with a hyphen—it's more difficult to read. Turn off your software's line-end hyphenation.

Slower readers may be able to sound out words with a clear shape—words like *Canadian* or *difficult*. Words like *that*, *there*, and *then* look very similar, though. Words with alternative sound changes (such as the *t* in *position*, or the *s* in *sure*) often cause trouble. Words that look similar, like *change*, *charge*, and *chance* can be hard for people with cognitive impairments.

Numbers: figures or words?

It's easier to read 8 than eight, so maybe ignore conventions about spelling out numbers under ten or 21. The only exception is 1, as it's easily confused with I. But when using numbers over 999, spell them out in words. A lengthy row of numerals is hard to work out, especially if there are many zeros. Unless exact numbers are really important, you can round a large figure into something easier to read. Say *four million*, rather than *three million eight hundred and fifty thousand*.

Dates are more easily read as words plus numbers. For example, 11 November 2008 not 11/11/08. With the latter, readers have to interpret one of the elevens as a month. And don't contract the month to Nov.

For readers with cognitive impairments, percentages rarely work. Instead of 50%, use one half. Use one quarter or three quarters instead of 25% and 75%. Beyond that, just say *many*, *most*, *a few*, *hardly any*. It's not as accurate but it's better than leaving your reader behind. Don't use graphs but a simple pie chart is OK, clearly labelled and in bright colours. Both graphs and percentages are all right for educated new-comers to English.

Accuracy: gains and losses

Critics may say you'll lose accuracy. At times, this is true. The rewriting process often exposes obscurity, but some detail will have to go. Ask a cognitively impaired person about rights (as in human rights) and they'll usually first think of rights and lefts, or rights and wrongs. *Human rights* may need to become *what is fair*, which is by no means a legal definition (or even accurate), but the idea is easier to grasp.

In many cases, however, you'll improve accuracy. The best part of writing low-literacy material is that it forces you to be utterly lucid. Abstraction and euphemism are out. If you're struggling with fuzzy text that's hard to paraphrase, call the original writer and ask for clarification: it's not always your job to interpret the uninterpretable. In one situation, a clarified consent form for a school outing became unusable when staff realized it was so biased towards the school that no parent would sign it.

Comprehension is the key thing, not whether it passes a lawyer's or grammarian's test of precision.

Proofread carefully

Check and recheck the writing, as people with low literacy often blame themselves for being stupid when a typo makes the text confusing.

Type size and style

Use a good-sized font. In a typeface such as Times Roman or Arial, that will normally be 13- or 14-point. Sixteen is too big (except for those with vision loss), while 12 is often too small. While the usual advice is to use a serif typeface (see chapter 24), try sans serif for people who read slowly, especially for those who read word by word. The lack of serifs makes the words clearer. But if there's a lot of text, Arial can seem heavy, so a modified sans serif such as Optima is a good alternative. Avoid Comic Sans as its informality can undermine serious text, and people soon find it irritating.

Adding a contents page and summary to longer documents

Add a contents page to text of more than a few pages, as these readers can seldom skim-read a long document. Sometimes just a summary of main points at the start will be enough for basic readers. Or use parallel text, in which the full version is in a column headed 'Full text', and a short one-sentence summary of each paragraph is beside it in a column headed 'Short text'.

Examples: transforming text into low-literacy english

Original: If the State agency finds that an individual has received a payment to which the individual was not entitled, whether or not the payment was due to the individual's fault or misrepresentation, the individual shall be liable to repay the State the total sum of the payment to which the individual was not entitled.
New: If the State agency finds that it gave you money you were not meant to have, you must pay it all back.

Original (leaflet about adolescents with cognitive impairments): We empower youth to make the necessary choices to effect a positive transition to adulthood.
New: We support young people to make useful choices.

Original (booklet about choices in pregnancy): Whether or not you seek the support of others at this time, remember that *you* are the only person who can make the final decision about what to do, and your decision must be voluntary. No one has the right to try to pressure or force you into parenthood, adoption, or abortion against your wishes.

New: Remember, *you* are the only person who should pick what is best for you. You can ask people to tell you what they think. But no one should try to make you do something that does not feel OK for you, no matter how much they love you or how much you think they know. (Both examples by permission of Calgary Sexual Health Centre.)

Original (a medical consent form): I, the undersigned, have had the above procedure(s) explained to me by Dr. _____ and understand the nature and consequences of it (them), including any alternative/ additional procedure(s). Further, I understand that during the course of the procedure(s), unforeseen conditions may necessitate alternative procedure(s).

Let's unpack this example:

- This form needs splitting in two to avoid confusion. One part would be for people having invasive procedures such as surgery. The second would be for those having tests. Then, for accuracy, *procedure* could be altered to *surgery* or *test*.
- The plurals *s* and *them* in brackets are hard to understand, as is the slash between *alternative* and *additional*.
- *the undersigned* can be removed and a space left for the person's name.
- The passive voice can be made active: *Dr X has explained to me*, or *I have learned about the surgery Dr X will do.*
- *unforeseen conditions* can become *something may happen that was not in the plan.*
- *necessitate alternative procedures* can become *Dr X may then need to do something different.*

Pictures and gestures

Where feasible, pictures can help people read the words. Colour pictures are better than black and white, which are themselves better than nothing. Pictures also break up the text and make it look more inviting.

However, people interpret pictures differently according to their life experiences and background. So clear representational pictures work best, even if fluent readers find them dull. Don't remove facial features. Don't put in fussy backgrounds or irrelevant details. Explain any symbols: a crossed-through red circle is meaningless until people have learned to 'read' it.

Don't use cutesy or childish pictures as they can offend in a way that plain words don't. Try to find pictures that represent and include the readership. People with low literacy are more likely to be cleaners than airline pilots. They may be on meagre incomes, so holidays are more likely to mean a local seaside resort than skiing.

Try to show diversity if the pictures are for newcomers to English, but don't use those that label people just by their national clothing (unless, of course, the materials are meant only for a particular group and occasion), as it marks the readers as 'other' and quaint. Include real variety—not just one shade of black or brown to represent all. Avoid displaying gestures like the thumbs-up that are offensive or cause derision in other cultures.

Effects of plain English

It's hard to prove exactly how useful low-literacy plain English is for people with cognitive impairments. This would involve not only watching for changes in behaviour, but taking into account further variables like poor memory, physical disabilities, interest, and opportunities. For newcomers to English, again it's difficult to measure effectiveness, as their literacy skills improve all the time. As for people living on the edge of society or undergoing personal crisis, it's unkind to be trying controlled studies.

Getting professional help

Writing for low-literacy readers is harder than writing for average readers. Finding an author can be difficult. Most people working in the field are doing so for a particular organization or agency. So you may have to learn to do it yourself.

Children and young people

Norwood supports babies, children and other young people
with learning and physical disabilities and other problems.

Binoh

Some children find it hard to do well at school. Teachers at
Binoh give children extra help so they can stay at school and
be happy.

What did we do last year?

■ We helped children at 20 schools. We had never helped
children at schools in Redbridge before, but this year we
helped children at 3 schools there.

■ We had more than 200 phone calls from parents asking us
for help.

■ We started a new art class for children. In the class they can
use art to show how they feel.

■ We got a new teacher to make sure the work that children do
at Binoh helps with the work they do at school.

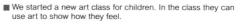

What will we do next year?

■ We will help children in the new Norwood nursery.

■ We will start a new scheme for children age 15.
We will help them to:
  ■ learn, and
  ■ get ready to do training, and
  ■ choose what job they want to do when they start work.

■ We will start another new art class because so many children
enjoy art.

What did children say about Binoh?

"Binoh makes me feel more confident." Alan

"My speech is getting better and I know where to put my
tongue when I speak." Stephanie

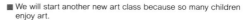

4

Norwood, a London-based charity, looks after children and adults with learning
disabilities. Formerly it published a version of its annual review written in
low-literacy plain English, helping service users to read about its work. In 2008,
though, Norwood began producing the review in the simplified style only. This
saves money and seems to be preferred by sponsors and supporters. Above is a
typical page: short sentences, active-voice verbs, and personal words are com-
plemented by line illustrations.

Web writing for low-literacy readers

Low-literacy users are less able to scan Web text for meaning. They tend to plough through it word for word and may miss peripheral page elements because they are focusing more narrowly. They often spend time puzzling over difficult words.

Jakob Nielsen found that they tend to accept their conclusions as 'good enough' based on scant information because digging deeper demands too much work. 'As soon as text becomes too dense, lower-literacy users start skipping, usually looking for the next link. In doing so, they often overlook important information.' (www.useit. com/alertbox/20050314.html)

Put your main point at the top of the page, where even readers who may give up after a few lines will see it. And, as with pages for more able readers, put other important information high up, to minimize the risk of users losing their place as they scroll.

Static text is easier to read, so avoid text that moves or changes, such as animations and fly-out menus. Avoid fussy additions around the edges of the screen (like advertisements). And if buttons are used to direct readers to other sites, make sure they're big enough to be easy for people with poor hand–eye coordination.

In *Writing Matters: Getting Your Message Across*, Janet Pringle, who works with low-literacy readers in Canada, says:

It is as important for readers with literacy barriers to be able to take part fully in society as it is for people who are blind or use a wheelchair.

In my ideal world, two aspects would be different. There would be fewer literacy barriers. And someone would be able to say 'Please be more clear. I have difficulty reading' just as easily as someone else would say 'Speak up. I'm hard of hearing.'

Hard-to-understand documents can mean the writer needs to try again, not that the readers are failures.

24 Basics of clear layout

Guideline: *Use clear layout to present your plain words in an easily accessible way.* Plain English needs effective layout otherwise only half the job has been done. At its simplest, in a letter or short report, this might mean using easily legible type and putting ample space between paragraphs. At its most complex, in instructions, detailed official forms, or Web pages, effective layout might require the manipulation of hundreds of variables such as different typefaces, headings of various sizes, colours, and illustrations.

Not so long ago, layout was largely outside writers' control. Typesetting was an expensive mystery guarded by layout professionals. Now, with the advent of desktop publishing (DTP) and Web-design software, many writers have access to sophisticated layout tools. But if these tools are not used with a reasonable degree of skill, if there is no sense of what makes a page look good, or if readers' strategies for tackling a document are ignored, then the results can be dire—poor layout can negate many of the benefits of plain English.

There is no simple checklist for good layout, but this chapter summarizes key points that you may like to bear in mind when preparing a layout or getting others to do so. Naturally, for important or high-use documents, you may need help from layout and printing professionals who have undergone rigorous typographical training.

Some of the guidance here is more appropriate to the highly flexible DTP and Web environments than to word processing, though these fields increasingly overlap. The points are intended to supplement the technical guidance that software manuals tend to cover. For simplicity I've set out the points in question-and-answer form.

What's the best way to get a feel for good layout?

Study layout critically—books, reports, letters, Web pages, forms, and your car and life insurance policies. Every line of type on every page or website, every ruled line, and every white space is the result of someone's conscious layout decision, for good or ill. The sum of those decisions is what gives a page its distinctive look. By going through the document yourself—say by filling in a form—you can see whether it is usable as well as legible.

Consider which documents are easy on the eye, and why. Which organize the material well, and how do they do this? Economy is often an important factor, so if a large number of words has been squeezed into a page, what has been done (or not done) to make the result easily legible?

Consider how different layouts fulfil different purposes—to attract attention, to sell, to summarize main points, to ask questions, to act as reference material, to save space. Consider whether the layout styles fulfil their purposes.

In paper documents, what's a good page size to use?

This depends on many things such as the amount of information, how the readers use the document (do they need, for instance, to carry it around with them on a building site or to follow a route?), whether it's to be stored and filed, or whether it needs to be fed through photocopiers or laser printers.

In Europe the commonest range of sizes—and therefore the most economical—are the 'A' sizes such as A3 (297×420 mm), A4 (210×297 mm), and A5 (148×210 mm). Each of these is formed by folding in half, along the long edge, the next biggest 'A' size. All the sizes offer an infinite number of layout possibilities. Most business letterheadings are A4, and a single column of type is the obvious layout choice. But an information leaflet might have two columns to the A4 page and be double-sided; this allows a great number of words to be fitted in. An A4 page could be divided into one narrow column (perhaps for side-headings) and one wide column for the associated main text. Many leaflets are A4 folded twice on the long edge, producing a six-panel set-up—one panel for a front cover, perhaps, and five for other information.

The 'B' sizes offer other interesting possibilities, especially when you want to create a distinctive look to your sales literature. B4 is 250×353 mm, B5 is 176×250 mm, and B6 is 125×176 mm.

In the US, common sheet sizes are 25×38 in, 26×40 in, and 36×48 in, from which the sizes for booklets, leaflets, etc. can be derived. Common sizes for trimmed stationery are 8.5×11 in, 8.5×14 in (US legal), and 7.5×10 in.

What are the key variables to control for high legibility?

Three important variables are type size, column width, and space between lines ('leading', pronounced 'ledding'). These interact in ways that improve or impair legibility. While it's impossible to lay down rules for how these variables should be manipulated, some guidelines may help.

Type size: Type size is measured from just above the top of the capitals to just below the bottom of letters like y and j. The distance can be measured in points. (A point is about 1/72 inch.)

In many typefaces the sizes 9-point and above will be highly legible for large areas of continuous text on paper, though this will depend on how the other variables are handled. On Web pages, a bigger size will be needed (see chapter 21).

Point size alone is an uncertain guide to how big the type appears to be. Here are examples of 10-point type in two typefaces, Monotype Bembo and Monotype Nimrod ('typeface' means a set of lettering in a certain design):

Example of 10–pt Monotype Bembo, a widely available typeface based on a 15th–century Italian type.

Example of 10-pt Monotype Nimrod, designed in the 1970s for newspaper text setting.

Though both are 10-point, the characteristics of Nimrod make it appear bigger than Bembo. This is mainly because in Nimrod the x-height (height of the lower-case *x*, *o*, *m*, *n*, etc.) is great in proportion to the type size. So x-height is a better guide to legibility than point size. Provided the x-height is 1.5 mm or more, printed type will be highly legible to those with normal eyesight under good reading conditions. For a mass audience, though, 1.8 mm is more reasonable. Documents to be read from a distance—posters, say—will need a bigger type size. In a reference document you might be content to use a small point size, say 7-point, for the sake of economy—but you would choose a typeface whose x-height was large enough to make the point size reasonably legible and you would use narrow columns.

If some of the audience are known to have poor eyesight, an x-height of at least 3 mm is good. An alternative is to offer large-print and Braille versions of documents. See chapter 21 for advice on websafe fonts and how to make Web pages accessible to visually impaired people.

Column width: For large areas of text on paper, most layout professionals reckon that the optimum column width is 50–70 letters and spaces. This means about 8 to 12 words per line, as in the column width you're reading now. In research with a sample of 4 000 people, Colin Wheildon found that 38 per cent thought text was hard to read if the lines extended beyond 60 characters.

Certainly a common mistake is to set small type across too wide a column, such as 170 mm on an A4 page. The result could be more than a hundred letters and spaces to the line unless the type is correspondingly big. And if the type is big, there'll be fewer words to the page so printing or copying costs could increase.

Leading: Normally there needs to be some leading, otherwise readers tire easily and make mistakes when locating the start of lines. The amount of leading depends on the trade-off you make between economy and legibility. As a guide, try to ensure that the leading is about a fifth of the type size. So 12-point type might have leading at 2.5 or 3 points. Generally, the wider the column, the more leading is needed. Typefaces with a large x-height relative to their type size (like most versions of Times, Helvetica, Arial, Plantin, and Palatino) tend to need the full allowance of leading; those with a smaller x-height (like Futura, Bodoni, and Bembo) tend to need less.

So which is the best typeface to use for high legibility?

What works well in one set of circumstances may not work well in another. Generally, the type for printed body text should be quiet, simple, and regular in form without the eccentricities of display type-faces such as those on the fascias of hamburger joints or on advertising hoardings. For booklets longer than, say, twelve pages, it's usually better to choose a serif type (that is, a type with tiny strokes or projections at the end of most of the letters). The serifs guide the eye horizontally and put light and shade on the page because the letters have thick and thin strokes. Serif types tend to look rather more authoritative, classical, and official. The main text type in this book is a serif, the Monotype version of Swift.

Highly legible serif types include Plantin, Garamond, Joanna, Pala-tino, and Times. These are their industry names; trade names may differ for commercial or copyright reasons. Samples of fonts are easy to find on the Web (e.g. www.adobe.com/type, www.linotype.com), and your computer may have many fonts you can examine too.

Times is available in most DTP and word-processing software, but its narrow character width tends to make it more suitable for newspaper columns. Its universality makes it an unusual choice for any layout professionals who want to create an individual look for their client's documents. In short, it is a little boring.

The sans-serif types (types without serifs) tend to be more useful as headings and in forms, catalogues, and flyers, though they can look good in almost any application if handled well. They have enjoyed a resurgence on websites as they seem easy to read on screen. Sans faces tend to be plain, unfussy, and very compact, so in bold weights they make a strong impact. Good sans faces include Helvetica, Gill, Franklin Gothic, and Frutiger. The Arial font, which is similar to Helvetica, is available everywhere, like Times.

Many documents combine sans-serif type for headings with serif type for body text. The opposite combination is less common but can still work well.

What about ways of emphasizing type?

Most typefaces can be used in weights such as roman (this weight), bold, italic, and bold italic. A popular type like Helvetica has as many as 28 weights. In a single document, it's usually better to use as few weights as are really necessary and to make sure there is ample difference in strength between them. In some typefaces, especially sans faces, the italic weight is merely a sloping version of the roman and may not be noticeably different, especially on Web pages.

Use highlighting weights sparingly—if you emphasize too much, nothing will be emphasized. If too many individual words are typed in bold, pages will look spotty or dazzling and the reader will find concentration difficult. This is a common fault in insurance policies where defined terms like 'we' and 'you' tend to be given bold type whenever they appear.

Most people with normal eyesight dislike reading long swathes of bold, italics, and capitals. Of these, capitals tend to be the most disruptive to reading and may seem aggressive. There's no harm in capitalizing a few words, but the usual mix of upper and lower case is best for legibility. There's no need to set headings in capitals; generally they'll look better in sentence case.

In typewriting, underlining was one of the few available ways of emphasizing text. The weight of rule corresponded to the weight of the type and the effect was pleasant enough in small doses. In DTP, underlining is probably the least attractive way because the line will usually slice through the bottom of the type unpleasantly, like this. Only do it if there's no other way.

Any hints on the use of white space?

Without wasting paper unnecessarily, you should allow generous margins and reasonable space between columns. Resist the temptation to fill white space with type. It's no tragedy if a section of a report ends halfway down a page or if the back of a leaflet has to be left blank.

If you are leaving space between paragraphs (a common alternative to indenting the first line), ensure the space adequately separates one paragraph from the next but don't allow the paragraphs to look like islands. The software will generally allow you to set up style-sheets to exert fine control over inter-paragraph space.

If headings appear in a column of text, be sure to put at least as much space above them as below them, otherwise they'll seem to be floating upwards to the previous paragraph.

If there are bullets, don't indent them excessively (or even at all), and don't unduly separate them from the text—5 mm is enough. Generally the space from the bullet to the type should be the same as or less than the space between lines.

Is it a good idea to reverse out the type?

Reversing out means printing the type in white out of a background colour. Usually this will only be highly legible if the type is at least 10-point in a bold weight and if the background colour is dark. Sans-serif faces tend to reverse out better than serif. Only reverse out small areas of type.

Should type be printed on a coloured background?

Not if it destroys the clarity of the type. For most purposes, there needs to be strong contrast between foreground (the type) and background. If you use dark green type on a pale green background, you're asking for trouble, especially as about eight per cent of males are colour blind for green and red and may see these colours as grey.

Is it a good idea to track or scale the type?

Tracking means adding or taking out space between letters. There comes a point when excessive tracking disrupts the readers to the extent that they start to look at individual letters instead of reading words by their shape and in sweeps of four or five words at a time. If done at all, tracking needs to be sensitive and to respect the design characteristics of the typeface.

Similar points apply to the ability of some software to scale the type to compress or expand it. Don't overdo this: be sensitive to the design of the typeface and to your readers' eyesight.

The term 'hierarchy of headings' is often used. What does it mean?

A document may need to use several sizes or weights of heading to signify, for example, chapter headings, subheadings, and paragraph headings. This range of sizes or weights (or both) is the hierarchy of headings. In general, the strength and position of headings should reflect the job they are being asked to do. So chapter headings will usually be considerably stronger than subheadings, which will in turn be stronger than paragraph headings. This is similar to the arrangement used in this book. The hierarchy of headings should be applied consistently—readers get confused if the same signal is used with different meanings.

Should I use justified type?

Justification means inserting spaces between words (and even between letters) so that all the lines of type take up the full column width. Hyphenation at line-ends may also be needed to make this work. The main reasons for justification are economy and, according to some, greater neatness.

There's no clear-cut evidence that competent justification impairs the reading performance of literate adults. Sometimes, though, mechanical justification tends to produce rivers of white space running down the text as well as very uneven letter-spacing. If you dislike the justified type your machine produces, your software manual may offer help. For example, you should be able to adjust the program so that it applies line-end hyphenation only to words of seven letters or more and so that it bars more than two successive line-end hyphenations.

Unjustified type ('ranged left' or 'flush left') tends to produce a more relaxed, informal look. Word-spacing remains constant. The hyphenation program can be switched off if you dislike line-end hyphenation, though the drawback is a more ragged right-hand edge to the column. With unjustified type you'll want to avoid breaking up the left-hand edge of the column by excessive indentation. Try to use the left-hand edge as the starting point for as much text as possible.

By editing or other adjustments, try to remove widows (single words forming the last line of a paragraph), especially if they appear as the first line of a page. They waste space and look unsightly.

Does colour help?

Cost may prohibit the use of a second colour (or several colours) on anything except pre-printed stationery, external publications with long print-runs, and websites. But if colours are available, don't spatter them throughout the text. Use them mainly to help people navigate through the document, perhaps by applying the same colour to all headings or to one level of heading. Use colour also to add impact, say on a front cover. In forms, a second colour is now common (perhaps as a percentage tint) to surround white completion boxes; this helps them to stand out.

What paper should I use?

This depends on your budget and the conditions under which the document will be used. If possible, take advice from a printing professional. Heavy gloss papers tend to be expensive and may make the type hard to read in certain lighting conditions. Thin papers create an unacceptable amount of show-through when printed on both sides. Certain weights and finishes are treated unkindly by photocopiers and laser printers. Papers with a high recycled waste content are gradually improving in quality and in their range of weights, finishes, and colours.

Doesn't decent layout cost more?

The work has to be done, so it might as well be done properly. A poorly laid-out form, for example, may substantially impair readers' performance and this adds to administrative costs if it has to be returned for re-completion. Government departments reckon that the cost of laying out and printing a form is as little as half of one per cent of the cost of administering it after completion. A life insurance policy might cost a few pence to print, yet the first year's premiums could easily be several thousand times that. So good layout is unlikely to add significantly to costs.

To showcase most kinds of essential information, nothing more than decent competence is needed in the layout. Often the best results come from quiet, unshowy pages that the readers hardly notice. There's no need to shout. Colin Wheildon says, 'Typography must be clear. At its best, it is virtually invisible.'

The next few pages show the layout features of pages from several documents. All are shown at much reduced size. Colours other than black are shown in greyscale. Most of the documents from which these pages are taken display the Clear English Standard from Plain Language Commission.

Other **useful contacts**

Abandoned vehicles
020 8379 1000

Age Concern (Enfield)
020 8351 1322

Animal welfare
020 8379 3695

Anti–social behaviour (ASB)
freephone 0800 40 80 160

ASB out of hours
020 8379 1000

Asbestos advice
020 8379 3661

Care & Repair
020 8379 1000

Childline
freephone 0800 1111

Citizens Advice Bureau
0870 126 4664

Community Alarm
020 8367 3521

Community Safety Unit
020 8379 4612

Crimestoppers
freephone 0800 555 111

Domestic violence helpline
0808 2000 247

**Elder abuse
(safeguarding adults)**
020 8379 8052

**Enfield Racial
Equality Council**
020 8373 6271/2

Environmental Health
020 8379 1000

**Federation of Enfield
Community Associations
Ltd (FECA)**
020 8245 3593

Gas leaks
freephone 0800 111 999

Hate Crime Forum
020 8379 4612

Housing assessments
020 8379 4377

Housing/council tax benefit
020 8379 3798

Legal advice
020 8807 8888

Local police
020 8807 1212

National Debtline
0808 808 4000

NHS Direct
0845 4647

Noise nuisance
020 8379 1000

Pests
020 8379 1000

Recycling
020 8379 1000

Refuse collection
020 8379 1000

**Street lighting
(David Websters)**
freephone 0800 032 6788

Thames Water (water leaks)
freephone 0800 714 614

**Three Valleys Water
(water leaks)**
freephone 0800 376 5325

Victim Support
0845 30 30 900

15

A contacts list needs to be easy to scan so that readers can find the name they want. Good layout can help, as shown here in a page from Enfield Homes' tenants handbook. The names are in alphabetical order and bold type, while the phone numbers are in roman type. There's space between all the items, too. It looks so simple that someone must have spent quite some time thinking it out. (Design by The Bridge Group. By permission of Enfield Homes.)

Part of a series of fifteen on housing and council tax benefit, this leaflet from St Albans District Council adopts a clear hierarchy of headings and good use of bold and italic type. Note the use of the bottom left of page 2, traditionally a graveyard area, for reference information (the contents list). The six-page 1/3 A4 gatefold layout makes economical use of an A4 sheet and gives a good column width (about 48 characters). Bespoke themed illustrations (in full colour in the original document) add a touch of class. The cost of this kind of high-quality design work was spread among ten local councils, with pages 1 and 6 carrying details unique to each council. (Design by M & IM Frost. By permission of St Albans District Council.)

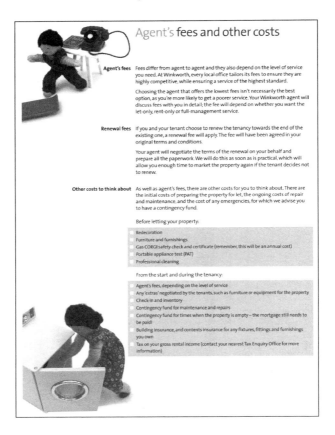

Agent's fees and other costs

Agent's fees   Fees differ from agent to agent and they also depend on the level of service you need. At Winkworth, every local office tailors its fees to ensure they are highly competitive, while ensuring a service of the highest standard.

Choosing the agent that offers the lowest fees isn't necessarily the best option, as you're more likely to get a poorer service. Your Winkworth agent will discuss fees with you in detail; the fee will depend on whether you want the let-only, rent-only or full-management service.

Renewal fees   If you and your tenant choose to renew the tenancy towards the end of the existing one, a renewal fee will apply. The fee will have been agreed in your original terms and conditions.

Your agent will negotiate the terms of the renewal on your behalf and prepare all the paperwork. We will do this as soon as is practical, which will allow you enough time to market the property again if the tenant decides not to renew.

Other costs to think about   As well as agent's fees, there are other costs for you to think about. There are the initial costs of preparing the property for let, the ongoing costs of repair and maintenance, and the cost of any emergencies, for which we advise you to have a contingency fund.

Before letting your property:

- Redecoration
- Furniture and furnishings
- Gas CORGI safety check and certificate (remember, this will be an annual cost)
- Portable appliance test (PAT)
- Professional cleaning

From the start and during the tenancy:

- Agent's fees, depending on the level of service
- Any 'extras' negotiated by the tenants, such as furniture or equipment for the property
- Check-in and inventory
- Contingency fund for maintenance and repairs
- Contingency fund for times when the property is empty – the mortgage still needs to be paid!
- Building insurance, and contents insurance for any fixtures, fittings and furnishings you own
- Tax on your gross rental income (contact your nearest Tax Enquiry Office for more information)

This page, from Winkworth's *Letting your property* booklet, uses side-headings and full-colour illustrations (in the original) to help make good use of the A4 size. The side-headings mean it's important to keep the text ranged left ⁃ there are no paragraph indents. Subheads are placed in the main
   The line length is about 70 characters, and to compensate for this there
      of leading. (Design by M & IM Frost. By permission of Winkworth
         g Ltd.)

And everyone

YHA accommodation is open to all. People of all ages are able to stay with YHA, to enjoy the great locations and the friendly relaxed atmosphere of our accommodation.

Even though you no longer have to be a member to stay in our hostels, the number of people joining YHA increased in the last year by 10,000, reversing a trend from recent years.

Two million families in the UK cannot afford a week's holiday. YHA's affordable accommodation is an attractive option for many. The number of families staying with YHA increased by almost 18% in the last year.

Families enjoy the opportunity of getting out to new places, in the countryside and in cities. The social mix YHA offers is great for families. Children have an opportunity of making new friends, giving their parents a chance to relax.

Some accommodation is particularly suited to families. YHA Hartington has a children's play area and a small pets corner.

Families are able to take part in activities at YHA Edale in the Peak District and Okehampton in Devon. At YHA Treyarnon, Cornwall, and YHA Broad Haven, Pembrokeshire, families can enjoy coastal activities together.

The Mosaic Partnership is a project designed to increase participation of people from black and minority ethnic (BME) communities in four National Parks (Peak District, North York Moors, Yorkshire Dales and Brecon Beacons) and YHA.

Our involvement with Mosaic proves our commitment to improving BME community access to the National Parks and the wider rural environment. Staff at YHA sites that have hosted Mosaic groups benefit from interaction with new users. BME groups are now independently using our hostels. This

raises our figures for overnight stays, and our involvement in the scheme can give us access to funders who want to know more about our commitment to community cohesion.

Case study

"The atmosphere (was) relaxed and security tight enough to enable mums and dads to relax and let their children use the games room and mix with other kids. Our boys... were never short of playmates during our half-term trip"

Dale Williams,
Birmingham Mail

12   Annual Review 2008

Annual reports don't have to be dull. The 32-page booklet from YHA (England and Wales) uses 89 colour photos to show the changing nature of youth hostelling, with emphasis on fun and outdoor adventure—no more helping out with the chores. The layout uses three columns to the A4 page. Few pages have more than 500 words of text. It makes for a bright, entertaining document that's clearly written and easy on the eye. (By permission of YHA (England & Wales) Ltd.)

Housing and Council Tax Benefit

Sunderland City Council

Application for a Pre-Tenancy Determination   18

A Pre-Tenancy Determination will tell you the maximum amount of Housing Benefit we can pay on a property. It does not tell you how much Housing Benefit you will get and it is not a claim for Housing Benefit. If you complete this form, you must ask your landlord or property agent to sign and date the form at question 3.

You do not need to complete this form if your Housing Benefit is paid under the Local Housing Allowance scheme. See the notes at the back of this form.

Local authority stamp and date

1. About you

Name:		Date of birth:	
Partner's name:		Date of birth:	
Current address:			
		Postcode:	

| Are you single and under 25 years of age? | Yes ☐ No ☐ |
| Are you receiving Housing Benefit at the moment? | Yes ☐ No ☐ |

2. About the tenancy and property

Address (that you want a determination for):

What sort of tenancy will it be?

Shorthold ☐   Assured ☐   Licence ☐   Fixed ☐   Other ☐   If 'Other', please give details

How long will the tenancy be?

| Will this be a joint tenancy with any other person? | Yes ☐ No ☐ |

If Yes, please state their name:

What type of property is it?

Detached house ☐	Detached bungalow ☐	Semi-detached house ☐	Semi-detached bungalow ☐
Terraced house ☐	Terraced flat ☐	Flat in a block ☐	Flat in a house ☐
Flat above shops ☐	Maisonette ☐	Bedsit ☐	Room(s) in house or flat ☐
Cottage ☐	Other ☐	If 'Other', please give details	

Please continue overleaf

This form from Sunderland City Council is well organized vertically and horizontally, with good use of white-out boxes showing where readers need to give their details. Language is clear—the difficult phrase 'pre-tenancy determination' is unavoidable and has been explained by the time the reader gets the form. (By permission of Sunderland City Council.)

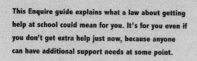

This Enquire guide explains what a law about getting help at school could mean for you. It's for you even if you don't get extra help just now, because anyone can have additional support needs at some point.

Everyone is good at different things. Needing extra help with something does not mean you are stupid.

call 0845 123 2303

So what does it mean?

Basically, if you need extra help to be able to get the most from school for any reason at all, then you have additional support needs and your school must help you.

You may need help for the whole time you're at school or you may only need it for a little while (maybe a few weeks or months).

log on to www.enquire.org.uk

These pages from a guide for secondary-school pupils use simple language and eye-catching graphics. The background is a flat colour to comply with guidelines for visually impaired youngsters. The text is consistently left-aligned to help those using magnifiers. (By permission of Enquire (Children in Scotland).)

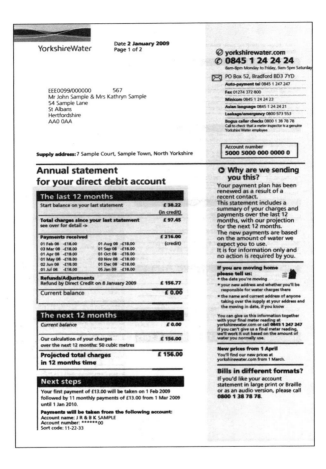

Customers of utility companies like bills they can understand. Good layout and clear language are vital.

On the front of this Yorkshire Water bill, three strong headings in the black horizontal bars divide the charge details and enable readers to find what they need. At the first fold, a strong horizontal rule acts as an important divider, and its weight is echoed in the three other rules in the right-hand column.

Bold type is used effectively throughout the page for headings and emphasis—for example in the smaller type at the top right.

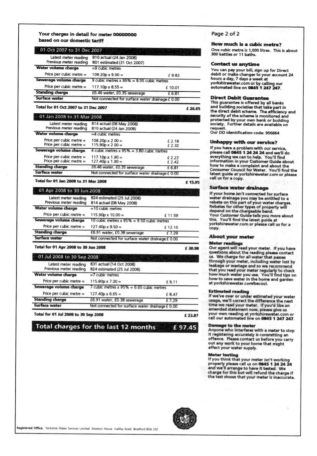

The back page has layout features that reflect the front. Again there are strong horizontal bars carrying important headings. The rules within those sections, and the invisible vertical grid line that is never breached by text, enable the reader to see the structure at once and read across easily. The right-hand column, broken up by numerous subheads, is held together and separated from the charging information by a pale tint (light blue in the original), which echoes the tinted panel on the front page. A sans-serif type has been used as this tends to be cleaner, simpler, and more concise in a document where tables predominate and space is tight. (Design by Boag Associates. Reproduced by permission of Yorkshire Water.)

25 Keeping errors in Czech: its time to Proof read

Guideline: *Check your stuff before the readers do.*
Seeing whether the bus driver has given you the right change. Ensuring you don't transfer £5 000 from your bank account instead of £500. Checking you've not left swabs and scalpels in the patient.

Only one of these things is a matter of life and death. The other two are just a bit boring and pedantic. Rather like proofreading, some think.

Yet proofreading matters. Without it your writing could soon be plagued by uninformed not uniformed police, marital not martial arts, infernal not internal disputes, and pubic not public affairs. And, as one hotel did, you could even find yourself keeping people abreast of events in the brasserie by telling them: 'We offer two restaurants, The Arctic and Scizzios brassiere.'

If you spend time clarifying your writing, it makes sense to invest a fraction more in a final check for errors before you send or publish. The most important thing about proofreading is to care enough to do it. Many documents, emails, and websites have errors in them, from misspellings to grammatical slips and factual blunders. Some readers won't notice or think any less of the author if they do. But plenty will regard a rash of errors, or even one gross error, as proof that the author's an idiot. They'll therefore reject what's being said.

So check and put things right. And when correcting the errors, try not to insert new ones. In a previous edition of this book, my last-minute changes included: 'Organizations that want to win the confidence of customers should give them incomprehensible legal agreements to sign.' The same kind of blunder created the so-called Adulterous Bible of 1631, in which the seventh commandment said: 'Thou shalt commit adultery.'

False negatives are easy to miss, as The *Times* showed in an obituary of the anti-apartheid activist Mike Terry: 'By then [1990] London had effectively become a global centre for opposition to anti-apartheid as well as a centre for exiled activists from the ANC (African National Congress).' For 'anti-apartheid', read 'apartheid'.

What is proofreading?

Proofreading is about being remorseless in attending to detail: checking things like spelling, punctuation, double or missing word spacing, use of upper- and lower-case letters, grammar, layout, and highlighting. So it's about getting things right, making them consistent, and avoiding the burrs and blots that may distract or derail the rushing reader. It corrects mistakes before they embarrass you.

Proofreading is not like other reading where we skim-read for information, usually in a hurry. To proofread well, go slowly. Make time for two checks, if you can. That's one for the big picture—layout, headings, type—and one for sense, spelling, grammar, and punctuation.

Proofreading on screen

If you're proofreading on screen, try to adjust the image size and brightness so that the type, including the punctuation, is highly legible. You can get some help from the computer program's automatic spell-check and grammar-check, too. The program will show where you've typed an extra space by mistake, failed to type a space, or omitted an initial capital. And it can help check consistency—the search-and-replace feature in Microsoft Word, for example, can quickly find all uses of '9' and change them to 'nine'. But the human brain will tend to beat computers at spotting homonyms (words that sound the same but are spelt differently)—*there* for *their*, *to* for *too* or *two*, *ball* for *bawl*, and *sun* for *son*.

Proofreading on paper

If you're proofreading on paper, first make sure the lighting is right. Then run that potent weapon, your index finger, beneath the lines of type so that your eye concentrates on each word (or use a ruler to cover everything except the line you're reading). This helps because in normal reading you're too clever—your brain sees the way the pattern is going and jumps to conclusions without spotting the detail.

Common sources of error

Depending on the nature, length, and importance of the document, you also need to check—separately—at least fourteen things:

1 Conformity with any house style your organization has: it will often prescribe certain preferred spellings (e.g. *organize* or *organise*) and how vertical lists are to be punctuated.

2 Alignment: check margins, bulleted lists, and everything that is supposed to align horizontally or vertically.

3 Captions: check captions on photos and illustrations. Often they'll have been added late and retyped by a designer in a hurry, rather than cut-and-pasted from the author's work.

4 Contents list: check that the listed chapter or section headings are identical to the way they appear in the rest of the document and have the correct page numbers. If the contents list seems error-free, you may not have looked hard enough.

5 Dates are often wrong: when a day of the week is given, check it matches the calendar. The date error in this council letter was missed by the author: 'Having visited the site on 28 March 1007, a visual inspection showed the complaint to be justified . . .'. (King Ethelred himself may have been Unready that sunny springtime, but his officials were keeping busy.) The layout of dates should also be consistent, e.g. in the pattern *10 January 1954* or *January 10, 1954*, not both.

6 Phone numbers and Web addresses: check them if that's part of your brief.

7 Headlines: check these separately. They may have the authority of bigger type, but errors will often lurk. A headline in The *Times* spoke of 'A salutory tale of greed, adventure, and unlikely characters'—read 'salutary'. Another headline referred to a famous Chelsea goalkeeper as Thompson though his name was Thomson. A ramblers' magazine spelt Lake Waikaremoana correctly, which takes some doing, but the headline above said 'Plunging into the Maori lengend'.

8 Numbers and prices: it's easy to mistype numbers, so check them carefully. An article about the tanker Braer running aground off Shetland in 2007 referred to its carrying 85 tonnes of crude oil. A sceptical proofreader would have realized this was practically a thimbleful—the real tonnage was 85 000. *The Guardian*'s review of a book on English usage began by saying it was priced at £00.00—clearly a snip.

9 Spelling of names: these are mainly the author's responsibility, but be alert for oddities that may be mistakes; they're often easily checkable via the Web. For example, 'St Margrets Road' is probably St Margaret's Road; the 'Princess Louse School in Blyth' is probably the Princess Louise School; and if a Restoration poet is referred to as Ben Johnson, he's probably the famous Ben Jonson (whose tombstone in Westminster Abbey needed proofreading as it says 'Johnson'). If you're lucky enough to be a proofreader in Wales (which some may regard as a guarantee of full-time work), the aqueduct near Trevor is spelt Pontcysyllte.

10 Names of organizations: these change. In the UK, ministry names change remarkably often, though not as often as the politicians leading them. The Department of Education and Science now exists only in Ireland, a separate country. What used to be a UK department of that same name became first the Department for Education and Skills in 2001 and then, in 2007, was split into the Department for Children, Schools and Families, and the Department for Innovation, Universities and Skills. The Royal National Institute for the Blind became in 2002 the Royal National Institute of the Blind, and then in 2007 the Royal National Institute of Blind People. Helpfully, it has remained 'RNIB' throughout. Stay alert for similar names becoming confused, as in this TV review in *The Times*: 'There was good news about education, however. Not from *Panorama* but on *Teen Mum High* (BBC Two) which found an Ofcom-lauded secondary school in Stockport ... '. For Ofcom, the UK telecoms and broadcasting regulator, read 'Ofsted', the education inspectorate.

11 Footnotes, paragraph numbers, page numbers, running headers and running footers, and all cross-references to page or chapter numbers: all need a separate check. The title on the front page of a booklet may differ from the title in the running footers because the designer has used an old template unamended.

12 Homonyms: commonly confused words are principle/principal, compliment/complement, it's/its. Errors involving the last two came together in this example from a furniture brochure: 'Every home is unique with it's own character and style. We listen to you and provide carefully considered solutions that are

engineered to compliment your home and your lifestyle.' In an unusual example of a near-homonym, *The Guardian* managed to confuse military takeovers with hen-houses when it said that early TV sports commentators were 'confined to glorified chicken coups lashed to an outer extremity of a grandstand'.

13 Consistency in punctuation: lists of opening times are a common source of error, e.g. 'The office opening hours will be 8 am to 6p.m. on Mon to Friday and Sat from 9am–1pm.' Tidying up the inconsistencies of spacing, abbreviation, wording, and punctuation might give:
'Office opening hours: Mon–Fri 8am–6pm, and Sat 9am–1pm.'

14 Alphabetical order: check that the items really are in order.

The Society for Editors and Proofreaders (www.sfep.org.uk/) offers a helpful page on the proofreader's role and what to look out for.

Checking against copy

The now-rare activity of checking against copy means making sure that a piece of typesetting replicates what the author wrote. If you are checking on paper, it helps to use a ruler or a blank notepad to screen everything except the line you are reading, as you're constantly referring from one document to another. The job needs total concentration. Checking numbers in a set of accounts or calculations can be especially tricky: ensuring the layout is right is all-important, and proofreading other people's figures reminds you to set out your own neatly and methodically.

For the professionals

If you're marking up copy for professional typesetters to correct, then using the standard proofreading marks may help—though many a typesetter will just tell you to make yourself clear, mainly in the margins, without using all the fancy notation. Conrad Taylor's free guide to about 45 of the main marks is available from www.ngomedia.org.uk/proofmarks.pdf, and there are similar sources on the Web for British and American proofreaders. The BSI website sells the standard on which many British guides are based (BS 5261C:2005).

When in doubt

For doubtful spellings, use a good dictionary. If you can't spell, get someone else to proofread. And yes, since you ask, there were four mistakes in this chapter's title. Well spoted.

Proofreading blunders that chill the blood

- 'The UK's education ministry reprinted 48 000 posters promoting literacy in schools after spelling mistakes were spotted by teachers. The blunder cost £7 000 and was blamed on 'proofreaders'.' (*Daily Telegraph*, 29 January 2000)
- 'A music exam paper taken by 12 000 pupils in the UK had the answers printed on the back, enabling pupils to gain 30% of the marks if they read the information.' (*Daily Mail*, 23 May 2008)
- *The Independent* (16 March 2007) reported that 'thousands of young people taking A-levels and GCSEs [in the UK] were especially baffled last summer... because of errors in the questions by exam boards'. A total of 36 question papers contained errors, 'which examiners had to take into account when awarding marks'.
- The first leader in *The Times* on 12 September 2008 referred four times to 'Professor Michael Weiss', apparently the Royal Society's director of education. The news item on the opposite page named him correctly—again, four times—as Professor Michael Reiss.
- 'Four years ago this May... the University of Wisconsin awarded nearly 4 000 diplomas with the name of the state spelled "Wisconson." Amazingly, six months passed before anyone noticed and brought it to the University's attention.' (*Minneapolis Star Tribune*, 3 April 1992)
- For his benefit year, England cricketer Ashley Giles ordered hundreds of drinking mugs to be printed with 'Ashley Giles, King of Spin'. But instead the potters gave him royal status as 'Ashley Giles, King of Spain'.
- The BBC's website on Armistice Day 2008 included a picture captioned 'WW1 veterans laid reefs at Cenotaph'. (Read 'wreaths'.)
- The Typo of the Year award went to Reuters for this in 2005: 'Quaker Maid Meats Inc. on Tuesday said it would voluntarily recall 94 400 pounds of frozen ground beef panties that may be contaminated with E.coli.' (Read 'patties', presumably.)

Appendix: commonest words

This appendix shows, in priority order, the most commonly used nouns, verbs, adjectives and adverbs in written and spoken English, according to data derived mainly from the British National Corpus of 100 million words. The website http://ucrel.lancs.ac.uk/bncfreq/ (Leech, G, Rayson, P, and Wilson, A (2001) *Word Frequencies in Written and Spoken English* (London)) also shows the frequency with which the words are used. Frequency is not the same as understandability. But if most of the words in your writing are from these lists, you should find that most readers will be familiar with them.

Top 150 nouns	week	market	society
time	member	court	figure
year	end	effect	police
people	state	result	city
way	word	idea	need
man	family	use	million
day	fact	study	community
thing	head	name	kind
child	month	job	price
Mr	side	body	control
government	business	report	process
work	night	line	action
life	eye	law	issue
woman	home	face	cost
system	question	friend	position
case	information	authority	course
part	power	road	minute
group	change	minister	education
number	per cent	rate	type
world	interest	hour	research
house	development	door	subject
area	money	office	programme
company	book	right	girl
problem	water	war	moment
service	other	mother	father
place	form	person	age
hand	room	reason	value
party	level	view	force
school	car	term	order
country	council	period	matter
point	policy	centre	act

health
lot
decision
street
patient
industry
mind
class
church
condition
paper
bank
century
section
hundred
activity
table
death
building
sort
sense
staff
team
experience
student
Mrs
language

Top 300 verbs
be
have
do
will
say
would
can
get
make
go
see
know
take
could
think
come
give
look

may
should
use
find
want
tell
must
put
mean
become
leave
work
need
feel
seem
might
ask
show
try
call
provide
keep
hold
turn
follow
begin
bring
like
going
help
start
run
write
set
move
play
pay
hear
include
believe
allow
meet
lead
live
stand
happen
carry

talk
appear
produce
sit
offer
consider
suggest
expect
read
let
require
continue
lose
add
fall
change
remember
remain
buy
speak
stop
send
receive
decide
win
understand
develop
describe
agree
open
reach
build
involve
spend
return
draw
die
hope
create
walk
sell
wait
shall
cause
pass
lie
accept

watch
raise
base
apply
break
learn
explain
increase
cover
grow
report
claim
support
cut
form
stay
contain
reduce
establish
join
wish
seek
achieve
choose
deal
face
fail
serve
end
occur
kill
used
drive
represent
rise
discuss
place
love
pick
prove
wear
argue
catch
enjoy
introduce
eat
enter

present	prepare	protect	**Top 150**
point	improve	adopt	**adjectives**
arrive	fill	confirm	other
ensure	mention	let's	good
plan	fight	stare	new
pull	miss	demand	old
refer	intend	imagine	great
act	drop	beat	high
relate	push	attempt	small
affect	hit	born	different
close	discover	associate	large
manage	refuse	marry	local
identify	prevent	care	social
thank	regard	voice	important
compare	teach	collect	long
obtain	lay	employ	young
announce	reveal	issue	national
note	state	release	British
forget	operate	mind	right
indicate	answer	emerge	early
wonder	record	mark	possible
maintain	depend	deny	big
suffer	enable	aim	little
publish	complete	shoot	political
express	cost	appoint	able
avoid	sound	supply	late
suppose	check	order	general
finish	laugh	observe	full
determine	realise	reply	far
tend	extend	drink	low
save	arise	strike	public
listen	notice	settle	available
design	define	ring	bad
treat	fit	propose	main
share	examine	ignore	sure
control	study	link	clear
remove	recognise	press	major
visit	bear	respond	economic
throw	shake	survive	only
exist	hang	arrange	likely
encourage	sign	concentrate	real
force	attend	lift	black
reflect	fly	cross	particular
smile	gain	approach	international
admit	perform	test	special
assume	result	experience	difficult
replace	travel	touch	certain

open
whole
white
free
short
easy
strong
european
central
similar
human
true
common
necessary
single
personal
hard
private
poor
financial
wide
foreign
simple
recent
concerned
American
various
close
fine
English
wrong
present
royal
natural
individual
nice
French
following
current
modern
labour
legal
happy
final
red
normal
serious

previous
total
prime
significant
industrial
sorry
dead
specific
appropriate
top
soviet
basic
military
original
successful
aware
hon
popular
heavy
professional
direct
dark
cold
ready
green
useful
effective
western
traditional
Scottish
German
independent
deep
interesting
considerable
involved
physical
left
hot
existing
responsible
complete
medical
blue
extra
past
male

interested
fair
essential
beautiful
civil
primary
obvious
future
environmental
positive
senior
nuclear

Top 150 adverbs
so
up
then
out
now
only
just
more
also
very
well
how
down
back
on
there
still
even
too
here
where
however
over
in
as
most
again
never
why
off
really
always
about

when
quite
much
both
often
away
perhaps
right
already
yet
later
almost
of course
far
together
probably
today
actually
ever
at least
enough
less
for example
therefore
particularly
either
around
rather
else
sometimes
thus
ago
yesterday
home
all
usually
indeed
certainly
once
long
simply
especially
soon
clearly
at all
more than
further

better
before
round
forward
please
finally
quickly
recently
anyway
a bit
suddenly
generally
nearly
as well
obviously
exactly
okay
maybe

a little
immediately
easily
though
earlier
through
up to
above
tomorrow
highly
eventually
fully
slightly
hardly
no longer
below
otherwise
directly

like
completely
normally
best
slowly
relatively
apparently
early
merely
instead
alone
for instance
largely
possibly
nevertheless
carefully
hard
mainly

currently
somewhere
along
entirely
previously
tonight
extremely
fairly
in particular
increasingly
equally
all right
surely
ahead
twice
straight

Sources and notes

General sources

Butcher, J (2006) *Copy-editing* (Cambridge).

Carey, G V (1971) *Mind the Stop* (London).

Dumas, J S and Redish, J C (1993) *A Practical Guide to Usability Testing* (Norwood, New Jersey).

Eagleson, R D (1990) *Writing in Plain English* (Canberra).

Felker, D B and others (1981) *Guidelines for Document Designers* (American Institutes for Research).

Gowers, E (1986) *The Complete Plain Words* (London).

Greenbaum, S (1991) *An Introduction to English Grammar* (Harlow).

Hart's Rules for Compositors and Readers (1983, Oxford).

Howard, G (1993) *The Good English Guide* (London).

James, N (2007) *Writing at Work* (Crows Nest, New South Wales).

Manser, M (2007) (ed.) *The Good Word Guide* (London).

Miller, C and Swift, K (1989) *The Handbook of Non-sexist Writing* (London).

Swan, M (1993) *Practical English Usage* (Oxford).

Thomas, M (2000) *Tell All: a Guide to Inclusive Communications* (Birmingham).

Truss, L (2003) *Eats, Shoots and Leaves* (London).

Turk, C and Kirkman, J (1989) *Effective Writing* (London).

Williams, J M (1981) *Style* (Glenview, Illinois).

Legal language

Adler, M (2006) *Clarity for Lawyers* (London).

Asprey, M M (2003) *Plain Language for Lawyers* (Sydney).

Charrow, V R and Erhardt, M K (1986) *Clear and Effective Legal Writing* (Boston).

Cutts, M (2001) *Clarifying Eurolaw* (Stockport). Free online from www.clearest.co.uk.

Cutts, M and Wagner, E (2002) *Clarifying EC Regulations* (Stockport). Free online from www.clearest.co.uk.

Cutts, M (2000) *Lucid Law* (Stockport). Free online from www.clearest.co.uk.

Garner, B A (1995) *Dictionary of Modern Legal Usage* (Oxford).

Kimble, J (1994–5) 'Answering the Critics of Plain Language' *The Scribes Journal of Legal Writing*, vol 5.

Kimble, J (2006) *Lifting the Fog of Legalese* (Durham, N Carolina).

Mellinkoff, D (1963) *The Language of the Law* (Boston).

Wydick, R (2005) *Plain English for Lawyers* (Durham, N Carolina).

Specific sources and notes

Starting Points

page vi   Several of Sir Arthur Quiller-Couch's lectures, including *Interlude: On Jargon*, are available on the Web from the Literature Network at www.online-literature.com/quiller-couch/art-of-writing/5/.

page ix   Councillor Wilkinson's remarks appeared in the *Teesdale Mercury*, 23 November 2006, while those of Judge Openshaw were in *The Times* on 17 May 2007.

page xii   The UK justice minister's remarks appeared in the *Daily Mail* on 8 December 2008.

page xiv   The Associated Press report was carried by the *Sacramento Bee*, 14 January 1997.

page xvii   The booklet *Health and Safety at Motor Sports Events* (HGS112) is available from HSE Publications.

page xix   Work on the Clearer Timeshare Act is published in Cutts, *Lucid Law* (cited above). This and other efforts to clarify statutes are explored in *The Law-Making Process* by Michael Zander (London 1994).

Page xx   The quantity of recent UK law is stated in a letter to the author from Tom Levitt MP, 2 May 2008.

Page xx   The minister responsible for the Coroner Reform Bill was writing in *The Guardian* on 12 June 2006.

page xxii   The studies on jury instructions are quoted in Joseph Kimble's paper 'Answering the Critics of Plain Language' (cited above). The primary sources are Charrow R P and Charrow V R *Making Legal Language Understandable: a Psychological Study of Jury Instructions*, 79 Columbia Law Review 1306, 1370 (1979); and Benson R W *The End of Legalese: The Game Is Over*, 13 New York University Review of Law & Social Change 519, 546 (1984–5).

page xxiii   Work on the Social Security Administration form is thoroughly described in *Clarity*, issue 45 pp 2–4, www.clarity-international.net.

page xxiii   For the development of plain English, see the *Oxford Companion to the English Language*, edited by Tom McArthur (Oxford 1992).

page xiv   The remarks of Coode and Bentham are quoted in 'Writing Rules: Structure and Style', an unpublished paper given by David C Elliott to the International Conference on Legal Language at the Aarhus School of Business, 1994.

chapter 1

page 2   The analysis of American sentence length is included in *Computer Analysis of Present-day American English* by Kucera H and Francis W N (Providence, Rhode Island 1967).

chapter 2

page 20   The study referring to unconsciousness was reported in the *Daily Telegraph* on 24 February 2000.

page 21   The research study among scientists is described in Turk and Kirkman, cited above.

page 28   *The Living Word Vocabulary* by Dale E and O'Rourke J was first published in 1976. A copy can be borrowed from the British Library. Copyright is owned by World Book, Inc., US.

chapter 3

page 41   Strunk is quoted in *The Elements of Style* by Strunk W and White E B (New York 1979).

chapter 4

page 50   Orwell's prescriptions are quoted under his entry in the *Oxford Companion to the English Language* (cited above) and in his essay *Politics and the English Language*, included in *Shooting the Elephant and Other Essays* (London 1950).

page 56   Among those who recommend the use of 'I' and 'we' are Booth V *Writing a Scientific Paper* (London and Colchester, The Biochemical Society 1981); Sandman P M and others *Scientific and Technical Writing* (CBS College Publishing 1985); and Barrass R *Scientists Must Write* (London 1978).

page 58   Information on the passive percentage is drawn from a manual accompanying the software program *StyleWriter – the Plain English Editor* (Editor Software Pty Ltd 1994).

chapter 9

page 80   The role of punctuation in showing the construction of the sentence is described in *Mind the Stop* (cited above) and in *Eats, Shoots and Leaves* (cited above).

page 83   My dislike of the 'nameless thing' is shared by *Hart's Rules*, cited above.

chapter 10

page 98   A detailed study of readability formulas is given in *Predicting Readability of Data Processing Written Materials* by Ronald Guillemette (Data Base, summer 1987, pp 40–47). Another useful source is *Tackling NHS Jargon* by Sarah Carr (Abingdon 2002).

chapter 11

page 106   Nesfield's book, long out of print, was published by Macmillan, London. Updated variations are used in India.

chapter 15

page 129   The core statement is a variation of the core sentence described in *Write To Win* by Thomas McKeown (Clear Communications Press, North Vancouver 1987).

page 132   For the section on different approaches to planning, I have drawn upon *Writing Strategies and Writers' Tools* by Daniel Chandler (*English Today* 34, Vol 9, 2 1994).

page 133   Dr Flowers' work is reported in *Getting the Structure Right: Process, Paradigm and Persistence* by Christopher Balmford (*Clarity* 43 pp 14–23, May 1999). The original source is *Madman, Architect, Carpenter, Judge: Roles and the Writing Process* (44 Proceedings of the Conference of College Teachers of English 7–10, 1997).

chapter 17

page 151   The use of algorithms, flow charts, and other alternatives to continuous prose is thoroughly described in James Hartley's *Designing Instructional Text* (London 1991). Another excellent source is Doris Wheatley's *Good Business Communication* (London 1988).

chapter 20

page 166   The work by H Song and N Schwarz was mentioned in *Science Daily*, 31 October 2008, reporting on a paper in *Psychological Science*, October 2008.

page 173   The US figures on 'child restraint systems' are given at www.cdc.gov/ncipc/duip/spotlite/chldseat.htm (Centers for Disease Control and Prevention, Department of Health and Human Services). The Derbyshire (UK) figures come from the *Buxton Advertiser*, 5 June 2008.

chapter 21

page 176   A valuable source for this chapter was *Writing for the Web* by Susannah Ross (Edinburgh 2007).

page 179   Dr Jakob Nielsen's work is quoted from www.useit.com, with permission.

chapter 22

page 187   Mark Adler was writing in the *Information Design Journal* 7/2 (1993): *Why Do Lawyers Talk Funny?*

chapter 23

page 207   Janet Pringle's book *Writing Matters: Getting Your Message Across* (2006) is available from http://library.nald.ca/research/item/7031.

chapter 24

page 211   Colin Wheildon's work is described in *Type and Layout: How typography and design can get your message across – or get in the way* (Strathmore Press Inc., Berkeley, California 1995).

Index